Family and Community
in the ~~Kibbutz~~ KOLONY

D1369374

FAMILY AND COMMUNITY IN THE KIBBUTZ

by Yonina Talmon

Harvard University Press
Cambridge, Massachusetts

Second Printing, 1974

Library of Congress Catalog Card Number 72–76561

SBN 674–29276–6

Printed in the United States of America

Introduction

BY S. N. EISENSTADT

This collection of essays by the late Yonina Talmon on the major aspects of social life and development of the kibbutz represents a landmark in development of the sociological study of the kibbutz movement in Israel. It presents a full report of the first and most comprehensive sociological analysis of the kibbutzim.

Truly enough, the kibbutz has been for a long time—probably since its very beginning—a focus of great intellectual, ideological, and sociological interest and criticism. Thus, for instance, the plan for the first cooperative village (moshav) in Israel—differing in principle from that of the kibbutz—which was drawn up in 1912 by the renowned German sociologist Franz Oppenheimer, analyzed several aspects of the kibbutz, young as it was then. In the twenties and thirties of this century, with development of the Jewish settlement in Palestine, many socialist and left-wing intellectuals evinced great interest in the kibbutz, often comparing it to the more coercive and state-controlled Russian kolkhoz. It was naturally the more "utopian" socialists who were especially drawn to the kibbutz—a tradition transplanted to Palestine by Martin Buber who, in his *Paths in Utopia*, has singled out the kibbutz (and moshav) as the only case of such utopian settlements that has not failed. At the same time, the broad economic and social trends of development and problems of kibbutzim and moshavim were being analyzed by Arthur Ruppin—the first Professor of the Sociology of the Jewish People at The Hebrew University and the Director of the Jewish Agency's Settlement Department—in the context of his studies of Jewish sociology and of the different types of Jewish settlements in Palestine.

It was but natural that this type of interest, rooted in social or national ideological premises and concerns, tended to evoke similar ideological responses from within the kibbutz movement; and indeed in the first heroic phase of the establishment of the kibbutz its members were always ready to join ideological and political battles with members of moshavim, members of the labor movement, and outsiders.

But with the passing of time, with the settling down of the kibbutz, the whole tenor of this discussion has greatly changed. On the one hand the kibbutz became more and more accepted, even if not always with great enthusiasm, as a part of the reality of life in Jewish Palestine. It also became more and more a focus of scientific sociological concern. For instance, with the growth of the second generation in the kibbutz, great interest was shown in the whole problem of communal upbringing of children, an interest later taken up by many psychologists and psychoanalysts; Bruno Bettelheim is one recent example. Similarly, several aspects of the social organization of the kibbutz—especially egalitarianism and communalism—became foci of inquiry by sociologists and social anthropologists.

Thus since the middle forties, scholars from outside Israel, such as Eva Rosenfeld, Melvin Spiro, and S. Diamond, have taken up studies of the kibbutz. Some of the most important aspects dealt with were the problems of egalitarianism, investigated by Eva Rosenfeld; the upbringing of children and intergenerational relations, studied by Spiro; and some broader general problems of communal life taken up by Spiro and Diamond. Whatever the specific theoretical problem on which these studies focused (for example, possibilities and limits of egalitarian allocation of role) they were on the whole greatly influenced by ideological orientation toward communal life in general and toward some of the specific Zionist implications of such life in Israel in particular.

At the same time there became evident within the kibbutz a greater recognition of the need for introspection and self-examination, a development stemming from the expansion and stabilization of the kibbutzim as viable economic structures, with all the problems connected with specialization and routinization of communal life.

But this self-awareness did not necessarily lead to a ready acceptance of sociological research undertaken by outsiders. Indeed, most of these scholars and the results of their work were on the whole not very well received by the members of the kibbutzim, who felt they were studied from afar, as sort of guinea pigs, by unsympathetic or curious strangers who did not understand the real problems of the kibbutz. This attitude toward sociological research was not just a passing phenomenon to be explained as aversion toward "strangers." It became actually even more articulate in the reactions to research by "local" scholars, for instance, to the work of S. Landshut, a renowned German sociologist who came to Palestine in the thirties and published a book on the kibbutz in the early forties. It was based on a suspicion of any "bourgeois" study of the kibbutz, and on a doubt that any "objective" observer not committed to the basic ideological premises of the kibbutz could understand its problems.

This attitude was closely related to premises common to other parts of the labor movement, and to some degree to other socialist or revolutionary societies—namely, that they do not have any real "social problems," that in a sense they have solved them; and that therefore the conceptual and methodological tools developed to cope with the problems of bourgeois society are not applicable. This conviction was often coupled with a fear that sociological investigation would disclose the weak spots in the structure of the kibbutz, either such simple human weaknesses as the craving for some individualistic or material goals, or more important problems stemming from the very process of implementation and institutionalization of the original communal pioneering vision and ideologies. It was suspected that analysis of these problems by outsiders would necessarily stress weaknesses and belittle the importance of the original vision or its feasibility.

Yet the very factors that made for the initial closure and antagonism to foreign and Israeli researchers also created the potentialities for some mutual opening, with the growing recognition within the kibbutz movements of the necessity to reexamine its own problems.

An important indication of such a potential opening up of the kibbutzim and moshavim to a dialogue with the scholarly community about their problems was the first symposium on the communal villages in Israel organized and presided over by Martin Buber, which took place in 1946 at The Hebrew University on Mt. Scopus. For the first time leaders and members of the kibbutz and moshav movements discussed with scholars the problems of social organization in the kibbutz and moshav, a discussion in which Yonina Talmon, then a recent graduate, participated.

It was indeed Yonina Talmon's singular achievement to have been able to break through this mutual closeness, to tear down barriers, and to bridge the gap between the claims and interests of sociological analysis and the kibbutz's search for self-examination. This was not an easy task—it was often an uphill struggle. She was able to achieve this opening, to overcome the difficulties, by a combination of a high level of scholarship, the application of rigorous standards of scholarship and research, with an intense commitment to the examination of the critical problems of the kibbutz and its place in Israeli society.

She came from a family of old settlers in Petah Tikva, the first modern Jewish colony in Palestine. In 1940 she enrolled as a student at The Hebrew University, where she studied philosophy, history, and sociology (or rather, as it was then called and taught by Martin Buber, "Sociology of Culture"). Her attention turned to the possibilities of integrating philosophical, historical, and sociological studies and methods, and to sociological research. This twofold interest became manifest in the two major scholarly activities she undertook after graduation in 1945: her doctoral studies, and a research project on the moshavim, in which we worked together.

The topic of her dissertation under Buber was "Mythical and Historical Time in Primitive and Archaic Societies." It was chosen with the explicit aim of attempting to combine a philosophical orientation and philosophical concepts with the study of society, or, perhaps more accurately, to delineate those areas of social life and of sociological study in which philosophical orientations and concepts were most relevant. This study also brought to the fore another interest of hers, namely, social anthropology (especially as it had developed in Britain). Many of the materials she analyzed in her dissertation were taken from some of the major works of British social anthropologists—especially E. E. Evans-Pritchard, M. Fortes, M. Gluckman, and Nadel—although the study was not confined to the primitive societies studied by these scholars but encompassed many historical ones. British social anthropology had an even greater influence on Yonina's work after 1951–1952, a year she spent in England, at the London School of Economics.

The propensity to anthropological approaches was also evident in the other study she undertook, that on moshavim, never published in its original form as a result of the vicissitudes of the period just before and after the Israeli War of Independence. In that study she showed her great talent for intensive participation and observation as well as her finesse in analyzing intricate face-to-face relations and interaction in informal and formal situations. It was this combination of the philosophical, historical, sociological, and anthropological dimensions—as well as the continuous creative struggle to find ways in which they could indeed be best combined—that perhaps constitutes the major characteristic of her scholarly orientation.

The choice of the moshavim as a topic for study was indicative of another aspect of her intellectual commitment, namely, the search for central problems stemming from the socio-ideological roots of Israeli society, and the attempt to apply sociological analysis to some of its crucial problems. This search became especially pronounced in the last period of her life (from about 1953 till her death) when, on the one hand, she undertook the vast pioneering study of the kibbutz in general and of family patterns within them in particular; while, on the other hand, she developed her interest in the sociology of religion and religious movements.

The study of the kibbutzim she organized and directed was based on close cooperation with several of the kibbutz movements. She succeeded in establishing an ongoing research project in one of the central areas of Israeli society—an area that had demonstrated antagonism toward ("bourgeois") social science. It was among the most continuous and widespread sociological research projects then undertaken in Israel. It served as training ground for many of the younger generation of Israeli sociologists and was extremely important in shaping the general intellectual climate of opinion in the nation.

The project branched over many aspects of kibbutz life: family patterns, patterns of work and organization, leadership, and intergenerational relations. In all these spheres central problems of sociological analysis were confronted. In this context her two-year stay at Harvard, 1961–1963, was helpful in sharpening her general theoretical focus, as can be seen, for example, in her article on "Mate Selection" (Chapter 5), which tackles the old problem of incest prohibitions and exogamy with a fresh approach, combining functional and causal analysis in a unique way. Similarly, in her articles on family structure (Chapter 2) and aging (Chapter 6) many pivotal aspects of general and comparative studies of these problems are posed and analyzed. From these she went on to deal with the broad comparative problems of family and aging, and problems of crisis situation in social life, as can be seen in her article on aging in the new *International Encyclopedia of the Social Sciences*.

Her study also included analysis of the development of the kibbutz structure as a process of transformation of a great ideological movement, which, in its attempts to create a new man and a new society, itself became transformed, routinized, and organized, and yet managed to keep its elitist element and orientation, and to maintain—even if in a changed way—its prominent place in Israeli society. In a way the study of all the other aspects of the kibbutz was preparatory for this major undertaking, of which she was able to complete only some parts, such as the study of secular asceticism presented here (Chapter 8). She approached this central problem not in an ideological way—as perhaps many kibbutz members might have wished—but with the same painstaking scientific analysis she had used in other areas. It was in her approach to this central problem that the nature of her own personal commitment became most evident. Here also is the raising of general issues concerning analysis of religious movements that can be seen in the brilliant article on millenarian movements she prepared for the *International Encyclopedia of Social Sciences*.

Yonina Talmon died in her prime, with many of the works she had planned still undone—although what she accomplished in the study of the kibbutz, the family, problems of aging and crisis situations, and religious movements are great achievements.

In the six years since her death the sociological study of the kibbutz in Israel has acquired a momentum of its own. The kibbutz movements have established an institute of social research, in close cooperation with various universities and research institutions in Israel. Truly enough, the tensions between "bourgeois" research and the ideological commitment of kibbutz members are still there—but by now they constitute minor dissonances in a setting of mutual acceptance, interest, and even trust.

In the development of this setting Yonina Talmon played a decisive role. Many researchers in the kibbutz are her students or students of her students; and much of the work has been greatly influenced by her own studies. Her impact stems from her personality as a teacher, the high quality of her scientific work, and above all the characteristics that determined her work: commitment, intensity, continuous critical self-appraisal, search after perfection of content and form alike. Her work not only opened up the kibbutz to sociological research, but put the study of kibbutzim in the forefront of sociological thinking and analysis.

Preface

This volume on the "Family and Community in the Kibbutz" constitutes part of the unfinished work of my late wife, Yonina Talmon-Garber. For over a decade Yonina had been involved in a large-scale research project on the kibbutz. She initiated the project and directed it until the very last weeks before her death in April 1966. The project was cosponsored by the Federation of Kevutzot and Kibbutzim, one of the four kibbutz federations in Israel, and by the Department of Sociology at The Hebrew University of Jerusalem. It was to encompass all major aspects of life in the kibbutz—the most significant expression of collectivist ideology in modern Israel—so as to assess the degree to which its organizational set-up and ideological bases were affected by the processes of social change. The ultimate intention was to widen the scope of the project in order to bring under scrutiny also the other three federations. This would have enabled the author to complement the development patterns that emerged from the initial investigation by comparing them with the patterns of change that obtained in kibbutzim subscribing to different socialist and religious convictions. The research was meant continually to observe and record the dynamics of kibbutz life, and possibly to formulate guidelines for further development of collective-communal organization. There was no time for her to pursue these comprehensive plans; even parts of the initial study remained unfinished at the time of her death.

Fortunately, the completed sections of the research project had been fully written up and in part published in diverse journals during Yonina's lifetime. In recent years her colleagues and friends have been convinced that these merited publication in a form that would make them more readily accessible to a wider scholarly audience. Toward this end, essays previously printed in Hebrew were translated into

English for publication in the present volume. In this venture, I was continuously encouraged by Professors S. N. Eisenstadt, Max Gluckman, Seymour Martin Lipset, and Talcott Parsons, whose friendship and scholarly cooperation Yonina had enjoyed over many years.

This volume consists of a series of major studies that focus on the ideological and organizational bases of the relationship of the family and the wider community in a collective. The pertinent issues are dealt with both in their synchronic and diachronic dimensions, thus illustrating significant differences between various types of kibbutzim and dynamic transformations within a given type of kibbutz over a length of time. The results are set into more comprehensive frameworks of social and anthropological theory. This opens the door for their possible application to the analysis of other societies. Such issues are the primacy of the family, "natural" or "social" bases of exogamy, status of the sexes, social equality, patterns of communal production and consumption, social elitism, and consciousness of social responsibility. Initially written as independent pieces, these essays are nevertheless interconnected. In their presentation here, an effort was made to highlight their internal cohesion by a sequential arrangement. In the process of preparing the manuscripts for publication some revising and editing was required, especially with respect to Chapter 3 in which two initially independent studies were combined because of their topical relatedness. Neal Kozodoy edited the manuscript expertly and with the utmost care so as to remain true to the author's intentions and style, as far as possible. However, even loving care cannot fully make up for the unavoidable inadequacy inherent in posthumous publication. Obviously we fall short of the perfection Yonina's hand would have achieved.

I wish to acknowledge my gratitude to the individuals and institutions who in one way or another helped in making the publication of this volume possible.

The team of researchers was drawn from among the author's students and assisted at various stages in the implementation of the project: Uri Avner, Hanna Adoni, Bath-Sheva Bonné, Rivkah Bar-Josef, Esther Breimann, Rachel Guttmann-Shaki, Shelomo Deshen, Uri Horowitz, Tamar Horowitz, Erik Cohen, Elazar Leshem, Zippora Stup–Ben Zimrah, Amitai Etzioni, Yohanan Peres, Rivkah Rahat, Menachem Rosner, Eli Ron, Leah Shamgar, Josef Sheffer, and Moshe Sarel. Mrs. Zippora Stup–

Ben Zimrah co-authored the essay that forms Chapter 8. Uri Almagor checked bibliographical references. Eric Cohen, Emanuel Marx, Aviva Rosen, Menachem Rosner, and Leah Shamgar read parts of the manuscript and checked the accuracy of the translation against the original.

For permission to reprint, thanks go to *Human Relations* and the Plenum Publishing Company for "Social Structure and Family Size" (Chapter 2), *Niv Hakevutzah* for "Children's Sleeping Arrangements (Chapter 3) and "The Sociological Study of the Kibbutz" (Appendix), the Henrietta Szold Institute in Jerusalem for "The Parental Role in the Occupational Placement of the Second Generation" (Chapter 4), the American Sociological Association for "Mate Selection" (Chapter 5), the *American Journal of Sociology* and the University of Chicago Press for "Aging in a Revolutionary Society" (Chapter 6), the Magnes Press of The Hebrew University in Jerusalem (who first published a Hebrew version of the material included here) for "Differentiation and Elite Formation" (Chapter 7), the editor of Sefer Bussel and Ihud haKevutzoth wehaKibbutzim for "Secular Asceticism" (Chapter 8).

My thanks are due to the staff of the Harvard University Press, to Martha Greenberger for retyping the worked-over manuscript to make it ready for the printer, and to Margaretta Fulton for shepherding it through the various stages of the publication process with expertise and unlimited patience. The unfailing support and friendship of Ann Orlov helped me overcome the many difficulties that arose over the years and ultimately paved the way for the publication of the volume.

Shemaryahu Talmon
June 1972

Contents

Family and Community
in the Kibbutz

1. The Family in Collective Settlements

The kibbutz offers a unique and invaluable test case for the study of family organization in revolutionary and collectivist movements. There is very little reliable or systematic evidence on changes that have occurred in the position of the family in societies like the Soviet Union and China. What scanty information is available for these societies concerns major changes in institutionalized patterns and official ideology. We have only limited access to data on the more subtle transformations going on within the system and can only speculate on what such modifications mean to the people involved (118, 21, 50, 51, 138, 20, 58, 149). But in the kibbutz we can examine at close range the position of the family in a recently established collectivist society. Moreover, kibbutzim are small-scale and cohesive communities that can be grasped in their totality as coherent social systems. The family may be studied in its intricate interactions with other institutions, and the data on it are amenable to rigorous structural and ideological analysis. A study of the kibbutz may thus help to shed some light on the position of the family in revolutionary and collectivist societies elsewhere.

Another important reason for studying family organization in the kibbutz is the fact that we have here an extremely nonfamilistic society. The study of similarly sharply defined cases has often proved particularly productive in the comparative analysis of kinship. It leads inevitably to an attempt to formulate a minimum definition of the family and to isolation of its root functions (62, 81). The kibbutz has often been adduced as conclusive evidence against the assumption that the family is universal and that no society can possibly function without it. It is sometimes also considered indicative of future trends of development, and is taken as proof that the family is destined to disappear.

1

Our study provides a favorable opportunity to examine and test these allegations.[1]

The main features of the kibbutz (131) are common ownership of property, except for a few personal belongings, and communal organization of production and consumption. Members' needs are provided for by communal institutions on an equalitarian basis. All income goes into the common treasury; each member gets only a very small annual allowance for personal expenses. The community is run as a single economic unit. It is governed by a general assembly which as a rule convenes once a week. The executive agencies are a secretariat and various committees. Kibbutzim may vary in size from 40 or 50 members in newly founded settlements to more than 1000 in larger and longer established ones. The settlements are usually started by a nucleus of settlers. Additional groups and individuals join the founders at later stages of community development. The groups of settlers are recruited by youth movements and undergo a period of intensive training in longer established kibbutzim (128).

The process of change in kibbutzim may be described as a transition from "bund"[2] to "commune." The main characteristics of the kibbutzim during the bund stage are: (1) Dedication to an all-pervasive revolutionary mission. (2) Intense collective identification. (3) Spontaneous and direct primary relations among all members. (4) Informal social controls. (5) Homogeneity. Kibbutzim are established by young unattached individuals who share a comparatively long period of social, ideological, and vocational training. The social and economic systems are in a rudimentary, almost embryonic, stage, so that there is also little functional differentiation. The processes that bring about the emergence of the commune are: (1) Differentiation. The original homogeneity of the bund stage is disrupted by the differentiation of functions and of groups that perform them. Most important in this context is the division of labor in the occupational sphere and the establishment and growth of families. Another major source of differentiation is the persistent internal solidarity of the various nuclei of settlers who join the core of founders at later periods. (2) Attenuation and accommodation of the

1. See the Appendix for the design and methods of the study on which all the essays in this volume are based.
2. For lack of a better term, I use here the term "bund," which was coined by the German sociologist Schmallenbach for similar purposes.

revolutionary ideology. (3) Decline in the intensity of collective identification. (4) Standardization of norms of behavior and formalization of social controls.

This process of institutionalization may be observed in the history of the collective movement as a whole as well as in the development of any single kibbutz, and it of course affects the position of the family and family relationships. In what follows I have attempted to assess its impact by comparing the patterns of family organization and role images which were operative in the initial stage of the kibbutz movement with those which obtain at present.

THE REVOLUTIONARY PHASE

Let us first deal with the initial phases of the collective movement. Structural considerations have led to the hypothesis that there is a certain fundamental incompatibility between commitment to a radical revolutionary ideology and intense collective identification, on the one hand, and family solidarity on the other (69, 70, 11). Kinship is based on the maintenance of intergenerational ties and a certain basic continuity of transmitted tradition. Rejection of this continuity leads to revolt against the authority of the older generation and disrupts cross-generational kinship ties. Kinship is essentially nonselective and non-ideological. Members of a revolutionary elite substitute for the ascriptive, natural kinship ties a *Wahlverwandschaft,* an elective kinship, based on a spontaneous communion of kindred souls and on identification with a common mission. Ideology becomes the dominant unifying factor. Although solidarity among comrades is very intense and is a highly significant integrating factor, it must be viewed in context: it is firmly embedded in the commitment to the revolutionary cause and is subsumed in it. Fellowship is rooted in a common idea and a common will. Relatives and friends who do not share this commitment become outsiders, almost strangers.

The urge of the first settlers to immigrate to a new country and establish a kibbutz was the outcome of a kind of conversion that entailed a total change in outlook and way of life. This overpowering urge did not affect either whole communities or whole families; it cut through and disrupted both kinship and local ties. The pioneering ideology appealed mainly to the young and unattached. It induced them to sever their relations with parents, to discard their former attachments, to disengage themselves totally from their social setting. The young pioneers immigrated either on their own or with a group of comrades; they were usually not accompanied by parents or other relatives. The intense primary relations developed in the youth movements, and later in the kibbutz, replaced the discarded family ties. Fidelity to a set of ideals and intense collective identification checked any tendency to renew contact with relatives. As long as commitment to the cause was all-absorbing and defined every aspect of life, one's duty toward the kibbutz took clear precedence over kinship obligations. External ties and conflicting loyalties were not allowed to interfere with internal cohesion.

The formation of families and the birth of children within the kibbutzim confronted the collectives with the problem of internal family attachments. From the point of view of a bund, new families are a source of centrifugal tendencies. Family ties are based on an exclusive and discriminating loyalty which sets the members of one's family more or less apart from others. Families may easily become competing foci of emotional involvement that can infringe on loyalty to the collective. Deep attachment to one's spouse and children based on purely affective interpersonal relations may gain precedence over the more ideological and more task-oriented relations with comrades. Finally, inasmuch as they act as buffers and protect the individual from the direct impact of public opinion, families may reduce the effectiveness of informal collective control over members.

The antifamilistic tendencies inherent in the revolutionary and collectivist ideology were enhanced by the conditions under which the kibbutz developed and by the nature of the functions it performed for the society as a whole. The kibbutz acted as a vanguard of the emergent society. It was a unique combination of agricultural settlement, training center, and military outpost. Each new settlement marked a further step into more outlying and more arid frontier regions; it fought its way against great odds—eroded and barren soil, a severe scarcity of water, inadequate training of the settlers, and lack of capital resources for basic investment. On top of all this lay the heavy burden of self-defense in a hostile environment. Settlement entailed in most cases a long preparatory period of entrenchment, land reclamation, and experimentation, during which cultivation yielded little or no profit.

The kibbutzim overcame these almost insurmountable difficulties by channeling most of their manpower and capital into production, and by restricting consumption and services to the bare minimum. The non-familistic division of labor was to a large extent a matter of economic necessity. Centralized communal organization of the nonproductive branches of the economy enabled the kibbutzim to reduce investment in these spheres and to utilize fully the productive capacity of the members. It also made it possible to reduce the number of women engaged in social services and to draw many of them into active participation in the effort to advance production.

The tendency to attend to the needs of members directly on the community level rather than by means of family households was strongly reinforced by the demographic characteristics of the kibbutz and by its function as a training center for youth movements. A large proportion of the members were, as mentioned before, young and unmarried. Each kibbutz accommodated, in addition, a transient population of youth-movement members who got their basic training there or helped out during the busy seasons. The presence of a considerable number of young members who did not have a family of their own and the constant turnover of temporary trainees made the development of communal service institutions imperative.

Another factor operating in the same direction was the function of the kibbutz as a defense installation in outlying regions and in the area of more vulnerable settlements.[3] Settlement in remote frontier regions was a semimilitary undertaking which required a flexible combination of activities directed toward economic development on the one hand and defense on the other. The nonfamilistic, communally organized division of labor enhanced the effectiveness of the kibbutz in the sphere of defense. In cases of emergency, the kibbutz was able to mobilize most of its members without delay and temporarily shift the main emphasis to defense activities. The care of production and service institutions could be entrusted to skeleton teams. The ability to combine activity in both spheres and to switch from one to the other could be maintained only by means of central control and coordination. Settle-

3. Material on military organization clearly indicates that there is a certain inherent incompatibility between a strong emphasis on military duties and family commitments. The tension is sometimes resolved by prohibition of marriage until completion of army service. For an interesting case in point see Gluckman (55) and Bryant (18).

ments composed of organizationally and ecologically independent family farms were much more difficult both to tend and to defend in times of emergency. The nonfamilistic structure of the kibbutz facilitated the task of merging semimilitary and economic functions.[4]

The inherent tension between the collective and the family and the exigencies of the community's situation led to far-reaching limitations on the functions of the family. Kibbutzim curtailed family obligations and attachments and took over most family functions. Among the many devices used to prevent the consolidation of the family as a distinct and independent unit was the delegation of separate functions to family members. Not only were husband and wife allotted independent jobs; there was a strict ban on assigning members of the same family to the same place of work. Division of labor in the occupational sphere was based on a denial of sex differentiation. Women participated to a considerable extent in strenuous productive labor as well as in defense activities. All meals were taken in the common dining hall. Communal institutions and stores supplied goods and services on an equalitarian basis. The importance of consumption became minimized and neutralized so that it no longer was a means of self-expression. There was a very small personal cash allowance. Standards of consumption were austere and, by and large, uniform. Since there was very little scope for the exercise of consumer choice, there was no need for family budgeting and planning in this sphere. A couple looked after its small and simply furnished rooms but had few other household responsibilities. Each mate received his share of consumer goods and services distributed by the kibbutz; neither was engaged in economic activities directed exclusively to the satisfaction of the needs of his spouse or children. In the economic sphere, interaction between the sexes occurred on the level of the community as a whole and not directly between mates.

There was also during this stage a strict limiting of the functions of the family in the sphere of member replacement. The birth rate in the kibbutzim was for a long time far below the rate of replacement. Life in the kibbutz tended to lower the fertility norms of all families within

4. In this analysis of the position of the family in the bund, I place the main emphasis on inherent ideological and structural tendencies on the one hand and on situational factors on the other. For an analysis that derives antifamilism almost exclusively from an overreaction against Jewish tradition, see Diamond (24).

it. This seems surprising if we take into consideration the fact that the attitude toward children was very positive—they symbolized to the community the promise of the future. Children were highly valued and cherished; they were accorded much better living conditions than adults and were given excellent care even in the hard early days of the kibbutz. The apparent discrepancy between this child-centered position and the tendency to limit fertility can be partly accounted for if we take into consideration the hazardous environmental conditions in which the kibbutzim developed and their severe economic difficulties. Frequent pregnancies and confinements removed women from regular work. An increase in the number of children entailed the transfer of a growing number of workers to services and child care and significantly lowered the number of workers in productive labor. The setting up of children's houses and schools required considerable basic capital investment. The care and education of children until they reached full maturity was costly and time-consuming.

Yet this is only a partial explanation. There are many indications that ideological and structural pressures enhanced the tendency toward limitation of family size. During the revolutionary phase of development, kibbutzim put the main emphasis on recruitment by means of ideological conversion.[5] They ensured their continuity and growth by drawing reinforcements of volunteers from external sources rather than by means of natural increase. The role of both men and women required a wholehearted devotion to work and active participation in communal activities. The emphasis on activities outside the family orbit and the masculine-role prototype prevented any intense identification in women with the role of mother, and curbed the desire for children.

A partial abdication of the parents in the sphere of socialization is another aspect of the restructuring of family roles. The whole system was organized on the basis of a separation between the family and its offspring. The physical care and rearing of children were the responsibility of the kibbutz rather than of individual parents. In most kibbutzim children lived apart from their parents. They slept, ate, and later studied in special children's houses. Each age group led its own life and had its own arrangements. Parents were not completely excluded, how-

5. The history of both religious and socialist communes supplies us with many analogies: all such communes tend to limit the family, although they cannot ensure their continuity without internal natural increase (122). For an interesting discussion of the same problem in a different setting, see Lea (80).

ever. During the first months of their lives infants were nursed and fed mainly by their mothers, and the fathers came to see them in the nursery every day after work. When the infants were about six months old, most of the task of looking after them was transferred to a nurse, but they were taken to their parents' room for an hour or so every day. As they grew older, the amount of time that children spent with their family increased. They met their parents and siblings in off hours and regularly spent the afternoon and early evening with them. On Saturdays and holidays they stayed with their parents most of the time. In most kibbutzim, parents put their young children to bed every night. There were thus frequent and intensive relations between parents and children. The main socializing agencies were, however, the peer group and the specialized nurses, instructors, and teachers. The age group substituted for the sibling group. It duplicated the structure of the community and mediated between children and adults.

This system of socialization, which at first developed by trial and error, can be partly accounted for by situational factors. It enabled the mother to continue her communal work and reduced the number of workers engaged in the upbringing and education of children. Children could be accorded far better living conditions and could get specialized care. The children's houses were in more than one way an economical and convenient solution of practical problems. Yet there is much more to it than that. At the root of the matter lies the conscious intention of transferring the main responsibility for socialization from the parents to the community. Basically, the children belonged to the community as a whole.

The kibbutz did not have a clear-cut ideology concerning sexual relations, and the evidence on actual behavior in this sphere is scanty and very often contradictory. Here too we see at work a number of ideological, structural, and situational factors.[6] There was, first of all, a reaction against the set patterns of the "bourgeois" way of life and an attempt to do away with such restrictive conventional norms as the demands for chastity and lifelong fidelity and the employment of a double standard for women and men. It was felt that sexuality should be anchored in spontaneous love. Marriage was to be a voluntary union between free persons and was to be binding only so long as it con-

6. For a partly analogous development, see Dunham (29).

tinued to be based on sincere and deep attachment and both partners desired to maintain it. Sexual relations were considered a purely personal matter, strictly the business of the couple concerned. This doctrine had a strong formative influence on attitudes and actual behavior. Freedom of choice and informality became the norm. Premarital relations were considered legitimate and were not censured. The union of a couple did not require the sanction of a marriage ceremony. A couple that had maintained a stable relationship for some time and had decided to establish a family applied for a room and started to live together without ritual or celebrations. The formal wedding was usually deferred until after the birth of the first child, and then was performed mainly because by law it was the only way to legitimize children. Marriage did not change the status of the wife. Wives remained kibbutz members in their own right and many retained their maiden names. The right of separation and divorce was not restricted in any way.

This extremely liberal position, which put such a strong emphasis on personal autonomy and erotic gratification, was counterbalanced and checked by the deep-seated sexual modesty and reticence instilled in the members by their traditional Jewish upbringing and by the asceticism and collectivism of the kibbutz. Members who came to the kibbutz from comparatively small communities and traditional milieus could hardly eradicate the sexual attitudes of their childhood and adolescence. Indeed, these attitudes were reinforced by the strong puritanism inherent in the revolutionary worldview and way of life. Life in the kibbutz required a long-range postponement of gratifications. It was oriented to duties and responsibilities rather than to direct rewards, and it put a premium on rigorous self-discipline. A high regard for sexual gratification ran counter to the pervasive emphasis on ascetic dedication and self-abnegation. Equally problematical, from the point of view of the collective, was the potential divisiveness of individual love relationships. Romantic love, by its very nature exclusive, sets lovers apart from their comrades; based as it is on intense emotion, it is in addition not readily amenable to social control, and it can easily get out of hand.

Another factor to be considered was the scarcity of women. In the initial stages of most kibbutzim, women constituted a minority, 20–35 percent of the total membership. Many members had to forgo sexual gratification and postpone the founding of a family for lack of a partner.

This imbalance between the sexes had a dual effect. Inasmuch as the scarcity of sexual partners resulted in competition, it enhanced the tendency toward shifting relations and instability. At the same time, in an indirect way, it had the opposite effect of deepening the asceticism already prevalent in the kibbutz.

As we have noted, the doctrine of free love had a strong impact on emerging institutional patterns. Yet while maintaining their positive attitude toward erotic attraction, kibbutzim developed many ingenious mechanisms to check its potentially disruptive effects. This was achieved neither by avoiding discussion of sexual matters nor by restrictive norms or enforced segregation. Rather, relations between the sexes were de-eroticized and neutralized by the practice of dealing with sexual problems in a straightforward and objective manner and by minimizing differentiation between the sexes. Women adopted male styles of dress and male patterns of behavior. Beauty care and personal adornment were eliminated. The kibbutzim deemphasized physical shame between the sexes. Larger rooms that could accommodate three or more occupants were often assigned to unattached men and women, who shared the room as a matter of course; they were expected to take each other's presence for granted, and in most cases they did so. There were very few sex-differentiated activities. Men and women cooperated with each other closely in everyday affairs and were expected to treat each other in a matter-of-fact and sexually neutral manner. Couples attempted to keep the special ties between them secret as long as possible. They tried to be inconspicuous and discreet even when the fact of their being a "couple" was common knowledge and fully approved by public opinion. They avoided appearing together in public, and when with their comrades they refrained from any overt signs of affection.

The dual emphases on free love and on restraint operated simultaneously and served to check one another. This accounts for the fact that in spite of the complete absence of institutionalized restrictions, sexual relations were, generally speaking, not taken lightly. There was almost no promiscuous or indiscriminate mating, no wild and irresponsible experimentation. Only a small minority of kibbutzim experienced a high incidence of shifting relations, separation, or divorce, and it is probably significant that most members of these kibbutzim had been brought up in urbanized "emancipated" milieus and were not deeply imbued with Jewish traditions. In the absence of the restraining effects of a traditional upbringing, the permissive attitude toward sex sometimes gained an upper hand.[7] In such cases, permissiveness toward sexual gratification served as a counterbalancing mechanism that compensated members for rigorous restrictions in other spheres.

Internal relations among members of the elementary family were patterned to a large extent on kibbutz relations in general and emphasized equality and companionship. Husbands were expected to share the housework and the child care. Both conjugal and parent-child relationships were nonauthoritarian. The attitude toward children was very permissive. Parents tried to win a child's cooperation by implying, suggesting, or explaining their viewpoint but did not make demands or exert pressure. They were not entitled to unquestioning obedience, and a high-handed or domineering attitude on their part was severely censured. Children were not required to exhibit any special deference toward their parents. The relationship was easygoing and uninhibited.

The changes wrought by the kibbutz in family relations were mirrored to some extent in terminology. The Hebrew terms for husband and wife were abandoned since they connoted a concept of the family as a legally binding paternalistic institution. A man and woman in love were said "to become a couple." The term for establishing a family was "to enter a family room." The husband was referred to as "my (young) man," and the wife was called "my (young) woman." Even these terms were often felt to be too familistic, and members would try to avoid them by using proper names only. Children were encouraged to use their parents' proper names for both reference and address instead of "father" and "mother."[8] The terms "son" and "daughter" were extended to all children of the kibbutz, so that the only distinction was the occasional use of "my" when the parent was referring to his own children and "our" when referring to children of the kibbutz.

Segregation of family life was made almost impossible by housing policy. Capital was invested mainly in the expansion of productive enterprises and in the construction of communal buildings. Expenditure on living quarters was kept as low as possible. Couples often had to

7. Comparative data from kibbutzim affiliated with the Federation of Religious Kibbutzim confirm this interpretation. These kibbutzim rejected free love from the outset, and insisted on strict standards of reticence and modesty.

8. On the use of personal names instead of, or in conjunction with, kinship terms in order to de-emphasize ascriptive kinship affiliation and in order to negate an indication of asymmetrical distribution of authority, see Schneider and Homans (120).

wait many months before being allocated a room of their own. Families were routinely requested to accommodate an additional member in their one-room apartments whenever the scarcity of housing became acute. Although only temporary, these recurring violations of conjugal privacy expressed clearly the precedence of collective over personal considerations. Examination of the housing built in the first kibbutzim affords another indication of the same tendency. Rooms were arranged in a row and opened onto a long narrow corridor or veranda. Bathrooms and sanitary facilities were built in the center of the compound and were shared by all members alike. The baths and showers were important meeting places where members exchanged information, conducted informal discussions of local problems, and gossiped.

Any tendency to stay closeted in the family room and to build up a segregated family life was strongly condemned. Private radios and electric kettles were banned for a long time, among other reasons because they enhanced the attraction of the home and undermined full participation in communal affairs. As noted before, there was little or no regard for family relationships in work allocation. There was also very little coordination of vacations or days off. Each member of the family functioned independently and was pulled in a separate direction (133). Much of kibbutz life was lived in the public view, and members spent most of their free time as a group. They met every evening in the communal dining hall, in the reading room, or on the central lawn; committee work and discussions consumed large amounts of spare time. Spontaneous community singing and folk dancing were the main recreational activities. Public opinion discouraged the constant joint appearance of a couple in public. The husband and wife who stuck together and were seen often in each other's company were viewed with scorn.

The way in which festive occasions were celebrated symbolized the overall importance of the community. There were almost no family-centered celebrations. Weddings were brief and informal, and in most cases the ceremony was performed outside the community. Wedding anniversaries and birthdays meant very little and were not commemorated as a rule. The kibbutz also changed the familistic pattern of most traditional Jewish festivals, and adapted them to a new communal framework. On most such occasions children did not participate in the general celebration but had their own special festivities in which parents took part only as passive spectators.

It should be noted that although kibbutzim limited the functions of the family drastically, they did not abolish it altogether. Nor was the antifamilistic policy adopted in the kibbutz based on a preconceived or fully worked out ideology. Most early formations of ideological position did not propose to do away with the family. The imposition of restrictive norms was justified as a means of liberating the family, not of eliminating it. The family was expected to come into its own, purged yet renewed and strengthened by its liberation from extraneous duties and cramping legal prohibitions. Pronouncements of strong antifamilistic views were quite rare. Ambivalence was much more prevalent than outright hostility.

It should also be stressed that even during the earliest phases, when the antifamilistic bias was at its strongest, the family remained an identifiable unit. Families were regarded by their own members and by outsiders as distinct subgroups. There were socially regulated patterns of mating, and children were recognized as offspring of particular parents. While premarital sexual relations were permitted, there was a clear-cut distinction between casual sexual experimentation and the more durable and publicly sanctioned unions. By asking for a room of their own, a couple made public their wish to have a permanent relationship and eventually to have children. While children did not actually share a common domicile with their parents, they alternated between the nursery and their parents' room, and both were in a real sense home to them. Nor did the family relinquish its communal functions: parents contributed to the economic support of their children by working. Similarly, parents exercised a direct and continuous influence on the trained personnel who were in charge of their children. Since children's institutions were not segregated from the community either ecologically or socially, parents were able to supervise closely the way in which their children were raised. They also exercised considerable direct influence on their children during the time spent together every day (130, 5, 72, 106). While interaction among members of the same family was in many cases less frequent than interaction with outsiders, internal ties remained more continuous, more meaningful, and more intense. The emotional ties that bound husband and wife and parents and children were much more intimate and more exclusive than ties with other members of the community. The family combined physical and emotional intimacy and supplied close personal contacts which were partly independent of the community. By providing unconditional love and loyalty, the family helped to insulate its members from communal pressures and to enhance their sense of security.

THE PROCESS OF ROUTINIZATION

Extreme limitation of familial functions and relations was most pronounced during the initial phases of the collective movement. As kibbutzim expanded and became progressively stabilized, the position of the family became stronger and a partial restoration was made of lost functions.

The growth and consolidation of a kibbutz made it less vulnerable to physical attack. Military training and guard duty became less time-consuming. Kibbutzim gradually managed to stabilize their economic position. They became viable economic enterprises and sometimes even attained modest prosperity. The exigencies that had put a premium on a nonfamilistic division of labor became less pressing. Now, a certain amount of internal decentralization and flexibility could be allowed.

Consolidation and economic expansion likewise reduced the intensity of collective identification. A fusion of personal with collective aspirations often occurs during a period of revolutionary ferment and under conditions of emergency. Normalization blunts the sense of emergency and diminishes the possibilities for total collective identification. So it has been with the kibbutz. During the initial phases, economic activity served as an instrument for the realization of socialist and national ideals and was therefore imbued with high seriousness and dignity. The subsequent development of large-scale and specialized economic enterprises brought about a partial emancipation of the economic sphere from the ideals of pioneering. As enterprises came to be managed on an entrepreneurial basis, the criteria of profit and cost-efficiency became increasingly important. Divested of its special aura, economic activity turned into routine, and with routinization came a certain dissociation of the individual from the community: work was no longer as absorbing, meaningful, and satisfying as it used to be, nor could the individual member achieve complete self-fulfillment through it. Where a full merger between the private and the public spheres was no longer feasible, purely personal aspirations and purely expressive interpersonal relations began to attain partial autonomy.

Development and consolidation affected the position of the family in yet another way. Differentiation of functions, and the concomitant crystallization of the groups performing these functions, disrupted the original homogeneity of the bund. The various clusters of settlers who joined the core of founders at different stages of a community's development could not be assimilated fully but continued to maintain their internal solidarity. The community was gradually subdivided into overlapping subgroups that mediated between the individual and the collective. Kibbutzim became more tolerant of internal differentiation. The family then came to be accorded a certain measure of autonomy and was assigned a place among the subgroups.

The appearance of the second generation was of crucial importance in this context because children are the main focus of semisegregated family life in the kibbutzim. Marriage per se did not entail a redefinition of roles and a new division of labor; nor did it cause a perceptible cleavage between the couple and the rest of the community. The birth of children, however, made manifest the partial independence of the family. In addition, the appearance of the second generation introduced a gradual shift of emphasis from the disruption of intergenerational ties to continuity between generations. Children were expected to settle in the kibbutzim founded by their parents. The family was no longer an external and alien influence. Parents and children, members of the same kibbutz, lived in close proximity and, at least to some extent, shared the same ideals. Identification with one's family could thus reinforce identification with the collective.

Processes of routinization within the kibbutzim were intensified by processes of routinization in the society at large. During the prestate period, the collective movement performed many crucial functions for the emergent society. It realized and symbolized the society's formative values and was in many respects its pivotal elite. The establishment of the state precipitated and set in motion a series of social processes which to a considerable extent undermined this position of acknowledged leadership. Statehood lessened the dependence of the social structure on voluntaristic charismatic movements oriented to collective service. The implementation of collective values and goals was increasingly relegated to bureaucratic organizations like the regular army, settlement agencies, and the civil service. The accelerated process of institutional differentiation led to the proliferation of new administrative agencies. It enhanced the importance of political, bureaucratic, and professional elites and undermined the predominance of the pioneering elite.

Along with structural changes came an ideological reformulation. The achievement of independence weakened the strong collectivist emphasis as well as the orientation toward the future which had been so prevalent in the prestate period. This orientation toward long-term collective goals was superseded by a concern with short-term tasks and immediate personal satisfactions. A growing incongruity could be perceived between the values and mode of life of the kibbutzim and the values and mode of organization which gradually began to obtain in Israeli society at large.

The limitation of avant-garde functions and the partial isolation from society at large had a corrosive effect on the kibbutzim and undermined their confidence in the final outcome of their revolutionary venture. Collectivist values were eroded by alien influences and ceased to be self-evident and all-pervasive. Members were assailed by self-doubt and insecurity. The revolutionary mission no longer evoked the whole-hearted identification and unconditional commitment that made possible the virtually total merger between personal and collective spheres. As external pressures reinforced the process of internal routinization, the dissociation between kibbutzim and society as a whole came to be mirrored in the dissociation between individual members and their kibbutz.

As a result of these shifts and changes both within the kibbutzim and in the society at large, the typical kibbutz family in the recent past has become at least partially "emancipated" from the collective. To begin with home life: Most families now have their afternoon snack at home with their children. In some kibbutzim families sometimes have their evening meal at home too. Most families do this only occasionally, as a special treat for the children, but others eat at home regularly almost every evening. Though most clothing still goes to the communal laundry, many families tend to look after their best clothes at home so that there is a little extra washing, mending, and ironing now and then. Couples spend a considerable part of their personal allowances on their apartments. The housing policy of kibbutzim has changed considerably: whereas the houses built during the first phases of the movement were barrackslike, with the dwelling unit consisting only of one room, the typical dwelling unit now is a semidetached apartment containing one or two rooms, a kitchenette, and private bathroom. The style of the interior decoration has remained on the whole functional and uncluttered, but the number of items of furniture supplied to each unit has risen considerably, and the standard of equipment has improved. The apartment now requires more elaborate and more systematic care. Housework entails a fixed and repetitive schedule and has become increasingly time-consuming. The apartment serves in many cases as an important symbol of the family's cohesion and a physical manifestation of its separateness.

The attenuation of ascetic ideology and the change in patterns of distribution of certain consumer goods have had a direct effect on the family. Many kibbutzim have recently abolished the allocation of certain goods according to fixed and specific standards, and have introduced a more flexible distributional system. Every member has a claim on an average per capita share of the allowance for clothing, for instance, and within the limits of this allowance he is entitled to choose items of clothing according to his own taste and personal predilections. The same applies to the special allowance for personal supplies like soap, toothpaste, and razor blades. In most kibbutzim, members are not permitted to transfer money from one allowance to another or to use it for any other purpose than that designated by the kibbutz. Freedom of choice is thus narrowly circumscribed. But in spite of its restrictions, the new distribution system is more flexible than former systems, and it transfers some of the responsibility for planning to the family (111). Most families consider their allowance more or less inadequate. Increased autonomy in consumption has thus brought about the need for systematic and careful budgeting.

Examination of demographic data indicates a considerable increase in fertility in the kibbutzim. In longer established kibbutzim, economic considerations no longer play a large role in restricting the size of a family. The overall percentage of women has risen, and the age spread is wider and more varied than before. The partial exemption of pregnant women and nursing mothers from full-time or strenuous work does not undermine organization as much as it did in the past and as it still tends to do in younger kibbutzim; consolidation and diversification of the economic structure makes it easier to absorb them in lighter tasks.

Well-established kibbutzim are able to afford the expenses of child care and education. Even if they still struggle under economic difficulties they feel they must not jeopardize their long-range planning of family size.

The attitude toward fertility has also changed considerably. As long as the main emphasis was on recruitment, and reinforcements flowed mainly from the youth movement and training centers, natural increase was of secondary importance. The reduction in external sources of recruitment and the difficulties experienced by kibbutzim in absorbing new immigrants have greatly enhanced the importance of natural increase. Emphasis has shifted from recruitment of volunteers from outside to expansion from within. The family is now called upon to help the kibbutz ensure its continuity and growth.[9] The emergence of a more feminine role for women and the partial emancipation of the family reinforce the tendency toward a higher birth rate. It is felt that children consolidate the position of the family in the community and contribute to a richer and more varied family life.

Parents now tend to take a more active part in the socialization of their children. There is much closer cooperation among nurses, instructors, teachers, and parents. Parents help look after their young children; they take turns watching them at night and nurse them when they are ill; they help organize festivities for the children and attend most of them. There is considerably more parental supervision of children's behavior, choice of friends, and reading habits. Parents try to influence their children's choice of future occupations, and insist on their right to be consulted in this matter. Some kibbutzim have introduced a more radical reorganization: children no longer sleep in the children's houses, but return home every afternoon and stay through the night. Duties of child care and socialization have thus partly reverted to the family.

The functions of the family have shifted substantially from external to internal in all spheres except the occupational one. Although there has been considerable pressure to reduce the number of hours that women work in communal enterprises, only small concessions have been made in this respect—mothers of babies get more time off from work, and women shift to part-time work at an earlier age than men.

9. The closest analogy to the development reported here is the shift from a policy of limitation of family size to a highly publicized policy of expansion in the Soviet Union (87, 88).

Kibbutzim put the main emphasis on the occupational role, and it has remained the major focus of activity for both men and women. Yet even here we witness considerable modification. There is now a fairly clear-cut sex differentiation in work organization. Women are mainly concentrated in occupations more closely allied to traditional housekeeping like cooking, laundry service, nursing, and teaching. There are a number of intermediate spheres in which women participate alongside men: half of the workers in the poultry runs and about a third of the workers in the vegetable gardens and tree nurseries are women; to a more limited extent women are assigned to work in the dairies and with livestock as well. Yet many occupations are completely or almost completely sex segregated.

Sex differentiation in the occupational sphere was kept at a minimum as long as women were young and had few children, and as long as all efforts were concentrated in production and the standard of living was low. Today too, communal service institutions replace the mother very early on, but they cannot eliminate the special ties between the mother and her baby. Since mothers have to nurse and feed their young babies every few hours, it is more convenient for them to work in one of the service institutions situated near the children houses, and they usually take a leave of absence from productive labor. The birth of more children entails recurrent work interruptions. With advancing age, mothers usually find it increasingly difficult to return to physical labor in outlying orchards and fields. The birth of children affects work allocation in yet another way: it entails a growing need for more workers in service institutions and child care. This process is further enhanced by the rise in the standard of living. Nonproductive work now requires about 50 percent of all workers and absorbs most of the women, who usually number less than half of the kibbutz population. Since women cannot replace men fully in hard productive labor, it seems a waste to allow them to work in agriculture and at the same time to assign able-bodied men to services. When practical considerations of utility gain precedence, considerable sex differentiation in job allocation comes to be regarded as inevitable. Resistance to this trend is also undermined by the gradual emergence of a more feminine image of the role of women. Many members now feel that as a rule women should be assigned mainly to jobs that do not interfere too much with their duties as wives and mothers.

A similar trend may be observed in the sphere of voluntary participation in communal affairs. Differentiation in this sphere is less clear-cut than in occupations. On most committees both sexes are represented, and there are quite a number with proportional or near-proportional representation. Yet differentiation is far from eliminated. Men predominate in central committees and in overall leadership. Membership in bodies that deal with management of economic enterprises and security is almost exclusively male. Men have a small majority in those responsible for social and cultural matters. Women predominate mainly in committees dealing with consumption, education, health, and personal problems. In these areas they can draw on the experience they gain in their jobs and can give expert advice. Kibbutzim realize that joint participation in communal affairs is an indispensable bridge between the sexes and make many efforts to avoid underrepresentation and segregation. These efforts are only partly successful because many women are not very keen on nomination to committees and try to avoid it as much as possible. By the end of the day kibbutz women who work away from home usually crave a quiet evening with their families.[10] Active participation in committees encroaches on their family life.

Significant changes have occurred in the norms pertaining to sexual relations and marriage. During the first phases of kibbutz development, the movement combined an extremely permissive attitude to erotic attachments with far-reaching neutralization of relations between the sexes. Kibbutzim no longer resort so much to de-eroticization, and at the same time their attitude toward sexual relations has become considerably less permissive. Most of the de-eroticizing mechanisms have been modified or completely discarded. Kibbutzim now refrain from assigning members of different sex to the same room. Emerging sex role differentiation and the attenuation of the ascetic ideology have resulted in considerable differentiation of styles of dress and demeanor. Inconspicuous beauty care and personal adornment that discreetly underline femininity are permissible and are increasingly prevalent.[11] Attenuation of the collectivist orientation and a more balanced distribution of the sexes have changed the patterns of courtship as well. Couples are no

10. For housewives, on the other hand, participation in committee work is an important outlet from domestic isolation (compare Parsons on American patterns, 103).
11. It is significant that the Federation of Kevutzot and Kibbutzim has initiated a program to train members as hairdressers and beauticians. The decision was justified in terms of preserving "fitness" rather than in terms of beauty care.

longer expected to keep their relationship covert as long as possible. They are considerably less reticent and are not embarrassed to be seen together in public.

Modifications in the doctrine of free love have developed in the opposite direction. The general ideological position has remained basically liberal. When prompted to state their attitude toward sexual relations, most kibbutz members declare that they view it as a purely personal matter. Yet when it comes to more specific and more practical norms, they usually have many reservations. Practically all of them feel very strongly that adolescents should not be preoccupied with sexual matters and should refrain from sexual relations. After graduating from school, young members may engage in sexual relations with impunity, but they are enjoined not to be indiscriminate and not to treat sex frivolously. Promiscuous experimentation is viewed with open disapproval. Age at marriage has dropped considerably and premarital relations are often just a brief prelude to marriage. The time interval between commencement of sexual relations and the starting of a family is much shorter than it used to be. Normally, marriage now precedes the beginning of life together in a family apartment. Quite a number of couples postpone sexual relations until they marry. Most couples attach considerable importance to their wedding and want it to be a meaningful and memorable event. Wives now tend to discard their maiden name and to adopt their husband's name.

The prevailing attitude toward extramarital relations is more critical and restrictive than the attitude toward premarital relations. Members fully recognize that the attachment between spouses is not always durable and that extramarital relations are bound to occur occasionally. Yet they view such entanglements with considerable distaste. Although feeling that spouses should be understanding and tolerant and should not make too much fuss about a passing fancy or a temporary lapse, they maintain that extramarital liaisons endanger the stability and cohesion of the community and should be avoided. Most members regard the right of divorce as inalienable. However, they feel it should be exercised only in cases of very serious and persistent estrangement. Divorce in families with children is severely censured and condemned by public opinion. Officially, the kibbutz has no right to interfere in these matters and members may do as they please. However, many informal pressures are brought to bear on parents who contemplate divorce. They are constantly reminded of the potential harm to their children and of the probable adverse effect on interpersonal relations in the kibbutz. The image of the ideal family has changed radically. Life-long companionship, mutual trust, and understanding are emphasized much more than intensity of erotic attachment. Responsibility and loyalty are considered more important than spontaneity.

Both the community and the family have a vested interest in stability. Informal communication in such a closely knit and cohesive community makes it virtually impossible to keep an extramarital liaison secret—it soon becomes common knowledge. Since life in the kibbutz entails close cooperation and frequent contacts among all members, the neglected spouse is exposed to recurrent encounters with the rival. Bitter jealousies that tear members apart and breed drawn-out enmities have a corrosive effect on interpersonal relations and impair the functioning of the system as a whole. Similar considerations also affect the attitude toward divorce. Divorce is experienced by members of the family concerned as a major upheaval in their lives. It does not require economic reorganization and adjustment, but it does cut them loose from their most important sources of emotional support and security. If both husband and wife remain in the kibbutz, they cannot possibly avoid each other. This is very irksome when the dissolution of the family has left a residue of strong resentment. It is particularly painful to the rejected spouse. Small wonder that in most cases one of the couple tends to leave the kibbutz. In spite of the fact that children in the kibbutz have a number of primary socializing agencies and a host of secondary ones, the rift between their parents and the loss of one of them is felt to be very harmful. It is significant that in spite of the absence of legal restrictions and economic hindrances, the rate of divorce has dropped drastically even in kibbutzim that originally had a comparatively high rate of family dissolution. In most kibbutzim, divorce has become a rare occurrence, and some have not had a divorce in their community for many years. Families are on the whole cohesive and stable, and cases of severe and protracted conflict are rare.[12]

There are many signs of the emergence of a fairly clear-cut division of labor in domestic tasks, a division that, not surprisingly, follows the

12. The data on the stability of the family in the kibbutz do not corroborate the hypothesis that limitation of the role of the father in the maintenance and placement of his children leads to instability (125).

line of sex role differentiation in work assignment. Since they are concentrated in occupations that are closely allied to housekeeping and
child care, women find it easier to cope with such tasks at home. This
trend is accelerated whenever deeply rooted sex role images gain precedence and undermine the equalitarian ideology. The emergent division
of labor is flexible and fluctuating. The husband will usually help his
wife clean the apartment and prepare the afternoon tea. Some husbands do it regularly, some do it now and then, and some do it rarely—
in cases of emergency, when the wife is very tired, ill, or away. Clothes
are exclusively the concern of the wife. The husband does not take
much interest in clothes and almost never helps his wife look after
them. In most families the wife does the housekeeping and it is mainly
her responsibility. The husband is regarded as her assistant or as a
temporary stand-in but not as a coworker on equal terms.[13] Budgeting
of personal allowances of the whole family is almost invariably the responsibility of the wife. Officially, these allowances are personal and
not transferable, but in practice this injunction is overruled and the
allowances are pooled. Since men are less concerned with clothing and
other consumer goods, a considerable part of their allowance is in fact
transferred to their wives, who in many cases are entirely entrusted
with the planning and management of the family finances.

The tendency toward a more familistic pattern may be clearly discerned in the subtle transformation of informal relations and leisure-
time activities of husband and wife. Free time spent in public has
diminished considerably. There is still much organized activity on the
community level, and most members participate in committees, in
work-group discussions, and in various cultural interest groups; but
they are not so eager as they used to be to participate in public discussions or attend public meetings. Spontaneous dancing and community
singing sessions have become rare. Husband and wife spend much of
their free time together at home. They usually sit next to each other
during evening meals and on all public occasions. There is far closer
coordination of their work schedules as well as of vacations and holidays. Families get special consideration in this respect so that husbands
and wives are able to spend their free time together. Much of the in-

13. This seems to indicate that Bott's hypothesis, which relates conjugal role
segregation to degree of network connectedness, needs reexamination and revision
(16). In the kibbutz a growing differentiation between different types of social relations and a loosening of social control over the family enhance, rather than
diminish, sex role differentiation.

formal interchange among members occurs at home. Entertaining and visiting are becoming family affairs; it is now considered impolite to invite only one of a couple. Husband and wife may each have close friends of their own, but if a special friend is uncongenial to the other spouse, he or she is gradually dropped. It is significant that increasing sex role differentiation is accompanied by an increase in joint leisure-time activities, not by increased segregation.

In the sphere of child care, there is considerably more cooperation and interchangeability than in housekeeping.[14] This is clearly the effect of the system of socialization. As parents do not carry the main responsibility for either maintenance or socialization of their children, the emphasis is put on affective ties. Parents handle their small children in an affectionate, gentle way. The child is caressed and kissed often, and any reciprocal sign of affection on his part is richly rewarded. Expressions of affection become more restrained as the children grow up. Yet the parents continue to lavish loving attention, and do their best to be fully available while at home. The petty quarrels and persistent disagreements which often afflict parent-child relationships in other types of families are quite rare in the kibbutz. Parents endeavor to make the few hours that their children spend with them as pleasant and carefree as possible. They will abstain from making too many demands on their children and from severely penalizing misdemeanors, so as not to mar the happy hours of their daily reunion. The main function of the parents is to minister to their children's need for security and love. Both of them interact with their children in much the same way and play a common protective role. Fathers usually take a lively interest in their children and participate actively in looking after them: they play with their children, take them for walks, and put them to bed about as much as mothers do. Mothers have closer contacts with babies and small children, but fathers come into the picture very early.

In spite of the considerable blurring of differences between the father role and the mother role, there are some signs of differentiation even in this sphere. The mother is, as a rule, more concerned with the physical well-being of the children and takes care of them while they are at home; she usually has more contact with the children's institutions and the school, and supervises the upbringing of her children

14. For the factors that enhance the tendency to dedifferentiation of parental roles in the modern family, see Slater (124).

there. Whatever routine disciplining is done within the family, and that is not much, is more often than not the mother's responsibility. The child has to conform to certain standards of cleanliness and order. The living quarters of the family in the kibbutz are small. In many cases one room serves all purposes. While standards of tidiness are by no means very strict, there is a concern with the neatness of the apartment. Even with maximum permissiveness the child has to be controlled and restricted to some extent. There are also the problems of personal cleanliness and hygiene. The father is less involved in these problems, and the child may find him an ally in cases of exaggerated concern on the part of the mother. The father's main responsibilities lies outside the home—in the yard, on the farm, in dealing with communal affairs of the kibbutz as a whole. In the eyes of the growing child, the father gradually emerges as the representative of the kibbutz and its values within the family while the mother is primarily the representative of the family in the kibbutz.[15]

Parents emphasize the unity of the family and promote closer contacts among siblings. Older children are not burdened with heavy duties and are not compelled to look after the younger ones regularly. Yet they are encouraged to assume some responsibility and participate at least to some extent in the care of their younger siblings. Sibling relations are not devoid of tension and rivalry: constant sharing in the peer group often breeds a craving for complete monopoly over the parents and persistent demands for individual attention. Still it seems that the atmosphere at home is less competitive than in the nursery. The sibling group is as a rule smaller than the age group and, unlike it, is age-graded. Births are usually planned with an interval of at least two years. That means that the parents have enough time for intensive care of each child during his infancy, and that needs and claims for attention can be graded according to age. Conflict situations are minimized by the segregation and differentiation of activities in different age groups and in different children's houses. Having siblings enhances the

15. Our data disprove the hypothesis that the mother figure is always the more permissive and supportive, and the father more denying and demanding, as far as the administering of specific disciplines and everyday relations are concerned. They reinforce the hypothesis of "positional" differentiation. The mother is the representative of the family whereas the father is the representative of the community at large. For the distinction between role and position, see Berger (10), Parsons and Bales (104). This is discussed further in later chapters.

prestige of the older child in his age group—he will often assume a protective role toward his younger sibling and take care of him of his own accord—while for the smaller child an older sibling is a mixture of the parental and peer-group figure.

The consolidation of the family unit and the emerging sex role differentiation within it have a direct effect on the family's internal authority structure. Discussions and disagreements are usually kept within the family, and there is a strong tendency to maintain a common front toward outsiders. We have already noted that there is a "regional" division of spheres of authority. Family authority is determined by the manner in which obligations and responsibilities are distributed between marital partners. There are also many indications that, while the wife has more say in routine matters, the husband exercises more influence in matters of principle. Analysis of family decisions shows that husbands are usually more strict in their adherence to community norms and that they exert pressure on their wives in this respect. Public opinion ridicules a weak husband who gives way to his wife or allows her to deviate from the accepted norms. It should be stressed that although the emergent pattern indicates a certain division in spheres of authority, and favors a husband who takes a firm stand in matters of principle, the pattern is not clear-cut and does not enforce an institutionalized position of pivotal authority for either one of the spouses. The authority balance in each family therefore depends primarily on the interaction of the personalities of husband and wife and on the influence they exercise on each other at different stages of the family cycle. The family has remained basically nonauthoritarian, and neither of the spouses is felt to be entitled to give orders or disregard the views of other members of the family.

In the sphere of parent-child relations, we witness an interesting dialectical process. The extreme limitation of family functions in the sphere of maintenance and socialization of children has not led to disruption of family solidarity. Paradoxically, the curtailment of obligations has reinforced rather than weakened parent-child relationships and has enhanced emotional ties. Insofar as the family has ceased to be the prime socializing agency, parents need not play the dual role of ministering to the children's needs on the one hand and of thwarting their wishes in various ways on the other. Since they do not carry the main responsibility for disciplining their children, they can afford to be easy and loving parents. Interaction between children and parents is restricted and intermittent, but it is warm and permissive.

The role system in the children's houses is, from several points of view, the reverse of the role system of the family. There is a considerable turnover of attendants, which prevents the child from forming a strong and permanent identification with any of them. The relations in the nursery are, in addition, less affectively toned: they focus on the maintenance of a certain routine, and are regulated primarily by professional criteria of competence; diffuse general friendliness is emphasized more than love; the nurse is usually kind, but she cannot attend to the needs of one child exclusively. There is a narrow margin of legitimate variation in the individual attention given to each child, but this is curbed by the work schedule and by the need to take care of several children of approximately the same age who often make the same demands all at once. Any attempt to monopolize the nurse is bound to fail; the child has to learn to wait his turn and share with his peers. While the family is focused on diffuse gratification and the release of tension, the nursery and the school are task oriented and emphasize performance. Autonomous activity in the nursery is rewarding because it shortens the time span between a need and its gratification. The child is encouraged to do things for himself and is pushed toward learning and maturation. The child brings the new skills and capacities to his parents who are always ready to acknowledge and praise him. This allows the child to experiment in a noncompetitive atmosphere where any level of performance is appreciated. There is in the family a permissiveness toward slow development which balances the process of accelerated maturation in the nursery. Each child is, in a sense, an only child to his parents. He has an ascribed place in his family and receives his share of uncontested love and attention.

The position of the child in his age group is prescribed only to a limited extent. In spite of the fact that educators emphasize coordination of needs and cooperation, competition is not eliminated. The age group furnishes a setting for acting out dominance-submission problems. The child tests his powers in his relations with his peers. He competes with them for position in the group and for the approval of the adults in charge. A certain degree of outgoingness and self-assertion is functional to the child and promotes his adjustment. Children who are shy, less advanced, or less bright than the other members of their group are at a considerable disadvantage. The family redresses the balance by providing the child with unconditional love and loyalty. It is mainly within the family that both parents and children have intimate relations which are largely unpatterned by their positions in the age group or the community.

The countervailing functions of the family in the socialization process account for the overall importance of the parent-child relationship. Young children are deeply dependent on their parents. Children very often come to occupy the emotional center of their parents' life, and are a major preoccupation with most mothers. In the kibbutz, children eventually outgrow this intense involvement with their parents, and gradually become attached to their peers with whom they share uninterruptedly all the formative experiences of infancy, childhood, and adolescence. Solidarity in the kibbutz is focused primarily on horizontal ties among age peers rather than on vertical ties among successive generations.[16] Age grading serves as a major mechanism of organization and control in the social system as a whole, and especially so in the educational system. Intense loyalties that cut across age and generation differentiation are problematical in such a system and are eventually partly overridden and superseded by bonds with age mates and siblings. Adolescents gradually become firmly embedded in their group and drift away from their parents. The relationship with them remains straightforward, unconstrained, and in many cases exceedingly friendly, but it is no longer very intense and intimate. Parents resent this shift in the patterns of solidarity and often blame it on usurpation by the communal institutions. Many feel bereft of purpose and crave closer contact with their children. It is this process that is at the root of a recent reorganization of patterns of socialization (40, 107).

The emerging role relationships in the elementary family are partly mirrored in a change of terminology. The terms "my young man" and "my young woman" are now felt to be inappropriate, especially when the couples concerned are past their prime. There are no fixed, fully legitimized terms, but there is a growing tendency to refer to a husband as "my man" and in the case of the wife there are alternative terms such as "my woman" or "the woman"; members sometimes laughingly

16. For the effect of the emphasis on horizontal ties in family relationships in modern society, see Cumming and Schneider (22).

employ the rather poetic biblical "my beloved." Quite often one notices a reversion to the traditional terms husband and wife, which were strictly taboo in the past. These terms are employed self-consciously, and in a half-apologetic, half-defiant way. Almost invariably children now address and refer to their parents by the terms father and mother, adding "my" when using the terms for reference. Small children also tend to add "my" when they use the parental term for address, thus emphasizing the intimacy and exclusiveness of the relationship. Parents often use the kinship terms son and daughter instead of proper names when addressing and referring to their children.[17] Another significant change is the development of technonymic patterns. Children refer to and address other children's parents by adding the name of a child to the parental term. Thus, most adults are designated by the children as the father of ____ or the mother of ____. The children use either the name of the child they know best, or the name of the first-born in the family. So prevalent is this pattern that children will often refer to unmarried or childless adults as "father (or mother) of no one." This tendency to identify people by underlining their role as the parent of a certain child is not confined only to children but often penetrates adult society as well.

The most important feature of the process of change from the point of view of future development is the gradual reemergence of wider kinship ties. As long as the generation structure of the kibbutz remained truncated, most members did not have any kin beyond members of their own elementary family living with them in the same community. A gradual process of change set in when the children of the founders established families and the kibbutz developed into a full-scale three-generation structure. In addition, kibbutzim have accepted social responsibility for members' parents who are aging or sick and take in many of them to live with their children in the kibbutz. These elderly parents live either in separate dwellings or in small semidetached quarters adjoining their children's apartment. Relatives who live in the same community maintain close contacts through frequent visits and mutual help. There are many indexes of the emergence of cohesive kinship

17. Since proper names are used for address and reference in interaction among all members of the community, the use of such names becomes undifferentiated and neutralized, and ceases to denote a special intimacy or exclusiveness.

groupings. Relatives very often tend to cluster and form united blocks which have a considerable influence on communal affairs.

Wider kinship ties serve also as connecting links with the outside world. Members tend to renew their contacts with relatives who live outside the kibbutz. They will stay with their relatives when they go to town and will invite them to visit the kibbutz. They accept personal presents from kin and reciprocate by sending farm produce. The wider kinship categories have, however, remained amorphous and fluid. There is a vague sense of obligation to maintain amicable relations with all kin, but actually contacts with kin outside the kibbutz remain selective. The congeniality of a relative depends on many factors: political allegiance and degree of sympathy toward the collective movement, potential of mutual help, geographical accessibility, mutual compatibility on a purely personal basis (43, 16).

It is perhaps significant that, unlike the kinship terms denoting relationships within the elementary family, wider kinship terms remain undifferentiated and classificatory. The terms grandfather and grandmother are used for both address and reference. Grandfather and grandmother are used also as classificatory terms to describe all adults of the grandparents' generation, and in this use the identifying mark is either the proper name of the aging adult or the name of one of his grandchildren. There is comparatively little differentiation among different categories of relatives and usually one refers to them by the general term relative. The terms uncle and aunt are sometimes used for reference but not for address, and are employed indiscriminately to refer to more distant relatives as well. Small children sometimes designate by these terms any elderly stranger. Occasionally young people use uncle and aunt for the same purpose, but in this case the terms are employed to tease or poke mild fun at the stranger.

The process of emergence and consolidation of kinship groups within the kibbutz has been partly held in check by the patterns that determine the choice of mate in the second generation. With very few exceptions, members born and bred in the same kibbutz do not intermarry. We have found no case of marriage between members of the same peer group.[18] Since marriage brings about a rearrangement of the

18. Our data on erotic attachments and sexual relations among members of the second generation are rather scanty. As far as we could judge, although such in-

social structure, and determines to a large extent the structure and functions of the kinship groups within it, the phenomenon of spontaneous out-group marriage in the second generation calls for detailed analysis.[19] Classification of the marriage alliances contracted by members of the second generation according to group supplies a typology ranging from extreme endogamy (marriage between members of the second generation in the same kibbutz) to extreme exogamy (marriage between a member of the second generation and an outsider who does not share the kibbutz ideology). These polar types are in fact quite rare. Much more prevalent are the intermediate patterns in the continuum, which include marriage between a member of the second generation in a given kibbutz and (a) one who has joined the kibbutz at a later period; (b) a resident nonmember or hired worker; (c) a member of another kibbutz, either well established or newly formed. These intermediate patterns of marriage have the effect of safeguarding the internal cohesion and continuity of the local community and of the kibbutz movement as a whole.[20]

The tendency of second-generation members to seek a mate outside their own immediate peer group has developed spontaneously and is not buttressed by any clearly formulated and widely accepted norms—there are certain preferences but no explicit proscriptions or prescriptions. We can account for the emergence of this pattern on the motivation level only by examining it within the wider ramifications of the relationship between the first and second generations. The prevalent patterns of marriage are, in fact, an outcome of two opposing pressures. Parents have a vested interest in endogamy; their major concern is to ensure that the new family will stay on in the kibbutz, and from the point of view of familial and local continuity, in-group marriage is the safest solution. The old-timers would have liked very much to see their children united in marriage. In the few cases where such marriages

---

group attachments are more frequent than endogamous marriages, they do not occur often. We will not deal here with the deeper psychological meaning of this phenomenon. It should be noted, however, that on the face of it, the relations among members of the second generation seemed neutral, and there were no signs of repressed erotic attraction. The few cases of in-group affairs and marriages were considered legitimate and fully accepted by public opinion. Such relationships do not incur any of the condemnation or intense horror which violations of the incest taboo usually evoke.

19. For a complete discussion see Chapter 5.

20. For an analysis of the functions of intermarriage, see Lévi-Strauss (82), Merton (91), Gough (61), and Parsons (102).

have actually occurred, the parents of both spouses accepted the decision with enthusiasm. By contrast, members of the second generation are strongly inclined toward exogamy; they are attracted by newcomers and outsiders much more than by members of their own group.

This predilection of members of the second generation for out-group relations in the erotic sphere stems, at least in part, from the patterns of social relations and of communication and control in the age groups. Age groups are based on a diffuse and all-embracing internal solidarity that discourages exclusive dyadic friendships within it. There is also the problem of privatization of love affairs. Members of the second generation are at the center of public attention, and an amorous attachment attracts immediate notice and incessant comment. Courtship is conducted with the whole community looking on. Privatization of the relationship is much easier when the prospective spouse is a newcomer or an outsider.

This is, however, only a partial explanation, and our material indicates that the exogamous tendency so prevalent among members of the second generation stems primarily from their ambivalent attitude toward continuity. The kibbutz is part of a revolutionary movement that puts a premium on discontinuity and creative innovation. Inasmuch as it still is dependent on reinforcements from youth movements, it encourages young people to dissociate themselves from their parents and continues to glorify rebellion. At the same time, it expects its second generation to stay on in their native villages and continue their parents' life work. Thus, the second generation is called upon to continue and persevere in a movement committed to innovation and discontinuity. Most of the members of the second generation accept a responsibility to their heritage, but they resent the fact that, in comparison with their parents' role, their own seems secondary. There is also the fear of closure. The duty to live in their native village all their lives engenders mild claustrophobia. The exogamous tendency expresses a craving for new experiences and new contacts. Most important, perhaps, it affords opportunities to explore on one's own, to initiate and experiment. In short, out-group marriage enables the second generation to escape the in-group closure imposed on them by their system of education and by their commitment to continuity.

It would seem from the point of view of those directly concerned that the intermediate patterns which combine exogamy with endogamy are compromise solutions. These composite patterns enable members of the second generation to reconcile their contradictory interests and to meet halfway the opposing pressures impinging on them. In addition, these patterns combine desirability with the accessibility of marriage partners. Members of the second generation in any kibbutz are mutually and fully accessible, but they normally do not evoke erotic attraction in each other. Complete outsiders are desirable but not readily accessible. Newcomers and outsiders in their own kibbutz and members of other kibbutzim are both accessible and desirable.

It should be noted that the intermediate patterns provide a functional solution from the point of view of the elementary family as well. Extreme homogamy is based on internal uniformity, which limits the possibilities of a fruitful interchange and complementation. Extreme heterogeneity is inherently unstable since it joins spouses with conflicting loyalties and incompatible norms and aspirations. The intermediate patterns combine basic homogeneity with manageable differentiation. They enable members of the second generation to contract marriage with newcomers and outsiders without disrupting their matrix of interpersonal relations. It seems that the prevalence of the intermediate patterns stems from the fact that they perform important functions on both the motivation and social-system levels. Throughout the system and its subsystems they maintain a flexible balance between in-group unity and intergroup connectedness. It is significant that marriage patterns have come to serve as integrating mechanisms of major importance.

The change in the position of the family, and the growing importance of the kinship groups, are symbolized and made manifest by the patterns of celebrating festive occasions. Weddings have become important events both for the families concerned and for the community as a whole. They are celebrated by the whole kibbutz and are made the occasion of big and joyous parties. There is a tendency in most kibbutzim to celebrate a number of marriages together, but the couples who participate in this joint communal celebration are entitled to an additional, more exclusive party for their friends and relatives. Many families regularly celebrate wedding anniversaries and birthdays and attach considerable importance to such occasions. They invite their friends and relatives and are entitled to a special allocation of provisions for the purpose. There are reunions of relatives on all important family occasions. Celebration of communal and national festivals has become much more the affair of kinship groups. Members of each family tend to cluster and sit near each other. Members are entitled to invite relatives who are not members. Hundreds of such guests come from far and wide to spend holidays with their kibbutz relatives.

DIFFERENCES AND VARIATIONS

So far, I have concentrated on substantiating the hypothesis that the institutionalization of a revolutionary and collectivist movement leads to a progressive emancipation of the family. I have underlined the general trend and could only hint at differences among different types of kibbutzim and among categories of members within each kibbutz. Comparative analysis of our material clearly indicates considerable and patterned variation as to the rate and extent of change.

Let us first deal with typological differentiation. The contrast between the antifamilism inherent in the bund stage and the more familistic ideology and organization emerging in the commune manifests itself most clearly in the development of the movement as a whole. The differences among types of kibbutzim affiliated with the federation are bound to be less accentuated than the contrast between the initial and the later stages of development of the collective movement. The ideology and patterns of organization that evolved in longer established communes, and are upheld by the federation, cannot fail to penetrate newly established kibbutzim and modify their attitudes toward the family. Processes of institutionalization in the movement blur the typological differentiation between bunds and communes. There is much that is common to all kibbutzim. In certain notable cases there is even a reversal of positions, and members of the bunds who underwent their basic training after the movement had already discarded many of its antifamilistic tenets are more familistic than members of communes who underwent their training during the initial, antifamilistic stages of the movement. Yet in spite of the leveling effect of the process of institutionalization in the movement, typological differentiation does not disappear; this is in line with our hypothesis. On the most important counts, communes were found to be considerably more familistic than bunds.

Closely related to the differentiation between bunds and communes is the differentiation between subtypes of communes. The kibbutzim of the commune type fall into two major subtypes—unified and federated communes. Our main criterion for the distinction between these subtypes is the extent of amalgamation of the various groups of settlers in each commune. A federated commune is an aggregate of distinctive and clearly distinguishable subgroups. Each group of settlers retains its identity and constitutes a semiseparate unit within the framework of the kibbutz. The members of each subgroup have a strong "we" consciousness and a distinctive subculture. They have comparatively few close contacts with members of subgroups other than their own. A unified commune is one in which the subgroups have assimilated and have lost their separate identity. Interpersonal relations cut across the lines between the groups and the boundaries between them become almost indistinguishable.[21]

Persistence of subgroup identity is closely related to the initial cohesiveness of the nuclei of settlers. Cohesive nuclei of settlers who have undergone together a long period of preparation and indoctrination tend to continue to maintain their internal unity more than do less cohesive groups. Another important factor in this process is the extent of differentiation between the subgroups in terms of seniority in the kibbutz, age, country of origin, and level of education. A strong tendency toward maintenance of semiseparateness appeared in kibbutzim in which there was considerable differentiation according to most of these criteria and in which the groups were akin in several aspects.

Our material indicates clearly and persistently that changes in family norms and behavior are more prevalent in unified than in federated communes. In federated kibbutzim the subgroup is the focus of social relations. Members of each subgroup maintain numerous and close contacts with each other and identify with their group. Their identification with the subgroup is often much stronger than their identification with the kibbutz as a whole. Nevertheless, the subgroup mediates between the individual and the kibbutz and operates against the splitting up of the community into semiclosed and loosely connected family units. Friends are more important than relatives. The family is an integral part of the group. The stronger the internal cohesion of the subgroup, the more stubborn the opposition to the familistic trend and the slower the process of change within it.

Unified kibbutzim are basically aggregates of families intent on

21. It should be stressed that kibbutzim do not fall into sharply differentiated types. Some kibbutzim approach one type, whereas others come closer to the opposite one.

guarding against any encroachment on their privacy and autonomy. Husband and wife work in communal enterprises and institutions and use their services. They maintain friendly relations with other families, but relations with members of their elementary family and with relatives take precedence over relations with outsiders. The kinship groupings emerging in unified communes are more cohesive and far more influential than kinship groupings in federated communes. Family life and relations with kin are gradually becoming a major focus of community life.

In addition to the federated and unified types, there is a secondary subtype of commune which we have dubbed the "split" or "factional" commune. Much like the federated commune, the factional commune is an aggregate of clearly distinguishable subgroups. The internal division is in fact more clear-cut than in the federated commune. The resemblance between factional and federated communes misled us at first, and we identified the two kibbutzim that represent the factional subtype in our sample as federated communes. It soon became evident that there is a radical difference between the two. The distinctiveness of the subgroup in federated communes is based on internal cohesion and strong solidarity among its members: the subgroups are not very sharply differentiated as to seniority, age, country of origin, or cultural standards; they cooperate with each other, and there is comparatively little tension between them. The closure of the subgroups in factional communes is based primarily on their sense of opposition to other subgroups: there is very little internal cohesion in each subgroup, and uncommonly sharp conflict with others; the community is in fact split into sharply differentiated and bitterly opposed factions which reject each other and constantly compete for supremacy.

It is significant that on many important issues the members of factional communes have proved to be the most familistic in our sample. A closer and more detailed examination reveals, however, that their position in this respect is not unequivocal. Their attitude toward many important problems is individualistic rather than familistic, they are self-centered rather than family-centered. This is particularly noticeable in the reasons they proffer for their familistic preferences. It very often becomes evident that the particular interests of each spouse comes first, and there is no strong sense of duty and commitment to the family as a whole. The same tendency manifests itself in the patterns of interpersonal relations: most members do not maintain close and frequent contacts even with members of their own subgroup. There is also comparatively little cohesion among relatives.

Parallel to the structural differentiation we have just outlined is a pattern of ideological differentiation in which three main types of kibbutzim may be distinguished: the pioneering, the economic, and the consumer. The pioneering type of kibbutz is dedicated to serving the nation and to the complete reform of society. The economic type stresses economic stability and profitability. The consumer type emphasizes raising the standard of living. The extreme pioneering type and the extreme consumer type stand at either end of a continuum along which a number of various combinations of types may be perceived.

The process of institutionalization naturally cannot be separated from the evolution of ideals. In our comparative analysis we found that pioneering and economic kibbutzim were less familistic than consumer kibbutzim. The pioneering and economic types demand identification with aims that transcend the individual and his family cell. These types make severe normative demands on a person and require deference to the collective. When the emphasis shifts to private and public consumption, the demands for identification with ideals become less severe. More attention is paid to comfort and enjoyment. "Natural" relationships, based on kinship and geographical proximity, become more important than those based on ideology and shared ideals. The individual turns to his family and to himself.

Up to this point we have dealt with different types of kibbutzim. We turn now to the discussion of internal family differences. The purpose of this analysis is to locate the main agents of familistic innovation within the family. Who initiates changes in this sphere? Who is more familistic—husband or wife, first or second generation?

Structural analysis and examination of our data led to the hypothesis that women are more familistic than men, and this hypothesis was confirmed in almost all important issues. Generally speaking, women are less attracted to life in the kibbutz and find it more difficult to adjust. There are usually fewer women than men in the nuclei of settlers, and women are also more prone to drop out and leave the kibbutz. Girls are more firmly embedded in their families than boys and are more closely supervised and controlled by their parents. Girls consequently find it more difficult to dissociate themselves from their family and join a nucleus of settlers on their own. There is also usually more parental opposition to such a move in the case of girls, since many parents feel that girls are not fit for the arduous and hazardous tasks of pioneering.

Difficulties of adjustment stem also from pressures inherent in life on a kibbutz. The limitation of family functions has but little effect on the husband's role. It entails, however, a radical change in the role of wife and mother. The curtailment of family duties means, in the case of women, an almost complete transfer to "public" employment. Previous socialization and external influences prevent a smooth and whole-hearted acceptance of this radical change. Another important factor operative in this process is a certain disappointment with the results of the change. Women are mainly concentrated in occupations and tasks which are closely allied with traditional housekeeping, and they very often feel that they might as well perform these tasks within the confines of their own homes rather than within the framework of large-scale and specialized communal institutions.

The familistic pattern has a number of crucial advantages over the collectivistic pattern as far as individual women are concerned. The daily schedule of the worker in communal institutions is more uniform than the schedule of a housewife who combines, in each day, different types of activities—budgeting, shopping, cleaning, cooking, and child care. The collectivistic work schedule is in addition less flexible—it requires strict punctuality and careful coordination, whereas the rhythm of work of a housewife is more readily adaptable to personal inclinations. Workers in communal institutions are part of a team: they depend on the cooperation of their colleagues and are placed in a hierarchy of control. By comparison, the housewife is more independent in performing her tasks. There is also the difficult problem of rendering satisfactory service and measuring achievement. There are comparatively few objective and unequivocal standards of excellence in this sphere, and evaluation of the services depends to a large extent on subjective preferences. Criticism by "clients" is almost unavoidable and, since encounters with them are frequent and repetitive, intensive and immediate, it can be particularly painful. Communal service institutions vary considerably in this respect but the more frequent, regular, and direct the contact is, and the greater the intensity of involvement of "clients" with the service rendered, the stronger is the pressure of their discontent (37, 147). Intimate knowledge of every member of her family enables the housewife to comply with individual wishes. There is also less variation of tastes within one family than in the community at large, and it is therefore easier to find a common denominator. Most important of all, the familistic pattern is more personalized: the housewife renders services to those closest and dearest to her; her daily activities serve as a symbolic reaffirmation of a diffuse and comprehensive lifelong loyalty and affection. By comparison, the collectivistic pattern of service seems to be an impersonal routine. The difficulties inherent in women's roles are enhanced by the fact that, in spite of the equalitarian ideology, there is a considerable differentiation of occupational status, and service institutions rank lower than productive labor. Women are highly conscious of, and deeply concerned with, these problems and refer to them often. In many cases there is a tendency to idealize the domestic pattern and refer to it with nostalgic yearning.

It should be noted that the relative position of women and men varies in different types of kibbutzim. In the bunds women are only a little more familistic than men. In federated communes they are considerably more familistic than men. While men in federated communes are only somewhat more familistic than the men in the bunds, women are considerably more familistic than their counterparts in the bunds. The gap between the sexes narrows again in unified communes—both men and women tend toward familism, and men are only a little less familistic than women. The gap is almost closed in factional communes; both men and women advocate far-reaching changes of the position of the family, and there is hardly any difference between them in this respect. It is significant that all along the continuum from nonfamilism to familism women take the lead, and the gap between the sexes is closed only when the men catch up with the women and adopt a clearcut position in favor of the familistic innovations. Women are, in fact, the main agents of the familistic trend and initiate most of the changes in this sphere.

Comparative analysis of the first and second generations is yet another way of assessing initiation of change within the family (115, 116). In the category of second generation we include adult members who were educated in the kibbutz since early childhood. Most members of the second generation in our sample are comparatively young. Having only recently completed their education in communal institutions, they are still under the influence of the systematic indoctrination received there. They have not yet grown out of their age group, and tend to participate in its activities. The influence of communal socialization and the integration of the cohesive peer group counteract the familistic trend that is now so prevalent in the first generation. Generally speaking, and as far as most of the major issues are concerned, the second generation is less familistic than the first.

Comparison of the members of the second generation with members of the bunds links the typological with intrafamily analysis. This examination enables us to neutralize demographic factors that we could not isolate in the comparative analysis of bunds and communes. Both groups, second generation members and members of bunds, are almost identical as to distribution according to age and family status. Yet they are fundamentally different from the point of view of the process of institutionalization. Joining the collective movement entails, in the case of members of bunds, an act of conscious decision and a break with one's parents. Members of the second generation are born into their kibbutz and are expected to continue to live there. They are, in addition, influenced by the familistic trend emerging in their kibbutz. These considerations have led us to expect that members of the second generation would be more familistic than members of the bunds, and this hypothesis was corroborated on most major issues.

The hypothesis that the second generation will occupy an intermediate position between members of long-established communes and members of recently established bunds is based on the assumption that members of the second generation are under two influences pulling in opposite directions—recent collective socialization and identification with the peer group on the one hand, and the familistic trend emerging in their kibbutz on the other. That this analysis is basically sound is made manifest by the fact that the tendency to oppose familism is most marked in matters that are regarded as an integral part of the collective ideology inculcated by educational institutions. When it comes to matters that are not explicitly dealt with by educational institutions, members of the second generation take a much more familistic stand.

The role of communal education in temporarily holding in check the familistic trend is also made manifest by an examination of the social maturation of kibbutz-born children. Comparison of adolescents who are still studying in a secondary school with adult members of the second generation indicates that, generally speaking, the younger age groups that are still under the aegis of communal education are less familistic than the older age groups, and that the older the age group—the closer to full maturity—the more familistic it is. The waning of the influence of communal education and the progressive assumption of adult roles also bring about the sex differentiation in attitudes toward the family found in the first generation. There is little such sex differentiation in groups of adolescents and young unmarried adults. The pattern found in the first generation is reproduced in the second generation in a somewhat attenuated way. The differentiation is not very sharp, but second generation women seem to revert to familism earlier and are more familistic than men.

MAINTAINING COLLECTIVE PATTERNS

The transformation described above clearly indicates that the kibbutz has moved far from the antifamilistic pole. It should be stressed, however, that there are powerful internal pressures that block the trend toward familism. The tendency to revert to a familistic division of labor is held in check by two major restraining factors: (a) the continuing strength of collectivist emphasis, and (b) the tendency to rationalize and specialize organizational units. The attenuation of the collectivist ideology and the shift to intergenerational continuity ease the tension between the family and the community, but the basic rivalry does not disappear. Inasmuch as the family accepts the primacy of collective considerations, it may become a valuable ally; inasmuch as it resents a subordinate position and disputes the authority of collective institutions, it is still a potential source of conflict and competition. The collectivist emphasis is now much more moderate and more tolerant of differentiation, but the tendency to limit and control the family is still operative. Furthermore, the attenuation of the collectivist restraints is partly counterbalanced by a considerable increase in the emphasis on rationalization and specialization of the economic structure of the kibbutz. This accelerated process of rationalization counteracts the tendency to revert to a nonspecialized and small-scale domestic pattern.

The presence of such internal restraining factors accounts for the fact that, structurally speaking, the kibbutz has remained basically nonfamilistic. Both husband and wife work full-time in communal institutions, and most goods and services are supplied to members directly by the community. Parents make an extremely significant and indispensable contribution to the socialization of their children, but the center of gravity has remained in communal institutions. The main responsibility for preparing the children for their roles as adult members of the kibbutz rests with the educators. Parents have only a limited influence on the placement of their children and on their choice of occupation. The family in the kibbutz has a strong affective orientation; it emphasizes intimacy and exclusiveness. In itself, the family is hardly fit to prepare the child for life in the kibbutz, with its emphasis on togetherness and sharing and with its highly rationalized work-centered economic system.

There is also the problem of social control in adult society. The kibbutz makes many demands on its members, but employs only a few formal means of control. Allocation of material rewards is unrelated to position or performance, and there are almost no formal sanctions in cases of faulty execution of tasks or of deviance. The proper functioning of the system depends primarily on the voluntary identification of kibbutz members with collective aims and ideals. The family represents the private sphere. If it becomes an independent, largely self-sufficient and powerful unit, it is bound to undermine the primacy of collective considerations. Comprehensive ties among members which are based on a shared ideology and common objectives may be easily superseded by divisive and narrow loyalties based on kinship affiliation.

Kibbutzim are very much aware of the dangers inherent in the disengagement of the family from the collective. They have tried to check this trend by reinforcing the nonfamilistic division of labor and have gone about it in two apparently opposing ways. Most important is the drive to improve the efficiency of services by means of an intensive process of rationalization, mechanization, and professionalization of service branches. Until recently, collective organization of consumption lagged far behind production. At least part of the discontent that led to the resumption of family functions stemmed from the fact that service institutions were given very limited resources and were not effectively organized. Most service branches operated with a minimum budget and with inadequate and outdated equipment. Kibbutzim are now reorganizing and mechanizing all their service institutions. In doing so, they draw on the experience accumulated in the kibbutzim and on the advice of various experts from the outside. They make a persistent effort to develop scientifically tested techniques in the sphere of housekeeping and child care, and to turn these occupations into semiprofessions. Workers in these fields are sent to acquire professional training in institutions outside the community. The federations organize seminars and refresher courses in home economics, nursing, and child care in which members get some theoretical grounding and practical guidance. The training is kept up and continued by means of extensive reading in semiscientific literature and occasional lectures. These efforts have a considerable effect on services and children's institutions. A process of gradual but cumulative improvement sets in, and communal institutions are able to render much more satisfactory services.

The efficiency drive leads to the formulation of precisely defined and fixed regulations and to a certain formalization of communication and control. While raising efficiency, the process entails standardization and often also leads to rigidity and imposed uniformity. Specialized bureaucratic agencies are effective in coping with repetitive routine tasks, but are not equally capable of solving idiosyncratic personal problems (86, 94). There is an inherent tendency in such agencies to treat situations and people "by the book"; they tend to assume similarity of needs, and to disregard individual inclinations and tastes. The kibbutzim make a special effort to avoid undue uniformization and inflexibility. They have counteracted the dysfunctions entailed in the process of bureaucratization by widening the margin of permitted variation and by allowing their members more freedom of choice. The workers in charge of the communal kitchen and dining hall make special efforts to cater to different tastes by diversifying their menus and offering as many alternatives as possible. The range of consumer choice has become much wider than it used to be, and personal predilections are not disregarded. To cite another important example, the schedule in the children's houses has become much more flexible, and parents have more free access to them. Within certain clearly circumscribed limits, parents are given a free hand. Communal institutions consciously cultivate a homelike, pleasant atmosphere, and the workers in charge of them are enjoined to treat members in a considerate and attentive manner. The task of inducing a process of bureaucratization and starting a counteracting process of debureaucratization, both at the same time, is a difficult one,

but it is not insurmountable. Kibbutzim in which this policy was im-
plemented in a systematic way have managed to formalize their institutional structure and still to avoid many of the dysfunctions entailed
in such a process.

Rationalization and professionalization are also employed to remedy
the effects of sex-role differentiation. The discrepancy between equalitarian ideology and everyday reality is a source of severe strain. The
advantages of the collectivist pattern are lost sight of while the disadvantages loom very large. Reorganization can help to redress the balance. The communal pattern cultivates a variety of talents and capabilities by specialization and systematic training. It enables workers to
develop high levels of competence and encourages them to perfect
their mastery of certain spheres of activity. The work schedule in
communal institutions is more rigid than the domestic schedule. On the
other hand it is based on a clear-cut dichotomy between working hours
and off hours and does not drag on intermittently during the day and
evening. During off hours the wife is not overburdened by routine
duties and can use her free time for relaxation, for study, or for participation in public affairs. She may choose to use much of her leisure for
furthering her training in her special field. She may, on the other hand,
prefer to pursue and cultivate other interests in order to counterbalance
excessive specialization in her job. Domesticity constricts the wife and
limits her perspective on life in the community at large. Work in communal institutions gives rise to more varied and more comprehensive
contacts and opens up a wider scope for achievement. Inasmuch as
communal institutions foster experimentation with new techniques and
modes of organization, it provides her with many opportunities to
exercise her ingenuity and organizational capacity. Most important of
all, work in communal institutions enables women to make a direct
contribution to the community as a whole and not just to the few members of their family.

Professionalization and institutionalization are the most important
aspects of the process which makes manifest the hidden potentialities
of the collectivist pattern. The professional aura enhances the prestige
of jobs in housekeeping and child care and establishes them as full-
fledged occupations. The specialized training supplies certain objective
criteria of excellence. The position of these women as competent ex-

perts bolsters their status vis-à-vis their "clients" and protects them from excessive criticism. Since the rights and duties involved in each job are more clearly spelled out, there is less tension in the team and fewer complaints from clients.

Female occupations require different amounts of vocational training and are therefore not equally amenable to professionalization. This distinction also applies to the different tasks involved in each occupation. Some tasks are more specialized than others. Certain jobs resist the efforts of mechanization and professionalization and are not easily transformed into intrinsically satisfying activities. Certain aspects of women's work remain arduous, monotonous, or full of tension. There are also considerable differences in evaluation—child care and nursing are considered more valuable and more worthwhile than food preparation or care of clothes. Permanent assignment to any of the difficult and less desirable tasks entails a serious curtailment of chances for job satisfaction. In the past this problem was solved by means of job rotation and quick turnover. Professionalization of women's work entails the introduction of a more or less prolonged period of training as well as a systematic accumulation of experience. It precludes quick turnover and presupposes considerable continuity in job allocation. Professionalization resolves many of the tensions involved in women's work; yet, inasmuch as it enhances the tendency to permanent assignment, it sharpens the struggle over specialized occupations and imposes permanent deprivation on those assigned to unspecialized jobs.

This dilemma has led to the emergence of an intermediate composite pattern based on an ingenious combination of long-term and short-term assignments. The tendency to professionalization predominates, but it does not do away with job rotation. Recruitment for the hard core of unspecialized chores that most members regard as irksome and distasteful is still dealt with mainly by means of short-term rotation, and the workers engaged in performing them change in quick succession. The supply of workers to unpopular jobs that require more training and experience is managed by means of a temporary recruitment for longer terms of service. Assignment and training at permanent jobs are preceded by a fairly protracted period of trial. Before settling down in one specific occupation, each member tries his hand at a number of different jobs and has a chance to discover which of them suits him best. Assignment to a permanent job slows down mobility but does not stop it completely. Each member works most of the time in his special field, but he is expected to participate in the system of rotation and is transferred now and then to some other field. Moreover, choice of a specialized occupation is a decisive step toward stability and more specialization, though it does not close the door to further readjustments. If the worker gets into a rut and loses interest, or if he is no longer as good at his job as he used to be, he need not feel trapped in his career. The choice of a particular specialty is not irrevocable. Diversification of activities is combined with varying degrees of specialization, and continuity of career does not preclude controlled mobility.[22]

The reorganization of service institutions and the composite pattern of job allocation relieve the tension inherent in women's roles, but they do not provide a full solution. Sex-role differentiation is one of the major sources of strain, and attempts to cope with it have led to the emergence of additional secondary institutional mechanisms that partly bridge the gap between the equalitarian ideology and actual practice. Kibbutzim are making persistent and systematic efforts to diversify the job choices open to women. The opportunities available to them in the kibbutz are rather limited, but the range of choice is widened by branching out into new spheres of activity. A recent development in this area is the beginning of a training program in social work, psychotherapy, and counseling. Training in arts and crafts provides additional openings. A considerable increase of suitable employment opportunities results from the development of local industries and crafts.

Diversification of female occupations occurs also by means of a policy aimed at reducing to a minimum the number of exclusively feminine and exclusively masculine spheres of activity. Kibbutzim often develop new branches of work which are suitable for both men and women. They try to achieve proportional or nearly proportional representation in as many committees as possible, and pressure is put on the women to accept nomination. The nomination committee will often prefer a female candidate to a male one of equal or even better qualifications. This balancing mechanism serves as an antidote to the limiting effects of occupational sex role differentiation and overcomes to some extent women's reluctance to accept office. Apprenticeship in a committee enables women to gain experience and to develop new interests and new

22. For a discussion of patterns of job allocation which counteract excessive specialization, see Friedmann (48) and Riesman (109).

skills. Quite a number of women who were at first self-deprecating and very insecure in their new role have gradually become active and competent participants in the deliberations of their committee. Such an "equilibrating" system of recruitment helps to discover untapped energies and hidden talents, and opens up many new avenues of satisfying and worthwhile activity.

The persistence of specifically feminine and specifically masculine roles is partly neutralized by the participation of men in specifically feminine roles and vice versa. Kibbutzim make a point of assigning a number of men to specifically female occupations on a temporary basis. The most important example is participation of men in work in the kitchen and dining hall. They are drafted by a system of rotation in which each man serves a two- to three-month period. Most of the men serve in the dining hall where everyone can see them daily. Similar mechanisms operate in the family, too, for example when fathers take their children out for walks or put them to bed in the children's houses.

Participation of men in female tasks has a practical value, but its main significance lies in its symbolic meaning as "atonement" for differentiation. Essentially, it is a token interchangeability. Women participate in masculine tasks much more and for much longer periods than men do in feminine tasks. Young girls and women are assigned to work in male occupations for a number of years. When they grow older and have children they leave these occupations and settle down in services and child care. Work in productive labor is regarded as an indispensable rite of passage for most women. A more durable crossing of the lines occurs only in exceptional cases: kibbutzim encourage women who continue to work in administration and central committees to hold out as long as they can. These exceptions to the rule serve as living "proof" that there is no deliberate discrimination. The exemplary life stories of the women who have achieved equality in spite of serious difficulties travel far and wide in all kibbutzim and have become an important part of popular lore. Some of these women have become heroic figures.

In some kibbutzim one may discern signs of the emergence of a cyclic pattern. This pattern is based on an extension of the composite pattern of job allocation. It institutionalizes a sequence of changes of occupation during the woman's life coupled with patterned shifts from one institutional sphere to another. During the first phase of the cycle, the main emphasis is on joint participation in the occupational system. As long as they are young and have no children, women tend to concentrate on either predominantly masculine or joint occupations. After they bear children, they settle down in services and child care and become engrossed in family affairs. When the children grow up and the mothers have more free time, they put more emphasis on social participation. The second phase is based on considerable sex differentiation, but it is preceded and followed by more equalitarian stages. The cyclic pattern is not rigid and allows for many combinations and variations. It does not try to erase sex differentiation completely, but neither does it yield to polarization and segregation. It takes into full consideration the developmental aspects of family life and defines the interrelations between the external systems and the internal family system accordingly. It combines equality and differentiation in an ordered but continually changing pattern.

The familistic trend is very strong in most kibbutzim, and in many of them it seems to be gaining momentum. It is not easily curbed, but reorganization and a host of special devices lately evolved do have some effect. In some notable cases, reorganization has brought about a partial reversal of trends. Families have relinquished some of their newly acquired tasks and communal institutions are taking over again. This partial reversal of trends is particularly noticeable in the case of the communal kitchen and dining hall. In a number of kibbutzim we were able to witness a partial return to the dining hall. Before the reorganization, it was very sparsely attended during the evening meal and at times looked almost deserted. But prompt service, clean, comfortable, and cheerfully decorated new halls, and good and varied food made communal dining much more attractive than it used to be, and won over many of the adherents of the domestic pattern. Cooking and eating at home have not disappeared completely even after the reorganization; wives still like to cook or bake for their families on occasion. The communal kitchen is sometimes used as a take-out service: the food is brought ready-made to the home and consumed there after reheating and minor finishing touches. But most families now take most of their meals in the communal dining hall. Well-run flexible communal institutions make manifest the advantages inherent in large-scale and specialized organization, and can supply satisfactory services which do not compare unfavorably with home cooking. Under such circumstances, there is little tendency to turn preparation and consumption of food at home into a regular practice. Such a routine is felt to be burdensome, and too much trouble after a full day's work. Cooking and dining at home serve as an outlet for the occasional urge to experiment with food, or for the wish to enjoy the privacy of a family meal now and then. The familistic pattern ceases to be a competing alternative that makes increasingly large inroads into the collectivistic pattern; it becomes a secondary mechanism—a complementary rather than a competing solution.

Reorganization and progressive professionalization check to some extent the familistic trend in the sphere of child rearing as well. The mistrust and discontent that parents feel toward the communal children's institutions stem primarily from the tensions inherent in the collectivist pattern itself, but the uneasiness and resentment are enhanced by faulty organization and shortage of skilled and fully trained personnel. Collective socialization has been tried under far from optimal conditions. Maintenance of educational institutions on a high level and unflagging efforts to develop and improve them bolster the confidence of parents in communal socialization and decrease the pressure for familistic innovations. Building children's houses that are fully equipped and fully adapted to the needs of the children, careful calculation of the size of the groups and the adult-children ratio, modification of methods of recruitment and training of educators, critical appraisal and revision of educational methods—all increase the chances of success. Also of considerable importance in the same context are the attempts to regularize the contacts and improve the communication between parents and the specialized personnel in charge of their children. Special efforts are now made to draw parents into participation in activities in the children's houses and to enlist their cooperation in contacts with their children at home.

Kibbutzim vary appreciably in their capacity to withstand and arrest the tendency toward familism. The more persistent the efforts to evolve supplementary institutional mechanisms and the more systematic and determined their implementation, the more noticeable is the reversal of trends. Ultimately, the capacity to curb familism is related to the degree of intensity of collective identification. The less pronounced the primacy of communal ideals and the weaker the sense of togetherness, the stronger the appeal of familistic innovations.

Although the antifamilism of the revolutionary phase has abated, it has not disappeared altogether. It has been superseded by a moderate collectivism which regards the family as a useful if sometimes dangerous ally. Kibbutzim still try to control and limit the family and direct it toward the attainment of collective goals. The main problem of the kibbutzim from a dynamic point of view is how to allow the family more privacy and a certain internal autonomy without harming the cohesion of the community.

2. Social Structure and Family Size

The average number of children per family in kibbutzim was for years one of the lowest in the country. In the early 1940s it was in fact below the level of replacement.[1] Fertility of families in kibbutzim was somewhat lower than that among city dwellers and much lower than fertility of families in cooperative settlements. Families in kibbutzim who were originally from areas that showed high fertility had a much lower rate than the areas from which they had come. The kibbutz's mode of life leveled down and standardized fertility norms of all families within it.[2]

Examination of the data from the 1950s[3] shows a rapid and considerable increase in fertility, making the fertility rate in kibbutzim higher than that in towns. The upward trend seems to be cumulative and persistent and apparently cannot be viewed as just a temporary change typical of a postwar period.[4]

But here I shall not engage in a detailed statistical analysis of fertility in kibbutzim. I shall take more or less for granted the reversal of trends and shall try to account for it by relating it to processes of social and ideological change. My main emphasis will be on an analysis of the interrelation between the redefinition of ideological patterns and norms

NOTE. This essay previously appeared in *Human Relations*, volume 12 (1956).
1. In 1941–42 gross reproduction rate in kibbutzim was 0.8 as compared to 1.12 for the country as a whole. See Gil (52).
2. For a detailed analysis of fertility differentials in this period, see Bachi (2, 3, 4), Gabriel (49), and Talmon-Garber (133).
3. This trend is evident in a study conducted by R. Bachi in one of the Federations of kibbutzim.
4. In 1953–54 gross reproduction rate in kibbutzim was 1.75 as compared with the urban rate of 1.64. The gross rate for the population as a whole was 1.80 children per family. See Gil (52).

pertaining to family size on the one hand and major changes in the position of the family in the community on the other.

NORMS PERTAINING TO FAMILY SIZE

The different aspects of our problem were explored by means of questions in interviews with representative members of kibbutzim. I shall sum up the results of this inquiry for the sample as a whole, and then proceed to a comparative analysis.

The first question was formulated as follows: "In your opinion, what should be the number of children per family in the kibbutz?" It should be stressed that we aimed at isolating norms, not at ascertaining personal aspirations.[5] The respondent was asked to state what he considered a proper family size without necessarily referring to his personal plans in this respect. At the exploratory stage of our project we had included a question about personal aspirations but soon found that it very often aroused discomfort and embarrassment. Many respondents refused altogether to answer it or soon switched to a discussion of the problem in general. As we were anxious not to strain the atmosphere in which the interviews were held, we abandoned exploration of aspirations and confined ourselves to isolating norms.

The classification of answers to this question revealed a number of distinct normative patterns of ideal family size:[6] (a) A small family pattern: one or two children. (b) A medium family pattern: three or four children. (c) A large family pattern: five, six, and "the more, the better." Other categories of responses were: (d) Objection to establishing a general norm: "Should be decided by the couple concerned." (e) "Don't know": failure to establish a general norm, either because of inability to reach any definite decision or because of lack of interest. (f) No information.

Table 1 shows that the small family pattern is referred to by a very small percentage of the sample. A single respondent thought that there should be only one child per family. About half of the respondents opt for the medium and about a quarter for the large family pattern. Most of the last group object to any limitation on family size. Some do not

5. For an attempt to analyze personal aspirations and plans with respect to family size, see Groenman (63), Muhsam and Kiser (95), and Diels (25).

6. For a similar analysis, see Freedman, Goldberg, and Sharp (47). A full bibliography of articles and books dealing with this problem may be found in Westoff, Mishler, and Kelly (146).

Table 1. Distribution of answers pertaining to norms of family size (percent; $N = 415$)

Accepting a Kibbutz norm								Rejecting a Kibbutz norm	Don't know	No information
Small family		Medium family			Large family					
1	2	3	4	3–4	5	6+	++			
0.2	5.3	20.4	16.8	10.8	6	1.2	16.8	9.6	5.0	8.0
	5.5		48.0			24.0		9.6	5.0	8.0

mention any pattern, either because they are against fixing any general norm or because they are hesitant or uninterested. The pattern of the medium family predominates. The large family is much more favored than the small family and a little more common than refusal or failure to fix a general norm.

IDEOLOGICAL PATTERNS

Analysis of the reasons given for the preference of a certain norm of family size elucidates the considerations on which these norms are based. For the classification of these considerations we used two basic cross-cutting criteria. On the one hand we distinguished between arguments favoring limitation and arguments favoring expansion of family size. On the other hand we examined the context or orientation of the argument, that is, whether it is kibbutz-oriented, family-oriented, or individual-oriented.

In the category of kibbutz-centered considerations, arguments were advanced in favor of limitation as well as of expansion. Family-centered considerations all tended toward expansion, whereas individual-centered considerations were, with very few exceptions, in favor of restriction. Four distinct ideological patterns emerge from this classification: kibbutz-oriented limitation; kibbutz-oriented expansion; family-oriented expansion; individual-oriented limitation.

In the subsequent discussion it will be shown that the patterns of collective-centered and individual-centered limitation are based on diametrically opposed principles and that the pattern of kibbutz-centered expansion is fundamentally different from the pattern of family-centered expansion.

The pattern of kibbutz-oriented limitation. Kibbutz-oriented arguments for limitation of family size are rooted in social and economic considerations. Most of these arguments refer to the first stages of kibbutz development. There are, however, a few kibbutz-centered arguments favoring limitation that seem to be anchored in the structure and values of the kibbutz as such.

Let us look first at arguments based on social considerations. Limitation of the number of children seems in this regard to be a manifestation of the general tendency to limit the functions of the family and prevent its consolidation as a semiindependent unit. Children are of crucial importance here because they are the main focus of a segregated family life in the kibbutz. Inasmuch as intensive collective identification disrupts family solidarity, it seems also to curb the desire for children.

Birth of children raises problems in the kibbutz for yet another reason. Kibbutz ideology tended to disregard sex differentiation and set up a masculine image of the feminine role. The role model of both men and women requires wholehearted devotion to work in communal institutions and active participation in public activities. The emphasis put on activities outside the family orbit and the masculine role prototype would seem to prevent any intense identification with the specifically and typically feminine roles of wife and mother.

Very few members are aware of the impact on fertility rates of tension between the family and the kibbutz. Only occasionally is the issue hinted at in remarks such as: "Families with children tend to keep to themselves"; "Most parents are not as active as they used to be"; "Whether you admit it or not, the establishment of families at an early age and the birth of a number of children undermine the kibbutz. Without our noticing it the center of gravity has shifted considerably."

The quotations cited refer to the first stages of development of the settlements. Once or twice we find a more general and more explicit formulation: "Formation of large families is not compatible with our constant emphasis on participation in collective activities. Parents, especially mothers of a number of children, withdraw to their private sphere. They do not and cannot bother with communal affairs."

Let us now look at the economic aspects of the problem. A high birthrate is a liability to the kibbutz, especially in the first stages of building up a productive economic enterprise. The percentage of women in newly established kibbutzim is relatively small (20 to 30 percent of the membership); almost all are young and get married at approximately the same time. Pregnant women are transferred to lighter tasks; breast-feeding mothers work only part time. Frequent births are liable to remove most of them from regular work and seriously disorganize work assignments.

Moreover, the birth of children entails the transfer of workers to services and child care, and the number of workers employed in productive work is significantly lowered. The same is true for the direction of capital and resources to unproductive goals. The standard of living of adults is flexible and can be lowered to permit increased investment in expanding production. Children, on the other hand, especially infants, have indispensable needs which must be satisfied. The kibbutzim try to maintain a high standard of child care even in the most difficult circumstances. The building of children's houses and of schools requires considerable basic capital investment. Children are an economic liability for another reason. The process of socialization and social maturation is a prolonged one in the kibbutz. All children are granted a secondary school education. They combine study and some work all through their school years but their work is of limited economic value and therefore it does not contribute much toward their maintenance. Assumption of full-time work is postponed at least until completion of army service (two to three years). The kibbutz has to maintain the children until they reach full maturity.

Respondents who referred to economic considerations in this context were aware of most of the problems mentioned here: "The kibbutz cannot afford to allow members to have large families. Parents have to accept conditions as they are. We came here to build up our kibbutz in the midst of the desert and we have to stick to our job." "We will never get out of economic difficulties if most women are unable for years to do a full day's work." "A lot of children means a lot of work and expenses for the kibbutz—we have to be careful." "The economic situation determines the number of children the kibbutz can raise if we do not want to endanger its sound economic development and if we are to maintain the high standards of child care and education." "Families have to be fully aware of the economic position of their kibbutz and plan the number of children accordingly."

The distribution of collective-oriented arguments in favor of restriction of the number of children is presented in Table 2. Economic considerations were mentioned more than twice as often as social considerations. The social implications of restriction are latent and were noticed and commented upon only by particularly perceptive respondents.

Table 2. Kibbutz-oriented restriction pattern

Type of consideration	Number of references	percent
Economic	29	54
Social	12	22
Other	14	24
Total	55	100

The overt legitimation of the ideology of kibbutz-centered restriction rests mainly on economic considerations.

The pattern of kibbutz-oriented expansion. Most kibbutz-centered arguments in favor of restriction of number of children refer to kibbutzim in the first stages of their development. Most kibbutz-centered arguments in favor of a high birthrate refer to fully established and stable communities.

The thinking here is based predominantly on considerations of demographic-ideological continuity and expansion. These considerations are closely connected with the proselytizing spirit of the collective movement. The movement views itself as an avant-garde of a future society; it hopes to set an example and to convert large sections of the Israeli society. As long as the main emphasis was put on ideological conversion and as long as reinforcements to the kibbutzim flowed mainly from youth movements and training centers, natural increase was of only secondary importance. But the dwindling of external recruitment sources and the difficulties experienced by the kibbutzim in absorption of new immigrants have greatly enhanced the importance of natural increase as a means of ensuring continuity and growth. Emphasis has shifted from recruitment of volunteers from outside to expansion from within.

Many respondents are fully aware of this reorientation and commented upon it frequently. To quote just a few of these remarks: "A high birthrate ensures the future of the kibbutz—only children guarantee stable growth and continuity." "We must have many children—outside sources are drying up. The less reinforcement we get from outside the more important becomes the birthrate. On this we ourselves can decide and are not dependent on others." "Bringing up as many children as possible should be regarded as one of the basic duties of the family in the kibbutz—we need a large reserve to ensure our future."

A high birthrate is also regarded as a national duty. For some respondents this duty is derived from the fate of the Jewish people: "So many of our people have been massacred in the Diaspora—these losses must be made up." Some look at it from the point of view of the state: "The future of the state depends on it." Occasionally all these arguments are linked together. The need for more children is derived from the role the kibbutzim are to play within the state: "We need children not only to guarantee our own future; we must put part of our second generation at the disposal of the state. The army, guidance of new immigrants, border settlements, youth movements—we will be able to participate in all that only if we have many children."

Respondents who recommend expansion regard the family as a major ally of the kibbutz. The growth of the family helps a member to strike roots and feel at home: "The kibbutz becomes a real home, the place where my children were born." "A family with many children takes roots in the kibbutz; with each additional child the family becomes less mobile, less inclined to leave." Many are convinced that a large family has educational advantages over a small family and serves as a good preparation for membership in the kibbutz: "In a large family many antisocial traits are avoided. The children have to help each other whether they like it or not. Egoistical tendencies are thus weakened."

What about the economic considerations that were so prominent in the pattern of collective-centered restriction? Some economic considerations seem to be rooted in the structure of the kibbutz as such, notably those stemming from the organization of women's work and from the long process of socialization of children. It should be stressed, however, that most of these considerations lose at least part of their weight in long-established kibbutzim, which are better able to afford lighter work loads for pregnant women and mothers, and the expenses of child care and education. There emerge instead some economic arguments in favor of large families. Most prominent among them is the need to prepare a labor force for the future: "We always suffer from shortage of labor. Large families mean workers, many workers, for the future." The more economical use of educational facilities is also taken into account: "Children's institutions come cheaper when they are used by more children." "Our teachers teach half-empty classes. We do not make full use of existing facilities." "It is possible to build up efficient and well-organized children's institutions only when there are many children and well-balanced age groups."

Kibbutz-oriented respondents who favor restriction usually confine themselves to considerations of the interest of their kibbutz. Those who tend to expansion very often reinforce their kibbutz-oriented arguments with enumeration of the advantages that a large family enjoys in the kibbutz: "We have economic security—we need not be afraid of the future." "Our children are sure to get a good education, no matter how many there are." "Here one can raise a large family without giving up one's occupation and without shutting oneself off from the community." "Only in a kibbutz can one raise a large family without becoming completely enslaved to one's children—communal institutions share the burden." Prominent among the advantages mentioned in this context is the relative freedom of movement of the parents: "The evening is free for recreation and social activity—one is not tied down to one's room." "The birth of many children is not the end of everything. It is not necessarily a prolonged retreat. It is still possible to continue to study and to participate in the social life of the community." "It is not uncommon in our kibbutz for either of the parents to attend various short courses outside the kibbutz or even to get long-term leave for advanced study."

The comparatively frequent comment on the advantages enjoyed by the family in the kibbutz shows that the kibbutz-oriented policy of expansion is viewed as compatible with the interests of the family.

The distribution of references to kibbutz-centered considerations in favor of large families is shown in Table 3. Reference to the kibbutz predominates. It is mentioned more frequently than the state, the Jewish people, or the family. Ideological-social considerations are more frequent than economic ones.

The pattern of family-oriented expansion. The kibbutz-oriented argument for expansion puts a premium on kibbutz considerations. The

Table 3. Kibbutz-oriented expansion pattern

Reference to	Number of references	percent
The state or the Jewish people	48	27
The Kibbutz:		
Ideological-social considerations	68	39
Organizational-economic considerations	39	23
The reciprocal relations between the family and the kibbutz	20	11
Total	175	100

interests of the family are of secondary importance and are brought up only inasmuch as they are conducive to the common good. In the family-centered pattern, kibbutz considerations recede and disappear. The family is not seen in its reciprocal relationship to the kibbutz. It is treated as an independent and self-sufficient unit. The number of children is discussed only insofar as it affects the family.

From our point of view, the most salient feature of this way of thinking is the considerable importance attached to kinship ties: "One's most constant and true friends are one's brothers and sisters, nobody can take their place. Without relatives one is alone in the world." In many of the references to relatives there is either a covert or overt note of disappointment with interpersonal ties based on common membership and common ideals: "We used to think that the ties that bind us to our comrades are much more significant and lasting. It turned out that you cannot rely on your fellow members"; or "In the midst of intensive collective activity you often feel so alone, so insignificant. It is only in one's family that one gets individual treatment and security—we must strengthen the family as much as possible."

The fear of loneliness and isolation is a recurring theme and it is one of the main reasons given for the high value attached to kinship: "A large family is a safeguard against loneliness. It keeps parents from getting old before their time. The parents will not remain alone, their children will always be around them." Quite a number of respondents referred to the possibility of losing children in war as a reason for recommending big families: "Constant insecurity on the borders will probably be our lot for many years to come. One must always reckon with the possibility of losing a son in battle. The future of the family may be shattered and destroyed forever. When there are other children one gets over the loss—one has a hold left on life." Some mention the extinction of their families in Europe: "I am the only one of our family who survived the massacre. I owe it to my family to rear many children and save it from extinction."

Children become a major source of happiness and satisfaction. Many respondents point out that children contribute to a richer and more varied family life: "I am all for large families. There is nothing more satisfying and more enjoyable." "A lot of children, big, small, babies, of both sexes—every additional child rejuvenates the family." "There is nothing better and more worthwhile than children—a large family is a real family—a self-contained world." Many respondents feel that children have a stabilizing effect on the family: "The parents have a common responsibility. Many children are the best safeguard against family instability."

There are also educational considerations. The kibbutz-centered expansion pattern emphasized preparation for communal life. The family-oriented responses, on the other hand, are confined to the sphere of family life: "Children take care of each other, they have suitable company within the family and it is easier to cope with them. They get used to helping one another and become less demanding of their parents." "The bigger ones help the small ones. The older children will develop a sense of duty and loyalty and the younger ones will have more security."

Family-oriented respondents tend to be more critical of collective organization than are kibbutz-oriented respondents. They mention some of the advantages but are fully aware of all the difficulties. One of the main complaints against collective organization in relation to large families is the difficulty of combining full-time employment of both parents with the duties of bringing up a family: "The mother comes home completely worn out from long hours of work in communal institutions and finds her house full of children clamoring for her care and attention—the burden is very heavy." Even more numerous are the complaints against the splitting up into age groups and the limitation of contacts with children: "The separation of children of different ages makes things very difficult. You have got to run from one building to the next." "Each child lives in a separate group, each age group has its own arrangements, its own problems, its own schedule. There is no integrated care of all children and it is difficult to stay on top of everything." "The contact with the children is concentrated in a few short hours. You are being torn to pieces." "You pay for the free evening— the afternoon is hectic and full of tension." One of the respondents sums up: "The disadvantages of communal organization very often outweigh the advantages. A large family carries a heavy load—but still, it is worth all the trouble!"

The distribution of family-centered arguments for expansion is shown in Table 4. References are almost equally distributed among the four main categories.

Table 4. Family-oriented expansion pattern

Reference to	Number of references	percent
Stability	25	24
Security against loneliness	20	19
Richer family life	25	24
Educational considerations	22	21
Other	13	12
Total	105	100

The pattern of individual-oriented limitation. All patterns described up to this point are rooted in a sense of duty and commitment to a more comprehensive social unit—the Jewish people, the state, the kibbutz, or one's family. The pattern of individual-oriented limitation is self-centered. The wish for a comfortable life, for leisure, for unhampered personal development, predominates. Children are a welcome addition only insofar as they do not unduly restrict the freedom of their parents and do not prevent them from leading their own lives. The self-interest of the parents comes first. However, restriction is also recommended for the sake of the children. The main consideration is the undisturbed personal development of each member of the family. With a difference of emphasis and relative weight, we find here many of the arguments that serve as a rationale for family limitation in Western middle class families.[7]

Respondents who tend to individual-centered arguments for limitations are very often on the defensive: "I am in favor of a small family; I know that the kibbutz needs more children but nothing can convince me that it is one's duty to bring children into the world for the public good. That is one's own business; one has a right to live one's own life." Kibbutz organization minimizes the effect that the number of children has on continuity of work and on standard of living. Considerations of vocational training, continuity of work in one's vocation, and career advancement are rarely mentioned. References to apprehension concerning the possible lowering of the standard of living appear more often but are not very frequent either: "A large number of children will

7. See Welpton and Kiser (144), I, 1–137. A more systematic attempt to deal with the problem of family limitation may be found in Mishler and Westoff (93). See also Myrdal (97) and Jolles (73). An interesting and perceptive analysis of the emergence of a pattern of individual-oriented restriction in a primitive society is presented by Schneider (119).

make it necessary to lower the standard of living—we have suffered enough." "A large number of children means a heavy economic burden —we cannot afford that, it is time we had it a bit easier." Here concern is the standard of living and not sound economic development of the kibbutz.

The desire for convenience and the wish for more leisure are important elements in the arguments for limitation: "A large number of children make life difficult for the parents—the burden is too heavy." "Parents of large families are like beasts of burden—they have no time for anything else." "I want something out of life besides children—it makes one stupid; one is tied down, one has no time to have some fun or rest." It is often pointed out that the combination of work and family life imposes a necessary limitation on the number of children: "One is wrung out by one's work and does not feel like messing about with a lot of kids in the afternoon." "One has a right to some peace and quiet. A family where both parents work must be limited."

The effect of the number of children on the balance of relations in the family is another aspect of our problem. Very few are aware that in a large family the center of gravity necessarily shifts from the relations between husband and wife to their relations with their children. We found only a limited number of short yet penetrating comments: "Having many children affects the relation between husband and wife. The children slowly gain the center of the stage and the husband is neglected." "A woman should be a wife to her husband, not only the mother of his children."

The focus of the spouse-centered small family is the love relationship of husband and wife, and hence great emphasis is placed on the preservation of the youthful appearance of the wife by methodical beauty care. It is significant that in the kibbutz, considerations of beauty are hardly mentioned at all. It seems that the masculine role prototype still operates against an overt reference to cultivation of feminine charm.

We found a surprising amount of preoccupation with considerations of health. In fact, health reasons feature most prominently among the arguments against a large family. It is often taken for granted that "too many births have a very bad effect on the health of the mother." Sometimes the tone and wording of the argument suggest that reasons of health are used as a camouflage for considerations of preservation of a youthful appearance. "Frequent births ruin the woman completely—

they affect her health." "The woman becomes like a child-bearing machine—nothing is left of her. It is very bad for her health." Since cultivation of beauty is not quite acceptable and is usually met with ridicule, respondents prefer to put forward a "safer" argument, thus conferring a sort of objective legitimacy on considerations of personal appearance and convenience.

Recommendation of a small family pattern for the sake of the children is based on two arguments. Least mentioned in this context is the demand for the highest possible standards of education: "A large number of children lowers the standard of education." "Better to have fewer children and educate them properly."

Reference to the needs of children for individualized care and attention is frequent. This seems to be of particular importance to many parents: "A child needs personal care; it is impossible to give him individual attention in a family burdened with many children." The undivided attention and love of the parents is often regarded as an indispensable antidote to collective education. The child spends the greater part of his life in the age group of his peers. He is required to share with his peers almost everything he has. Only the parents belong to the child—and to him only. Only within his family does he cease to be one of many. Parents are often afraid that a large number of siblings will encroach upon the right of the child to be the center of attention: he should not have to compete with others while he is with his parents." "They get so little personal attention in their group. We try to make up for this deficiency. It would be almost impossible in a large family."

Limitation of the number of children is sometimes linked in demographic literature with an uncertain outlook for the future and with grave insecurity.[8] It is perhaps significant that pessimistic arguments are very rare here. Only one of our respondents sounded a note of anxiety and insecurity, saying: "Ours is an unstable world, cruel and essentially bad—we bring creatures into the world who are destined to be lonely and unhappy. We cannot do without them, but we must at least refrain from having many children." It should be stressed, however, that this type of argument was hardly touched on by anybody else. An atmosphere of optimism and hope prevailed throughout the interviews.

A last question remains to be asked: how does this pattern affect the

8. On an attempt to account in this way for the decrease of fertility of Jewish families in some European countries, see Bachi (2).

evaluation of collective organization from the point of view of the family? Respondents who tend to individual-centered limitation are on the whole critical of the kibbutz in this respect. They feel that engagement in full-time work by both parents and the task of trying to make up for the lack of individual attention in collective education impose a limitation on the number of children: "Even a small family has its difficulties here," says one of them.

The distribution of individual-oriented arguments in favor of limitation is shown in Table 5. Reference to the interests of the spouses is

Table 5. Individual-oriented limitation pattern

Reference to	Number of references	percent
Relationship between spouses	4	4
Beauty	1	1
Health	22	20
Convenience	20	18
Leisure and recreation	10	9
Standard of living	10	9
Vocational training and career	3	3
Individual care of children	20	18
Opportunity for better education	10	9
Other	10	9
Total	110	100

much more frequent than reference to the interests of the children. The individual-oriented pattern in the kibbutz is mainly based on considerations of the health and the convenience of parents and on considerations of individual care for the children.

Let us recapitulate our discussion by comparing the patterns of responses with respect to the evaluation of the position of the family inherent in each of them. In the pattern of kibbutz-oriented limitation the kibbutz reigns supreme. The kibbutz regards the family as a potential rival and limits its independent activities; the family accepts its subordinate position and limits its size for the sake of the kibbutz. The pattern of kibbutz-oriented expansion is also based on the primacy of collective considerations, but instead of a competitor the family here becomes a major ally. Identification with the family supports identification with the kibbutz; the family actively helps the kibbutz to ensure its continuity and growth. The family adopts the goals of the collective as its own.

It expands in order to strengthen the kibbutz and to ensure its future. The pattern of family-oriented expansion is family-centered. Kibbutz considerations become secondary. The family is considered mainly as an independent and self-sufficient unit. Kinship ties supersede the ties among members. The individual-oriented pattern of limitation is individual-centered. The undisturbed personal development of each member of the family is the main consideration.

Collective-oriented respondents who favor limitation are hardly aware of the problems of a large family; and those who favor expansion emphasize the advantages that the large family enjoys in the kibbutz. Family-oriented respondents, on the other hand, are aware of both advantages and disadvantages of the collective organization. A tendency toward individual-oriented limitation sharpens awareness of disadvantages. Perception and evaluation of objective conditions are thus directly affected by the respondent's perspective.

The distribution of references to the four patterns is seen in Table 6.

Table 6. Distribution of patterns of opinion

	percent *(N = 445)*
Kibbutz-oriented limitation	12
Kibbutz-oriented expansion	39
Family-oriented expansion	24
Individual-oriented limitation	25
Total	100

The table indicates that the pattern of kibbutz-oriented limitation is on the decline. The kibbutz-oriented expansion pattern is the most prevalent. Individual-oriented limitation is slightly more common than family-oriented expansion. The feeling for expansion of family size is at present much stronger than that for limitation. Reference to a comprehensive social unit such as the kibbutz or the society at large is more prevalent than reference to the family or to the individual.

COMPARATIVE ANALYSIS

So far we have presented findings for the sample as a whole. We are now able to turn to an analysis of typological and intrafamily differentiation, and to test thereby a number of hypotheses developed in theoretical discussion and through examination of our data. These hypotheses are, in brief: that communes are more familistic than bunds; that of the two subtypes of communes, the unified are more familistic than the federated; that women are more familistic than men and seem to be the main agents of the familistic trend; that the second generation will tend to be less familistic than the first generation, but considerably more familistic than members of bunds.[9]

Typological differentiation. The preceding discussion supplied two main indexes of "familism": advocacy of extension of family size; and reference to the family-oriented thinking pattern. Let us first examine the distribution of norms pertaining to family size.

As Table 7 shows, the pattern of the medium family predominates in

Table 7. Norms pertaining to family size in different types of kibbutzim (percent)

Types of kibbutzim	Small family	Medium family	Large family	Rejecting a kibbutz norm	Don't know	No information	Total
				Responses			
Bunds (N = 45)	18	37	4	6	26	9	100
Federated communes (N = 105)	13	46	12	11	6	12	100
Unified communes (N = 193)	—	47	37	7	2	7	100

all three types of kibbutzim. It is somewhat more prevalent in the communes than in the kibbutzim of the bund type. Very few respondents in the bunds refer to the pattern of the large family. This pattern is much more current in unified than in federated communes. Reference to the small family pattern occurs more often in bunds than in federated communes. It disappears completely in unified communes. Failure to establish a general norm because of inability to reach a definite decision or because of lack of interest is much more common in bunds than in communes.

9. For a discussion of the various terms involved, as well as of the general background against which these and other hypotheses were drawn up, see Chapter 1.

The medium family pattern seems to be gaining acceptance in all types of kibbutzim. There are considerable differences, however, among the three types as to the small family pattern, the large family pattern, and the category indicated by "don't know." In kibbutzim of the bund type the small family is more favored than the large family. About a quarter of the respondents were either hesitant or uninterested in the problem. In the federated communes references to the large family appear about as often as references to the small family while in unified communes the pattern of the small family has disappeared and more than a third of the respondents opt for the large family.

These differences are all in line with our hypotheses. The advocacy of expansion of family size is more frequent in unified communes; next in this respect come federated communes. It is least frequent in the bunds.

A pronounced typological differentiation emerges from a comparative analysis of patterns (Table 8). The kibbutz-oriented limitation pat-

Table 8. Patterns of opinion in different types of communes (percent)

Pattern	Bund (N = 40)	Federated communes (N = 135)	Unified communes (N = 193)
Kibbutz-oriented limitation	40	21	3
Kibbutz-oriented expansion	35	45	43
Family-oriented expansion	7	15	32
Individual-oriented limitation	18	19	22
Total	100	100	100

tern predominates in kibbutzim of the bund type. It is less common in federated communes and almost disappears in unified ones. The kibbutz-oriented expansion pattern predominates in both types of commune. It is second in importance in the bunds. The family-oriented expansion pattern is of slight importance in the bunds. It appears more often in federated communes and is most common in unified ones. Differences in distribution of references to individual-oriented limitation are very small and are probably not significant. Examination of references to individual-oriented considerations in favor of limitation leads to the conclusion that differences among the three types of kibbutzim in this respect are qualitative rather than quantitative. Members of the bunds who refer to this pattern mention mainly considerations like relations between the spouses and leisure. These considerations are not incompatible with the collective-oriented limitation pattern. References to convenience, health, and individualized treatment of the children loom large in the communes.

For the pattern of individual-oriented limitation, the qualitative differences among the types of kibbutzim are significant and in line with our hypotheses. We can see that the kibbutz frame of reference is most prevalent in the bunds; next in this respect come the federated communes; it is least common in the unified communes. The familistic frame of reference and the tendency to expansion appear most often in unified communes; next in these respects come federated communes. Both the familistic frame of reference and arguments in favor of expansion are least frequent in the bunds.

Intrafamily differentiation. We may begin this analysis by examining our hypothesis that women are more familistic than men. This hypothesis leads us to expect that the tendency to recommend expansion of family size and the tendency toward family-centered thinking will be more prevalent among women than among men.

Table 9. Norms of family size among men and among women (percent)

	Responses						
	Small family	*Medium family*	*Large family*	*Rejecting a kibbutz norm*	*Don't know*	*No information*	*Total*
Men (N = 226)	8	44	30	8	4	6	100
Women (N = 189)	5	51	16	14	6	8	100

Table 9 shows that the medium family pattern predominates among both men and women. The large family pattern appears more frequently than the small family pattern, and is more common than objection to establishing a general norm. The balance between the different categories is roughly the same for both sexes. Yet there emerges a number of small but interesting differences. Reference to the small family is somewhat more common among men than among women. Reference to the medium family occurs more often among women than among men. Reference to the large family is more common among men than among women. Objection to a general norm and indifference toward the issue are more common among women than among men.

It is significant that contrary to expectation support of the large family pattern is more prevalent among men than among women. Women, who carry most of the burden of child-rearing and child care, are more realistic in their discussion of the problem than the men. Most of them feel that it would be difficult to cope with a large number of children and that a family of three or four children is quite enough.

The stronger identification of the women with their families is revealed not so much by recommendation of maximum expansion of family size as by the reasons proffered for their desire for children. Table 10 shows that the pattern of kibbutz-oriented limitation is more

Table 10. Patterns of opinion among men and among women (percent)

Pattern	Men (N = 250)	Women (N = 195)
Kibbutz-oriented limitation	18	13
Kibbutz-oriented expansion	48	28
Family-oriented expansion	10	34
Individual-oriented limitation	24	25
Total	100	100

common among men than among women, and the same holds true for the pattern of kibbutz-oriented expansion. The pattern of family-oriented expansion, on the other hand, is much more frequent among women than among men. There is no significant difference between men and women with regard to the pattern of individual-oriented limitation. Men are thus more kibbutz-oriented while women are more family-oriented.

Let us now turn to the examination of our hypotheses that the second generation will be more familistic than members of the bunds and less familistic than the first generation.

Table 11 shows that the small family pattern is most prevalent in the bunds. Few supporters of this pattern are to be found in the first generation and it disappears completely in the second generation. The medium family pattern predominates; it is more common among members of the first and second generations than in the bunds. The large family pattern is more common in the second generation than in the first and considerably more prevalent than in the bunds. Sizable differences emerge in the category designated "don't know." Very few members of either the first or the second generation had any difficulty in

Table 11. Norms of family size in first and second generations and in bunds (percent)

| | | | Responses | | | |
	Small family	Medium family	Large family	Rejecting a kibbutz norm	Don't know	No information	Total
Second generation (N = 37)	—	47	40	5	5	3	100
First generation (N = 241)	4	47	26	13	4	6	100
Bund (N = 45)	18	37	5	5	26	9	100

stating their opinion on the matter. More than a quarter of the respondents in the bunds were either hesitant or uninterested in the problem.

As was expected, members of the bunds differ considerably from members of the second generation. Members of the second generation put the main emphasis on the medium and large family patterns. Members of the bunds emphasize the medium and the small family patterns. Contrary to expectation, support of the large family pattern is more prevalent among the second than among the first generation.

Comparative analysis of ideological patterns yields similar results (Table 12). The kibbutz-oriented limitation pattern is most common in

Table 12. Patterns of opinion in first and second generations and in bunds (percent)

	Kibbutz-oriented limitation	Kibbutz-oriented expansion	Family-oriented expansion	Individual-oriented limitation	Total
Second generation (N = 48)	2	45	32	21	100
First generation (N = 253)	11	47	17	25	100
Bunds (N = 40)	40	35	7	18	100

the bunds. Next in this respect comes the first generation. This pattern has almost disappeared among the second generation. The kibbutz-oriented expansion pattern predominates among first and second generation members; it is more prevalent among them than among members of the bunds. The family-oriented expansion pattern is most prevalent among the second generation. The first generation comes next. It is of slight importance in the bunds. Differences in respect to individual-oriented limitation are small and probably not significant.

There is a considerable difference between the second generation and the bunds in the distribution of references. Members of the bunds put the main emphasis on kibbutz-oriented limitation and on kibbutz-oriented expansion whereas second generation members emphasize the kibbutz-oriented and the family-oriented expansion patterns. The family-oriented expansion pattern is more common among the second than among the first generation.

Comparative analysis has thus confirmed the first hypothesis: members of the first generation are in fact much more familistic than members of the bunds. It has led to a refutation of the second hypothesis: the second generation is more familistic than the first generation. The hypothesis concerning the relation between the first and second generation has been tested and more or less confirmed in respect to all other indexes of familism examined in our study.

The hypothesis that the second generation would occupy an intermediate position between the first generation and the bund was based on the assumption that members of the second generation are under the influence of two forces pulling in opposite directions: recent collective socialization and identification with age group on the one hand and the familistic trend emerging in their kibbutz on the other. Educational institutions inculcate the nonfamilistic tenets of proclaimed ideology. However, the influence of collective socialization on the second generation is most marked in matters that are regarded as an integral part of collective ideology; it is less marked and sometimes it even disappears completely in matters that are not explicitly dealt with and prohibited by it. Restriction of family size was never formulated explicitly as a part of the officially proclaimed ideology of the collective movement. Hardly any trace of this idea may be discerned in the attitudes of the second generation.

Moreover, the movement has come to regard the low birthrate of the families in kibbutzim with grave anxiety and has started a wide campaign for higher fertility. The pattern of kibbutz-oriented expansion is in the process of becoming the accepted ideology.

The unusually extreme familistic position of the second generation in matters pertaining to family planning is thus partly accounted for.

Familism in this sphere is not curbed by ideological prohibitions. Moreover, it is by now anchored in the fully sanctioned kibbutz-oriented ideology of expansion. It gains additional support from widely accepted family-oriented considerations.

Let us sum up our discussion. Comparative analysis has on the whole confirmed our hypotheses concerning typological differentiation. Certain features are common to all kibbutzim: the medium-family norm predominates in all three types of kibbutzim; the pattern of collective-oriented expansion prevails in both federated and unified communes, and ranks second in the bunds. Typological differentiation is not accentuated, but by and large it is in line with our hypotheses.

Comparative analysis has led to some modification of the hypothesis that women are more familistic than men. The stronger identification of women with the family is revealed less by their desire for a maximum number of children than by the reasons proffered for this desire. The contrast between men and women, generally speaking, is not very sharp.

Detailed examination has refuted our hypothesis concerning the relation between the first and the second generation. The second generation was found to be more familistic than the first. We were able partly to account for this unexpected variation by further clarification of the ideological implications of our problem.

The hypothesis concerning the differential position of the second generation and the bunds was fully confirmed. These two groups of young members occupy diametrically opposite positions on the continuum. The difference between the two groups as to structural perspective emerges in spite of the similarity of distribution as to age and family status.

CONCLUSION

We set out to analyze the interrelation between the transformation of norms pertaining to regulation of births and processes of ideological and sociological change. We found that the norms pertaining to family size are anchored in more comprehensive patterns of thinking and that variations in the balance among these distinct patterns are correlated to variations in the position of the family in the community.

We should like to conclude by pointing out some of the wider implications of this study. It appears that the analytical framework set up here may be used for the analysis of recent fertility trends in both West and East. One result of our study is of particular interest in this context. We found the tendency toward family limitation at two extremes of a continuum—in extreme collectivism at one end and in extreme individualism at the other—whereas the tendency toward family expansion was anchored in moderate collectivism and in familism.[10] The desire for many children is thus rooted in the intent of the family to serve the community or in its wish to consolidate its independent position. The shift from limitation of family size to expansion now occurring in Western countries may perhaps be interpreted as a shift from extreme individualism to moderate familism. It may be regarded as a valuable index of the stabilization and consolidation of the family unit in Western society.[11]

The far-reaching transformation of the policy of family planning in the Soviet Union should apparently be interpreted in a different way. The shift from a policy of limitation of family size to an ingenious and highly publicized policy of expansion is primarily the outcome of the institutionalization of a revolutionary movement. The shift from intergenerational discontinuity to continuity and the development of the urge to demographic-ideological expansion seem to be the main factors operative in this process (118, 87, 88). The violent antifamilism of the extreme collectivist revolutionary phase gradually abates and disappears. It is superseded by a moderate collectivism that regards the family as a potential though somewhat dangerous ally and employs it for the attainment of collective goals.

These suggestions are put forward with the purpose of demonstrating the applicability of our analytical scheme to the sociological study of demographic patterns in other societies. We venture to suggest that a comparative examination of the distribution of ideological patterns pertaining to regulation of births and a detailed comparative analysis of the components of each pattern in different societies may shed further light on the interrelation between family and society.

10. Examination of such trends, which are most pronounced in middle class families, may be found in Gille (53), Bjerke (14), Shryock, Siegel, and Beagle (123), and Westoff (145).

11. A similar hypothesis is hinted at by Parsons and Bales (104).

3. Two Aspects of Communal Upbringing: The Family Evening Meal and Children's Sleeping Arrangements

The question of the evening meal and the question of children's sleeping arrangements are two foci of actual or potential tension in relations between the family and the kibbutz; since both questions, in addition, bear directly on the larger issue of public versus private interest in a collective society, they may conveniently be discussed together.

THE FAMILY EVENING MEAL

Attitude survey. We asked our sample of representative members of kibbutzim: "What is your attitude toward taking the evening meal in the member's private room instead of in the communal dining hall? Why?" We regard the attitude to the evening meal as an important indication of a family's relative inclination to single out special functions as its separate and proper domain, apart from the collective living of the kibbutz. We made supper the subject of the question because this is the problematical meal; there is virtually no objection to taking breakfast and lunch in the communal dining hall. Family tea, on the other hand, is customary in most of the kibbutzim, and is even officially sanctioned in some of them. Only the character of the supper has not been decided.

Figure 1 summarizes the responses.[1] A considerable majority of the members either oppose the family meal or are prepared to sanction it only occasionally. The percentage of those expressing unqualified ap-

NOTE. The second part of this essay, on children's sleeping arrangements, appeared in Hebrew in *Niv Hakevutzah,* volume 8 (1959).

1. Figures here do not add up to 100 since (a) we have not included a number of small residual categories; (b) we did not receive answers from all the people questioned; and (c) some figures are rounded off.

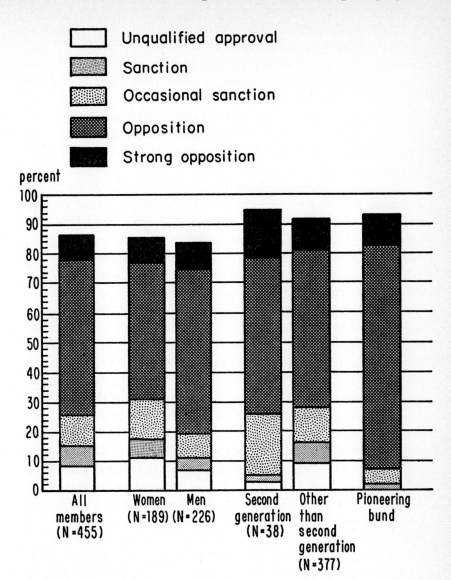

Figure 1. Attitudes toward a family evening meal

proval is relatively small. The percentage of those expressing strong disapproval, however, is equally small.

The graph shows a higher percentage of women among the sanctioners and occasional sanctioners, a lower percentage among those expressing disapproval. Though the differences are not great, they are mutually reinforcing, and we may conclude that women are more in favor of the private family meal than men. On this point, then, we have confirmation of our assumption that the female kibbutz member is more familistic than the male.

Let us now compare the second generation in kibbutzim with other members. The category here designated "second generation" comprises kibbutz members' children, and members who grew up and were educated in the kibbutz. We shall analyze only five of the sample groups, all of them containing grown-up second generation members.

It would appear that second generation members are more opposed to the family meal than all the other members of the kibbutzim, although not all the figures point to this conclusion. The opposition is most marked at the extremes, in the relatively small number of those expressing approval and the relatively large number of those strongly opposed. The percentage of those expressing opposition and strong opposition is slightly higher among second generation members than among the others. On the other hand, the percentage of those expressing occasional sanction—those opposed to the family meal as a regular practice, but prepared to countenance it from time to time—is higher among the second generation than among the others. We may sum up the evidence as showing that the majority of the second generation is either opposed to the family meal or is prepared to sanction it occasionally; only a small minority is ready to sanction it as a regular practice. This suggests that the second generation is less familistic than the first.

In order to determine the relation between the second generation and the kibbutz movement as a whole on this point, we shall compare the attitude of the second generation to that of members of young kibbutzim which are similar in type to the original pioneering bund.

The differences between the second generation and the pioneering bunds are not great on the whole. Most striking is the discrepancy in the percentage of those expressing occasional sanction. Like the members of young kibbutzim, the second generation is in favor of a communal evening meal, but a higher percentage of them sees no harm in an occasional family meal. On the other hand, a higher percentage of them expresses strong opposition. This seems to show that the second generation occupies a middle position on this question. They are less familistic than their parents but somewhat more familistic than the members of the pioneering bunds.

It is noteworthy that we found considerable variation in the attitudes of second generation members from kibbutz to kibbutz. In two of the five kibbutzim with a second generation, the attitude of second generation members is very similar to that of the members of the pioneering bunds. In another, the younger generation's attitude is close to that of its elders. In two of the sample kibbutzim the second generation is less strict on this point than the first.

The differences between those kibbutzim which, in our sample, represent the pioneer bund and those that represent a consumer community can be illustrated by a comparison of the attitudes in a single consumer commune with those in three pioneering bunds (Figure 2).

The differences are marked. In the consumer commune, a high percentage express approval or occasional sanction; a low percentage express opposition. The percentage of unqualified approvals is relatively high, and there is no strong opposition at all. The exact opposite is the case in the pioneering bund. In bund I which is the closest to the pioneering type, practically the whole population is concentrated in the category of those expressing opposition. In bund II, there is a minority who approve and a minority who sanction occasionally, but the overwhelming majority is opposed to the family meal. In bund III, the percentage of those opposed is smaller than in bunds I and II but this group contains the highest percentage of those strongly opposed. This comparison considerably strengthens our assumption about the non-family tendencies at work in a pioneering bund.

The differences between federated and unified communes are illustrated in figure 2 by a comparison of a federated commune with more or less unified communes.

The differences between federated and unified communes are most pronounced in the comparison between the federated commune and unified commune I. In the federated commune we found fewer unqualified approvers, fewer sanctioners, slightly fewer occasional sanctioners, and, conversely, more opposition and far stronger opposition. All the

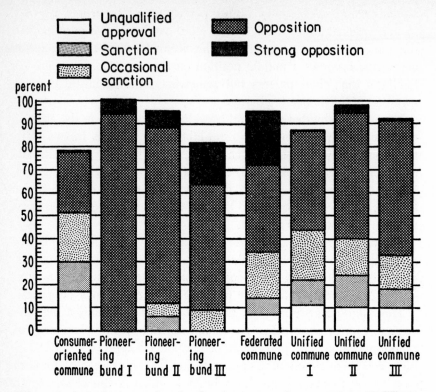

Figure 2. Attitudes toward a family evening meal: comparison of different kibbutzim

differences point in the same direction. The differences between the federated commune on the one hand and unified communes II and III on the other are less marked, nor do they all point in the same direction. The percentage of sanctioners is sometimes smaller in the unified communes than in the federated commune. The difference between the two groups is felt most in the relatively high percentage of approval in the unified communes and in the small percentage, or total absence, of strong opposition. This comparison would seem to provide some support for our assumption that the federated commune is less familistic than the unified commune. However, this conclusion should be accepted with caution, since in this matter it is difficult to separate the value factor from the structural factor.

No significant statistical summary of the arguments given by the respondents is possible: the arguments are too numerous, the answers too varied, and the differences in power of expression and readiness to justify attitudes too considerable. A quasi-statistical summary is feasible only for the distinction between attitudes adopted for organizational reasons and those adopted on ideological grounds, and even then not in all the points of the analysis employed in the discussion of attitudes adopted.

The main stress is on ideological arguments. Thirteen percent of the total sample raised only instrumental arguments, as against 30 percent who gave ideological arguments. Ideological reasons are more in evidence with men than with women. Second generation members place more stress on ideological arguments than all the other members. There are indications of a considerable difference between pioneering bunds and consumer communes.

Qualitative analysis reveals a number of recurring arguments. Organizational arguments in opposition to the family meal included: collective organization and operation of the kitchen makes for more economical and efficient use of manpower and goods; the domestic meal imposes a heavy burden on the woman which reduces her working capacity as a member of the kibbutz. In ideological arguments the stress is on considerations of what is good for the kibbutz: the family meal prevents the woman from playing her full part in the life of the kibbutz; the family meal encourages segregationism; the collective supper is a social occasion, hence the family meal has an adverse effect on the social cohesion of the kibbutz.

Organizational arguments in approval of the family meal include: disorder and noise in the dining room; unappetizing food, or food unsuited to individual taste; the distance of the dining room from the members' rooms and the children's houses; lack of coordination between the arrangements for putting the children to bed and the time of the parents' collective meal. In ideological arguments in approval the stress is on family and personal considerations: the wish to be alone with other members of the family; the desire for a quiet domestic meal as a relief from the strain of constant contact with other kibbutz members throughout the day; the desire on the part of the woman to express her talents and personal taste by looking after her family personally and directly. A considerable number of women emphasized that the activities connected with the evening meal, including supervision of the children and family conversation, provided them with an essential counterweight to the monotony or anonymity of their work for the collective economy.

We shall return to a consideration of these arguments when we analyze the results of actual observation.

Observation of communal meals. The special significance of supper and the problems connected with it become abundantly clear from careful observation of the patterns followed by kibbutz members at mealtime and of the formal arrangements made for meals. In some kibbutzim in the sample we made a systematic study of the ways in which table companions were chosen. We also tried to ascertain the type of communication entered into with these table companions and the principal topics of conversation at each of the various meals. From this study we concluded that there is a considerable difference between the morning and midday meals on the one hand, and the evening meal on the other. The first two are eaten hurriedly during work breaks, and conversation is frequently about work matters. The individual member does not spend much time in the dining hall—he usually hurries away, either to rest or to continue with his work. The evening meal, on the other hand, is as much a social gathering as when a family sits down to eat together. Members sit longer at table in the evening. They also linger in the dining hall both before and after the meal, talking at length about various matters.

It is clear, however, that the dining hall is no longer the general meeting place that it was in the past. Theoretically, each member is obliged to take the vacant seat next to the last person who has sat down; but in practice it is not difficult to disregard the instructions of the dining hall staff and choose the table companions one wishes. By waiting until all the places at a table where one does not want to sit are filled, and by making arrangements in advance with others, it is usually possible to ensure freedom of choice. At the morning and mid-day meals the individual member is not very particular about whom he sits with. His mealtime and the place he occupies at a particular table are determined mainly by work schedules in the various branches of the kibbutz economy. At the evening meal most of the members make a point of eating together with their families, and also try to sit near friends or the members of their own circle. It seems to us that the care taken to ensure that the whole family sit together is more pronounced in communes than in bunds, and more evident in unified communes than in federated communes. In federated communes the influence of group division on seating in the dining hall is sometimes clearly discernible: there are not many tables occupied by members of more than one group.

Social fragmentation into secondary groups, cliques of friends, families, and work teams is thus reflected, to a greater or lesser degree, in the seating patterns at meals. However, the divisive effect of this segregationism is in some measure counteracted by the commonly shared atmosphere of the collective dining hall. When the individual member enters the hubbub of the dining hall, he comes into contact with the whole kibbutz community. Whether he wishes to or not, he meets members with whom he does not come into contact in any other circumstance. In this way, his connection with the whole community is daily given overt symbolic expression.

The processes of fragmentation have affected supper more than other meals. The midday meal is taken in the dining hall almost without exception. A privately eaten breakfast on a weekday is extremely rare—to be noted occasionally in the case of night workers, or of some of the kibbutz officers who are late in getting to bed and therefore unable to get up early the next day. Occasionally we also came across a family breakfast on the Sabbath or on one of the festivals. But eating the morning or midday meal in private is exceptional: the collective morning and midday meals are an integral part of the kibbutz work schedule and way of life.

It is mainly in the evening that the tendency to eat separately as a family unit becomes operative. The custom of eating a private evening meal on specific occasions (such as on Saturday evening), or from time to time, is fairly widespread, and even those who are theoretically opposed sometimes indulge in the practice. On the other hand, it is noteworthy that only a few of those prepared to sanction the private meal in theory have actually made a regular practice of eating supper in their rooms. Most of the sanctioners go no further than an occasional family meal. Even those who wholeheartedly approve of a family evening meal and would like to change over to eating in their room find it difficult to realize their wish as long as the woman of the family works a full day for the kibbutz. In only two of the kibbutzim in the sample did we find a sizable number of families who were in the habit of eating in their rooms almost every evening.

The division of the kibbutz population in terms of actual conduct is thus different, in certain respects, from its division in terms of attitudes. Essentially, however, what emerges from both the attitude survey and the behavior study is that in most kibbutzim the evening meal remains a collective meal, with various degrees of permissiveness regarding an occasional family supper.

It may be asked how far the trend toward a separate family meal is affected by arrangements prevailing in the communal dining hall. When questioned about attitudes, members inclined to give prominence to value-based decisions and to cover up organization reasons. Those who said they ate separately because of poor arrangements in the dining hall formed only 1.9 percent of the total sample. When respondents were pressed to give reasons for their attitude, the organization factor was more frequently mentioned but was still not particularly prominent. But observation clearly shows that the organization factor is in fact extremely important. In some of the kibbutzim in the sample the arrangements in the dining hall were actually changed during the course of our study. Improvements in the quality of the food and in the preparation and serving of the meals markedly reduced the number of families eating regularly in their rooms. In several kibbutzim, on the other hand, we found a kind of vicious circle: the large number of families tending to have supper domestically brought about a lowering in the standard of the communal evening meal; since only part of the kibbutz population came to eat in the dining hall, the kitchen staff did not take pains with the preparation of the meal; the deterioration of the food and service then drove additional families to eat separately; and so forth. Efficiency and economy are among the main arguments brought forward in support of a collective supper, and therefore inefficiency raises doubts as to whether it is really worthwhile to continue with it. Moreover, faulty operation of the dining hall turns into a blatant demonstration of the weaknesses of collective organization. Instead of being a uniting factor, the meal becomes a divisive one.

Another problem which came to our attention in several kibbutzim in our sample, and one frequently mentioned as an argument against the collective supper, is connected with the problem of coordinating mealtime and the children's bedtime. (We shall return to this problem in the second part of this chapter.) Difficulty is encountered mainly in the case of children who are not yet asleep at suppertime but who do not eat with their parents in the general dining hall. During their meal, parents are disturbed by the children running about either outside or inside the dining hall, playing and making noise. Parents are often compelled to eat in turn, so that one of them can keep an eye on the children while the other has his meal, and this inconvenience leads quite a few families to have supper together in their room.

However, for all the importance that we attach to dining arrangements, it must be borne in mind that the main problem revolves about the relative emphasis placed by the individual on the collective and on the family. In this respect, observation confirms the conclusions drawn from the comparison made in the attitude survey between men and women members: the demand for a private evening meal comes from the women, despite the fact that it is on them that the work of preparation mainly falls. Observation similarly confirms in general outline the conclusions drawn from a comparison of second generation members with all others. At the same time, it appears that there are considerable differences among these members themselves on this question, and that these differences are connected in the main with the structure and values of the kibbutzim in which they grew up and received most of their education. Finally, observation fully corroborates the conclusions drawn from the comparison between bunds and communes, and strengthens the conclusions drawn from the comparison between federated and unified communes. In pioneering bunds a family meal is a rare occurrence; limited falling-off in attendance at the evening meal can be discerned only on particularly cold winter evenings, or after an exhausting work day. The family meal is not a frequent occurrence in federated communes but is fairly common in unified communes. In two of the unified communes in our sample most of the families eat supper together fairly frequently, and a number of families have adopted the custom of a regular family meal once a week.

Conclusions. Most members of the kibbutzim in our sample either disapprove of the family meal or are prepared to sanction it only occasionally. In most of the sample kibbutzim supper remains, to all intents and purposes, a communal meal. The occasional family meal is, however, a widespread phenomenon.

We found significant differences between male and female members, and also between second generation members and the rest. The demand for change in this matter comes principally from women.

We found significant differences between bunds and communes, and between federated and unified communes. Though it is difficult at this stage to separate the value system from the structural system, it seems probable that differences in the value system have more influence on the question of the communal meal.

The collective supper is an opportunity for social contact. Observation confirmed our view that in the absence of an equivalent substitute abolition of the communal meal will accelerate the processes of fragmentation and do serious damage to the social cohesion of the kibbutz.

In most kibbutzim we found that the family meal is a phenomenon of limited scope which does not do away with the collective pattern.

Proper management of the collective kitchen and of the general dining hall, and coordination with arrangements in the children's home, are largely effective in checking the spread of the separate family meal and its institutionalization.

CHILDREN'S SLEEPING ARRANGEMENTS

Personal relations between man and wife on the kibbutz are considered private, and are not subjected to open and direct supervision. This is not the case where relations between parents and children are concerned. As in every revolutionary collectivistic society, emphasis is placed on the continuity of the undertaking, and children are regarded as belonging chiefly to the society as a whole—a view that is incompatible with a strong emotional attachment to one's own children or with the tendency to consider them as belonging to one's private domain. Public interest and parental emotions here join issue: whereas the former would tend to remove children from the domain of the individual, the latter would tend to separate them from the authority of the community. The attitude toward the problem of sleeping arrangements is a crucial test in this regard, and can serve as a major index of the status of the family in the collective.

Sleeping arrangements and the demand for change. The attitude of those interviewed toward the problem of accommodations was examined by means of the following questions: (1) What is your attitude toward demands that children sleep in their parents' home? (2) If you are in favor of family accommodation, at what ages do you favor it? (3) Give your reasons. In analyzing the reasons given, we were aided by an analysis of the answers to a more general question: (4) What are the advantages and disadvantages of a communal upbringing?

The answers were classified and regrouped in a methodical framework, so as to achieve two main objectives: analysis of the choices, which would give us an idea of the strength and trend of the demands for change; and analysis of the ideological patterns, which would give us an idea of the whole range of considerations for and against change.

Table 13. Demand for family accommodation ($N = 415$)

Against family accommodation	42%
Occasional permission	2
Permission on Sabbath and holidays	1
No objections	2
In favor of family accommodation	42
No answer	11
Total	100

Table 13 summarizes the responses to the first question. It shows that the forces opposing and demanding family accommodation are evenly balanced, and noticeably polarized. The percentage of those taking a moderate stand is extremely small. The question provoked the respondents to extreme choices, either for or against, and few felt it necessary to qualify their reply in any way.

Most of the kibbutzim in our sample permit children to sleep in their parents' home from time to time. In most kibbutzim, parents accommodate their children at home whenever the children strongly insist on it, as an exception to the rule. Some kibbutzim formally permit children to sleep in their parents' home on birthdays and family occasions, and they do not mind when this happens on Sabbath and festivals. Rules are relaxed with regard to sensitive children who find it difficult to adjust to the children's house. There is also flexibility in the case of a child passing through an emotional crisis who needs to be close to his parents for a period.

As long as family accommodation is permitted occasionally, but not too frequently, and permissiveness is held within well defined limits, the principle of communal accommodation is not affected. However, family accommodation sometimes becomes widespread, and is no longer regulated by fixed rules. In some of the kibbutzim in our sample institutional disintegration had set in. We found that children whose parents had been allocated the superior housing reserved for veteran members frequently sleep in their parents' homes. Differentiation in housing thus permeates the children's society. In order that their children not feel inferior, parents who have only one room also tend to let their children sleep with them. The family sleeps crowded together in a small apartment, while many of the pleasant children's rooms are empty, and several children's houses remain almost unused at night. Each family does as it pleases and does not heed regulations or ask the permission of the children's nurse. Sometimes parents may prefer this sort of partial solution to more radical change. Some of them feel that they thus reap the benefits of both systems: they can either accommodate the children in their homes or return them to the children's house. They enjoy the proximity of their children, but do not prejudice the possibility of making alternative arrangements should the need arise.

Circumvention of communal accommodation relieves the pressure for radical change, but raises serious problems. Accommodation of children in their parents' homes whenever the parents feel like it is wasteful and hinders functional planning—the living accommodation designed for children is not fully used, and the parents' home, which was not designed for accommodating children, is overcrowded. The absence of compulsory rules applying equally to all children seriously undermines the status of the children's house and all efforts to improve arrangements in it. Institutional disintegration endangers communal upbringing more than a demand for change that seeks a stable solution.

The second question, put only to those in favor of family accommodation, asked at what ages sleeping at home was desirable. Some of those questioned were unable to distinguish precisely among age groups while others mentioned exact figures. The categories that most clearly describe the responses are: infants, newborn to 2 or 3 years; young children, 2–3 through 12–14 years; older children, 12–14 through 19 years. Table 14 summarizes the responses.

Respondents supporting family accommodation are by no means unanimous; there are many shades of opinion. Some of those in favor recommend it only for one of the three age groups. Some recommend it

Table 14. Ages considered appropriate for family
accommodation ($N = 196$)

Infants	21%
Young children	21
Older children	3
Infants and young children	23
Young and older children	18
All ages	14
Total	100

for two consecutive age groups (infants and young children, or young children and older children). A relatively small proportion (14 percent of all those in favor or 7 percent of the whole sample) want family accommodation for all ages.

It will aid us to estimate the relative weight carried by the demand for family accommodation for each age group if we calculate the number of times each age group is mentioned, irrespective of whether it is mentioned singly or jointly with other age groups. Infants are mentioned in 34 percent of the responses, young children in 45 percent, older children in 21 percent.

Psychological and educational considerations would lead one to assume that the demand for family accommodation would center mainly on infants, but this is not the case. The demand for family accommodation for infants is greater than for older children, but is less than for young children. The main emphasis is placed on young children. The significance of this distribution of attitudes can be brought out only by an analysis of the reasons given.

We observed in these reasons a clear distinction between the "conservative" collective ideology on which belief in communal education is based, and the familistic ideology which emerges when there is a demand for change. It should be noted that only in two of the "conservative" kibbutzim and in the one most "innovating"[2] kibbutz did we find a clear-cut and unqualified decision for or against communal ac-

2. The terms "conservative" and "innovating" are used in a sense internal to the movement. Those favoring communal accommodation aim at preserving existing patterns, whereas those favoring family accommodation demand change. It is obvious that from the wider social viewpoint, those in favor of communal accommodation are innovators in the sense that they are defending a revolutionary innovation, whereas those demanding change are conservative, adhering to accepted social patterns. In order to indicate the double meaning of these terms as regards a revolutionary movement, we put them in quotation marks. On the connection between innovation and conservatism, see Pareto (98).

commodation. In the rest of the kibbutzim in the sample, members pointed out that there were arguments pro and con, and explained the advantages and disadvantages of both systems. In many, the reasons for and against almost balanced. Only after classifying the explanations found in various parts of the questionnaire and piecing together their various combinations were we able to see two opposing viewpoints.

The reasons given within the scope of each competing viewpoint were classified according to two intersecting criteria. The first criterion was that of the frame of reference. We distinguished between considerations of the general good on the one hand, and considerations of the good of parents and children on the other. The second criterion was a distinction among emotional, organizational, and ideological arguments. It should be pointed out that these distinctions are not sharply defined. In the kibbutz, organizational considerations are founded on explicit or implicit ideological assumptions, and considerations of the common good are closely linked with organizational considerations. Moreover, discussions on the upbringing of children are not generally conducted in an atmosphere of calm and moderation; sometimes the parents become excited and it is difficult to estimate which factor dominates, ideological commitment or emotional reactions. Sometimes one is obliged to judge by the tone in which words are uttered or the order in which they are stated. In what follows the opposing arguments are described and their roots in the reality of kibbutz life analyzed.

The collective ideology: reasons supporting communal accommodation. Communal accommodation is generally defended indirectly, by attacking the demand for change. The "yes" to communal accommodation is often expressed as a "no" to family accommodation. The conservative line of reasoning is based mainly on practical and ideological considerations. Emotional arguments in favor of communal accommodation are extremely rare.

The organizational arguments touch on three problems: (a) rational planning to employ the labor force to its best advantage; (b) rational planning of buildings and their location in the settlement; (c) absorption of children and adolescents from outside the kibbutz into the children's society.

Those discussing communal accommodation from the aspect of work arrangements begin with the assumption that efficiency in work demands centralized organization of production, consumption, and services, and full exploitation of the female labor force. Family accommodation is seen as incompatible with having women share the labor in the public economy. The additional burden "would necessarily affect the female member's work" or "family accommodation demands a gradual reduction of working hours for the female member." Sometimes the matter is discussed mainly from the kibbutz angle: "the kibbutz would be the loser by altering the system—the change would certainly upset the women's work arrangements." Sometimes the parents' viewpoint is discussed: "collective accommodation is a good solution to the problem of working parents—a large part of the burden of looking after the children is removed"; and sometimes that of the children: "The children live an orderly life and do not suffer from the fact that both their parents work." In all these frames of reference, the work problem is central, and it is assumed that all other aspects of life must be arranged to fit in with it.

Those who discuss the organizational aspect of accommodation from the viewpoint of a rational planning of the buildings raise the argument that a change in sleeping arrangements would require an extension of the family living units and would greatly increase investment in housing. Great emphasis is placed on the fact that family accommodation does not lend itself to fair and flexible use of children's rooms. The children of one family would live in a room provided for its exclusive use. Living conditions for a small family would be better than for a large family: "The rooms of big families will be overcrowded, whereas families with only one or two children will not utilize their children's rooms sufficiently." There would also be the difficult question of separation of sexes and ages: "Children of different ages have different timetables and different interests. They will disturb each other at work and at rest. The little ones will be a nuisance." "It is undesirable for adolescent boys and girls to room together; we will be forced to increase the number of rooms at the family's disposal."

An additional focus of concern is the absorption of children and young people. Most kibbutzim maintain their own educational facilities and are not in need of regional or central educational institutions. However, the number of children is usually too small for an efficient use of the schools and the kibbutzim almost always have to supplement by bringing in children from outside. The absorption of youth groups is also important for the kibbutz as a source of extra manpower. It is of great advantage in this regard that the arrangements are identical for children inside the kibbutz and for those that come from the outside. In the words of the respondents: "Family accommodation will produce dangerous double standards in the organization. This would affect the kibbutz in two crucial matters—absorption of children to make up the school classes and absorption of youth groups as important reserves of manpower."

Arguments focused on the common good are generally confined to the internal sphere of the kibbutz and are founded on two distinct premises. There are those who view communal accommodation as a consistent and integral part of the value system on which kibbutz life is built, and there are those who view it as one of the educational means of handing these values down to the next generation.

In the first context, communal accommodation is regarded as the result of the internal logic of a value system based on cooperation, equality, and collective responsibility: "If we enjoin collective responsibility and cooperation, it goes without saying that we must see to it that the burden of looking after children is evenly distributed between large and small families." Many are convinced that the internal logic of kibbutz life obliges cooperation in all spheres and that cooperation in bringing up children is a necessary link in the chain. A very common argument is that family accommodation opens the way to a gradual decrease in cooperation: "The abolition of cooperation in one sphere would lead to its gradual abolition in other spheres—one thing leads to another."

The principal spheres which would be affected by family accommodation are sometimes enumerated. One conviction is that family accommodation would reinforce the already present tendency to relegate to the family many of the roles of which it had been deprived. The assumption is widespread that family accommodation increases orientation to family consumption. Too great an attachment to home life will, according to those in favor of communal accommodation, affect the complete dedication to work, especially in the case of women. No less widespread is the fear that family accommodation might make it harder to enlist members for voluntary office and committee work that is done after working hours. While family accommodation would interfere with the fulfillment of institutional functions in the spheres of work and public activities, it might be most damaging to informal social intercourse. There is a fear that considerable differentiation would arise between the way of life of a family member and that of an unmarried member.

Those who view communal accommodation as educational preparation for kibbutz life consider the structure of collective education to be suited to the structure of adult society, and well designed to prepare children for normal integration into adult life: "In the children's society, the child is trained for communal life, cooperation, and equality from the day of birth." "Collective accommodation is basic training in cooperation. Children learn the meaning of 'ours' before they learn 'mine'." Allied with this argument is the corollary line of reasoning, less frequently encountered, that the family is incapable of performing the educational role of ensuing continuity. The main argument here is that the educational trends of the family are not always compatible with those of the kibbutz: "Not all families can represent the educational orientation of the kibbutz." Parents may be suspect on a variety of grounds: extra-kibbutz upbringing; disillusionment with or lack of interest in kibbutz ideals; insufficient ideological training; self-interest.

In arguments supporting communal accommodation from the parents' point of view, many of the reasons already given from the kibbutz's point of view recur, but they are given different weight and appear in different contexts. Communal accommodation is viewed as permitting parents to work out a convenient routine and as a precondition for the combination of work and public office with orderly family life. In this connection communal accommodation is viewed as especially important for women: "The emancipation of woman depends on whether she is relieved of the burden of looking after the children in the evening." It should be noted that communal accommodation is viewed here as a means of liberating the woman for regular employment; thus, satisfaction with the existing arrangement is somewhat dependent on satisfaction with work.

The part played by communal accommodation in allowing social activity in the evenings is also mentioned. Communal accommodation leaves parents free in the evenings and permits men and women to participate in activities on equal terms. One female member said, "We are struggling with age-old traditions, against a reluctant society and the covert derision of men. But as long as there is communal accommodation, there is a chance of achieving something; family accommodation would put an end to the woman's chances of achieving equal status and holding public office."

In addition to allowing greater participation in public life, communal accommodation is also said to benefit the family and the individual. Communal accommodation leaves the parents free to engage in voluntary cultural activity and to further their education. No less important is a sense of balance in the family's internal relations. With communal accommodation, the children do not wholly dominate family recreation time. According to this outlook, family accommodation would lead to "too great a preoccupation with the children."

Supporters of communal accommodation also claim that it benefits the relations between parents and children. The relations are not clouded by the burden of housework and the bother of child care. As most of the burden of upbringing rests with the institutions, the parents need not be constantly exercising their authority. Above all, there is the advantage of a combined upbringing, both public and parental. The parents are largely relieved of the burden of upbringing, but can at any time influence and examine, criticize and supplement.

The main argument for communal accommodation from the point of view of the child's good lies in the benefit accruing from the professionalization of child care and education. There are a number of advantages to professionalization: selection of teachers ("not every parent is capable or suited for the task; it is better to reduce parental influence"); training (teaching demands proper training, and most parents do not have this training); objectivity (parents tend to be emotional, to spoil and play favorites with their children; by contrast, "teachers apply an objective yardstick").

Communal upbringing is based essentially on handing the child over to persons who give him their undivided attention, and whose expertise and experience assure that they will do the right thing in any situation. The supporters of communal accommodation attach considerable importance to the relations developing within the children's society itself. Here again, one can distinguish several advantages. (1) Communal upbringing ensures "a special children's world" suited both from the educational and the organizational points of view to the child's special needs. The physical dimensions of the children's house and the children's section of the kibbutz are adjusted to the children's ages. The equipment, implements, and buildings were designed especially for them. The child's routine has been fixed according to ideological precepts and educational considerations. These arrangements reflect adult society, yet are free of the defects inherent in real-life situations. (2) Companionship of peers in the children's society. Communal accommodation shared with age mates who have similar problems and common interests is, according to this outlook, preferable to the collaboration of persons of varying ages in the family. But in addition, contact with children of different ages is also possible in the children's society, as well as limited contact with siblings during the daily visit to the parents' home. (3) Stability is safeguarded by the permanent framework of the child's life and replaces the emotional twists and turns of fluctuating family relationships. (4) Centralization. Communal accommodation turns the children's institution into a real home, on which the child's life centers: study and work, social life and cultural activities, entertainment and rest.

To sum up: communal accommodation suits the structure and values of the kibbutz and is a necessary educational tool for ensuring inter-generational continuity. Communal accommodation also benefits both parents and children. It can be regarded as an original and effective solution of the problem of the parent-child relationship in the modern family. Contact is limited, but this loss is compensated for by over-whelming advantages.

The familistic ideology: arguments for family accommodation. The ideology on which the demand for change is based differs in many important points from that favoring communal accommodation. If in the "conservative" line of reasoning various considerations of the common good were decisive, here they are almost entirely absent; instead, one finds at the core of the argument considerations of the children's and parents' good. Whereas the collective ideology is almost entirely based on organizational and ideological considerations, here some emotional arguments also appear. In addition, references to extra-kibbutz life are more frequent.

The emotional arguments mainly articulate hopes and aspirations, and no attempt is made to justify them on organizational or ideological grounds: "When I returned from the hospital and brought my child to the children's house, I cried, and I still cannot get used to it. I am all in favor of abolishing communal accommodation." "Looking after a child and being close to him are sources of deep joy. Parents want their children." Some of these arguments are openly defiant: "They bring up all sorts of arguments and evidence, but I am clear about one thing—I miss my child and want him with me, and that's all there is to it!" Overall, however, we found emotional reasoning in only a few of the answers. As in the "conservative" viewpoint, the main emphasis in the arguments for change is placed on organizational and ideological reasons.

Organizational arguments against communal accommodation and in favor of family accommodation center upon the parents and children. Not one respondent referred to the common good. Even the most enthusiastic supporters of family accommodation do not, as a rule, argue that family accommodation suits the organizational structure of the kibbutz. They either ignore the problem, or argue that in such matters as education considerations of the good of the individual and the family are paramount.

The arguments against communal accommodation from the parents' point of view center upon the tension caused by compressing child care into a few hours after work, and by having the children living outside the home. There are serious complaints about the fuss and commotion involved in fetching a child from the children's house and then taking him back at bedtime. Concentration of most functions in the children's house, though economical and convenient for the kibbutz, splits the family up, since the children's house is often far from the home. This awareness of splitting up is aggravated by the difficulties of coordinating the arrangements for putting the child to bed and the communal evening meal, as we pointed out earlier. "All evening we shuttle between the parents' and the children's homes." "While they are small, they must be put to bed before the evening meal; when they are older they run about under the parents' feet at mealtimes, or one of the parents must stay behind and look after them while the other has to rush to finish his food."

More frequent are complaints about the procedure for putting the child to bed, which is the parents' job in almost every kibbutz in our sample. Only one kibbutz recently decided to give this task to the children's nurse. In a few kibbutzim, the nurses help the parents and supervise arrangements, but in general, the parents bear the full responsibility, and the nurse's task is reduced to a minimum. When the parents put the children to bed without supervision by the nurse, there are often wild outbursts, noise, and tension. Children try to put off the moment of parting as long as possible. There is a sort of covert competition among occupants of the room as to who can keep his parents there the longest. "It is hard to separate yourself from your child, and the thing drags on for hours."

No less serious, from an organizational point of view, is the problem of the overlapping of educational authority. In the parents' home, special treatment and permissiveness are the rule. In the children's house, the principles of general and obligatory order must of necessity prevail. When the parents put the children to bed, they bring with them something of the permissive atmosphere of the home, and it is difficult to restore order under such conditions.

The arguments against the procedure for putting children to bed also take in the possibility of damage to the children. When the parents put the child to bed, they can look after him before he goes to sleep and take leave of him gradually. In this way, a sharp and sudden transition from the parents' home to the children's house is avoided. However, these advantages are often outweighed by drawbacks. "This one leaves and that one enters; this one is undressing and that one is playing; this one is dozing and that one is howling—how could anyone fall asleep in such an atmosphere?" In the opinion of the supporters of family accommodation, putting the child to bed is "daily torture for the child." Their conclusion is not that the parents should refrain from putting their children to bed, or that a children's nurse should supervise the bedding down, but that communal accommodation should be abolished entirely.

The argument against crowded and disorderly bedtimes is reinforced by the argument that there is lack of supervision in the evenings. Parents complain of this lack of supervision, of noise and wildness, and also of the inadequacy of the night watch. "The children are afraid at night; they are alone in the dark. The night nurse looks in now and then, but this is certainly insufficient." Here again, the conclusion is not that the night watch should be expanded, but that communal accommodation should be abolished.

So far, we have presented arguments referring directly to accommodation arrangements. Many supporters of family accommodation would enlarge the scope of the debate to include communal upbringing. They argue that the theoretical advantages of communal education are in effect canceled out by its operational defects and severe educational drawbacks and that its influence on children should be restricted. In this context, the most common argument is against the use of unsuitable and inexperienced teachers. Not all the kibbutzim in the sample choose these workers after careful selection. In only a minority do they receive suitable training, and in only a few are they required to take refresher courses or read professional literature. A large number of kibbutzim are not strict in the selection of suitable workers, are negligent of their professional training, and are constantly changing personnel. These operational defects are said to invalidate the case for communal upbringing.

The complaints about educators appear side by side with arguments about the second major factor in kibbutz upbringing: the children's society. It is held that the age groupings are irregular and faultily composed. Many groups are incomplete and do not constitute educational units. There are more than a few groups containing difficult children, and these groups cannot function properly. For this reason, parents sometimes complain of a lack of space, of overcrowding, and of lack of suitable equipment in the children's houses. To summarize: The operational and organizational defects of collective accommodation are many, and the child needs a counterbalance in his family. The parents can give him his due, and can make up for the deficiencies of collective education, but only if he sleeps at home.

The ideological considerations supporting family accommodation are mainly based on a value system differing from the "conservative" ideology. There is a growing demand for more freedom, for the cultivation of individuality, for closer contact among family members. Only here and there do we find an attempt to examine the limitations of communal education according to its own standards, and an effort to suggest changes based on renewed and selective reference to the original communal values. The arguments relating to the good of the kibbutz are in a minority among the many considerations relating to children and parents.

We shall begin here by listing the main arguments from the parents' point of view. The most common argument is that parents are separated from their children. This type of argument is put emphatically and emotionally, and sometimes there is only a hair's breadth between an ideological and an emotional argument: "Motherhood is the major experience in a woman's life. It is an unforgivable sin to take her child away from her." "Communal accommodation entails the renunciation of the spontaneous attachment between parents and children."

A less common argument, but no less important, is that communal accommodation undermines family unity. Family unity largely depends on cooperation in daily affairs, and on a common way of life. The paucity of shared tasks weakens and undermines the possibilities for this kind of life, but "family accommodation would give the family a common field of action and interest."

Such are the main arguments from the parents' point of view. The arguments from the children's point of view are more numerous and far more weighty. Here again, they center mainly on opposition to communal upbringing in general, and consequently on a desire to reduce its influence or counterbalance its effects.

The supporters of family accommodation protest against too great an emphasis on ideology in kibbutz upbringing. The primary aim of this upbringing is to direct the young person toward carrying on the kibbutz movement; it cultivates the type of personality best suited to kibbutz life and most likely to perpetuate it. Instead of this obviously biased education, there is an increasing demand for education for its own sake, determined by the child's individual abilities and interests.

Children are said to have less privacy than adults. Adult life is divided into two domains—the public and the private. The public domain takes up a large part of the adult's life, but he has a place of his own, and he can retire to it in his free time. The child receiving a communal upbringing, however, has no place he can call his own and is always together with other children in the communal house. Contact with his parents and other members of his family is very limited, and even when they meet he is only one of several.

It is also argued that education is standardized according to a single formula, in which there is no shaping of personality or cultivation of individual differences. Group life demands subservience to uniform rules of behavior, whereas if the influence of the family were increased, variety and individuality would be encouraged; the intimacy, "togetherness," and permissiveness of family relationships encourage the child and help him to shape his personality.

Communal life demands more adaptation, more routinization, more coordination—and consequently more supervision. The peculiar nature of the kibbutz family also contributes to the intensity of supervision. The family is not isolated; the parents are in close contact with the teachers. There is constant pressure on the parents to support the trend toward communal upbringing and to identify with its demands. Isolation of the family, strengthening of ties between parents and children, and granting parents the right to bring up their children would give the child a partially independent domain, in which he would be protected from criticism and free from the supervision under which he is placed in communal education.

The child in his peer group is always one of many. His age mates are entitled to the same amount of attention as he. The child's status within the group depends on his ability to compete for the affection and admiration of his fellows and teachers. Those who complain of the pressure of competition prefer the multiaged structure of the family to the peer group. In their opinion, sibling rivalry is not as fierce as that between unrelated peers.

A lack of stability is noted in the child's life. Workers change in the children's house. The child passes from one teacher to another, and from class to class. Throughout these changes, it is important that there be a single continuous and permanent link with the family.

Where the supporters of communal accommodation emphasize the advantages of limiting contact with the parents, the detractors see this limitation as the root of all evil. They are often content to generalize: "The child needs his mother." The deep-seated fear of parental control among the supporters of communal accommodation disappears entirely, and its place is taken by unbounded confidence in parental capabilities. "The best children's nurse cannot take the place of a mother."

Others raise more specific arguments. They protest that communal accommodation artificially reduces contact to allotted hours, and consequently produces a forced and tense atmosphere between parents and children. Rationing of affection leads in turn to a sharp cleavage between the provision of reassurance and education, between affection and discipline. Day and night the children are subjected to a regime; they regard the meeting time with their parents as an opportunity to release their pent-up energies. Parents meeting their children briefly for an alloted time refrain from darkening the hour with unpleasant demands, moral preaching, or any sort of punishment. The child does not have to fear opposition to his desires during this time; his parents tend to be overly permissive.

Two further arguments appear here, which at first sight appear to contradict each other, but are in fact closely related.

First, the limited contact and the limited role of parents in the upbringing of their children cause emotional dependence and exaggerated sentimentality. The children want to stay with their parents and suffer from their absence, since only in the parents' home are they given unconditional affection, preferential treatment, and relief from supervision and criticism. Parents also miss their children and are not satisfied with the brief encounters. The child thus becomes the center of their world and the embodiment of their private lives.

On the other hand, communal accommodation encourages parents to abdicate responsibility for their children. The system thus has two contrasting results: the overly anxious mother and the mother who is not anxious enough. Some parents want communal accommodation because it is convenient for them. Their interest is sporadic, and is mainly at the expense of the children's nurse. Quite a few have relinquished their role as parents, and do not want to be bothered. As one member put it strongly: "Communal accommodation spoils them, and impairs their feelings of responsibility for their children."

This is the essence of the arguments and assumptions on which demands for family accommodation are based. The argument against communal accommodation stems from the nonfulfillment of minimal conditions that would ensure the success of communal upbringing. Unsuitable or insufficiently trained educators, irregular group structure, insufficient living space in the children's house, and a general atmosphere of neglect and incompetence—all these subvert communal upbringing and undermine the basis for its existence. Another source of resentment is the weaknesses inherent in communal upbringing even when it is properly designed and practiced. Many of these defects could be avoided through reorganization and effective planning. Problems arising from poor bedtime arrangements or insufficient night watch could be solved, if only partially, by increased supervision by nurses and by organizing a rotating night watch for parents. Friction stemming from strained relationships between parents and educators could also be largely avoided by increasing the parents' share in child care, by routinized patterns of contact, and by having definite rules regarding rights and duties. The same applies to tensions within the children's society, which could be considerably reduced by changing the age structure of the group and by appropriate arrangements in the children's house.

Irremediable structural defects which are an unavoidable accompaniment to the communal accommodation system should be viewed on a different level. Every educational system has its own structural weaknesses; one cannot benefit from its advantages without being to some extent affected by its limitations. Many parents believe that a communal education system should solve all the problems of upbringing while at the same time giving them all the advantages of other systems. Members have expected too much of communal upbringing and have made exaggerated demands upon it, which can only result in disappointment and defeat.

Only a few respondents distinguish among the different levels of the argument, and this lack of differentiation affects the clarity of the analysis. In general, no distinctions are made between unavoidable difficulties and defects which could be removed through organizational and educational improvements. A sober and realistic evaluation of the advantages and disadvantages is rather rare. Criticism thus leads not to a request for internal improvements but to a demand for radical change.

Arguments with reference to extra-kibbutz society. The debate on the problem of accommodation is generally based on arrangements customary in the kibbutz and does not depart from the kibbutz context. Few choices are made through conscious and detailed comparison with other ways of life. But even though explicit reference to extra-kibbutz society is uncommon, it is of interest for our purpose. Comparisons with patterns of family structure outside the kibbutz were alluded to in many of the interviews, although not stated expressly. An examination of these comparisons will throw additional light on the origins of the demand for change.

"It is impossible not to compare our family with our parents' homes. A family without children, without brothers and sisters living together, is not a home." Sometimes, on the other hand, the parents' home is recalled in anger and resentment: "We should not go back to previous systems; the members recall their parents' homes and it is hard for them to break away from old habits. They must be educated." Explicit reference to the parents' home are few, but attitudes toward it, either nostalgic or rejecting, filter through many of the arguments. References to the collective moshav are relatively common, since sleeping arrangements are a major and clear-cut difference between a kibbutz and this similar type of settlement.[3] "Family accommodation would give us one of the advantages of the collective moshav without our actually turning into one." And against this: "Family accommodation would lead to a blurring of distinctions—one step toward a collective moshav."

The urban family is frequently mentioned, and many refer to it by inference, though not explicitly. Several types of urban families are referred to: those in which the mother works outside her home, and those in which the mother is a housewife; here a distinction is made between the working class family and the affluent family.

References are few to the family in which the mother works outside her home, but generally the two main advantages of the working mother in the kibbutz are noted, namely that the child is well looked after during working hours, and that the mother is free to look after the child after working hours—the working mother on the kibbutz is released from the burden of housework, and can devote herself to the child.

The few references made to the working class family in which the wife is a housewife all emphasized the advantages of the kibbutz family as against the urban working class family with regard to continuation of the children's studies.

In the arguments both for and against communal arrangements the kibbutz family is compared with a well-to-do family which is able to give its children elaborate care. In general, only the advantages are stressed while the problems and difficulties are viewed unrealistically. Dissatisfaction with sleeping arrangements and communal upbringing is, in many cases, tied up with a comparison between the real-life family on the kibbutz and an idealized picture of an urban family.

A generalized argument that does not spell out specific claims but

3. A collective moshav is a cooperative settlement which consists of economically independent family units (houses and allotted plots). Buying and marketing is on a communal basis. Members give regulated amounts of time to communal affairs and enterprises.

expresses general dissatisfaction with communal accommodation is widespread. Many people justify their opposition to communal accomodation with phrases like "it goes against nature," "perverted and unnatural," "an inversion of the laws of creation." Many parents are aware that upbringing according to the kibbutz formula is not accepted anywhere else in the world, and view it as an experiment that should be treated with caution. Some of the respondents regard this experiment as important and take pride in it as initiators, but only a few are completely free of anxiety. Certainty and doubt are intermingled, even among the enthusiastic supporters. The lack of a sufficient ideological basis intensifies the insecurity which accompanies a deviation from customary behavior.

The uncertainty and fear that are the outcome of being unorthodox, the absence of long-standing traditions, the lack of experience, all engender too great a reliance on scientific and education theories. For example, we found many references to Freud in arguments on both sides. In a kibbutz containing members of American extraction, psychological and sociological theories are frequently adduced as evidence for the propensity to change. We shall briefly examine the relationship between accommodation arrangements and education and sociological theories.

In its day, kibbutz upbringing was a living embodiment of the demands of progressive education theory: education was in the hands of specially trained educators, the child was brought up in a world created exclusively for him, team spirit was cultivated, the children's society was self-governing, contact with parents was limited but regular and stable. Communal upbringing drew encouragement and security from being in accord with education theories, confirmed by scientific opinion.

This congruence has been partially undermined through the advent of new sociological and psychological theories that place great emphasis on the educational role of the family and regard contact between the infant and its parents, especially its mother, as the precondition for a stable personality. Many of the supporters of family accommodation regard these theories as clear-cut evidence against communal accommodation, and are convinced that the theories contain decisive warrant for change.

It should be noted that the use made of the theories is generally oversimplified, and in any case the evidence is not clear-cut one way or the other. But the propensity for change that is already present enlists the scientific theories in its aid. Latent emotional demands find objective justification in the theories. Supporters of family accommodation regard assumptions based on the familistic educational approach as a final, irreversible judgment. The supporters of communal accommodation reply halfheartedly to these arguments, but are in fact ridden with doubts.

The factor of age. We have so far presented arguments without referring to variations in the intensity of the demands according to stages of the child's development. An analysis of the responses shows that this factor is of the greatest importance and enables us to focus on a specific aspect of the argument.

There is little demand for a transition to family accommodation for all ages. Most respondents take it for granted that from the age of about twelve upward, communal accommodation is preferable. Only a relatively small minority demand family accommodation at an older age. The argument thus centers mainly on infants and young children. Although one would be inclined to believe that the demand for family accommodation would be the strongest with regard to infants, this is not the case; most of the emphasis is on young children. A further breakdown is to be observed between ideological arguments on the one hand and instrumental or organizational arguments on the other.

We found strong ideological pressure for family accommodation for infants, deriving mostly from considerations of the children's and parents' benefit. However, this tendency is counteracted by organizational pressure for communal accommodation, based mainly on considerations of benefit to both parents and the kibbutz. Organizational considerations counteract ideological considerations, and to a great extent restrain demands for family accommodation. For reasons of convenience and organizational coordination, parents also wish to delay family accommodation for several years. Collective considerations are thus supported by individual considerations.

Family accommodation is mainly favored for young children. The demand for family accommodation from the parents' and the children's point of view struggles with considerations of what is best for the kibbutz, but the tendency toward "innovation" is strong. A leaning toward family accommodation from the ideological viewpoint is supported by a similar tendency in the organizational sphere. The benefit which parents derive from communal accommodation is less than in the infant age group. The transition to family-individual terms of reference is thus connected with a tendency to "innovation."

The overwhelming majority of arguments favor communal accommodation for older children. A tendency to ideological conservatism is paralleled by a tendency to organizational conservatism. In some cases considerations of what is best for the kibbutz and for the children compete with the parents' desire to retain the children within their jurisdiction, but mostly those debating the problems of the older age group prefer communal accommodation.

Quantitative analysis of the arguments. The controversy aroused by the problem of sleeping arrangements resulted in a lively and varied debate. As stated previously, we did not find two opposing factions, one attacking existing arrangements and the other fiercely defending them. Both the supporters and the opponents of communal accommodation agree that there is more than one side to the question and mention both advantages and shortcomings.

Fifty-four percent of a sample of 753 argued for communal accommodation, 46 percent for family accommodation. Only 4 percent of the arguments presented were emotional; the effect of the emotional factor is negligible. The problem of accommodation is mainly viewed as a matter of ideology. Ideological arguments are far more numerous (57 percent) than organizational ones (39 percent).

Table 15 indicates the distribution of arguments on each side of the discussion. Most of the emotional arguments appear in the demand for change. The collective argument is almost entirely founded on

Table 15. Distribution of emotional, organizational, and ideological arguments on both sides of the question of sleeping arrangements (percent)

	Collective ideology (N = 343)	Familistic ideology (N = 410)
Emotional	1	9
Organizational	56	19
Ideological	43	72
Total	100	100

organizational and ideological reasons. There is also a significant difference with regard to the relationship between organizational and ideological arguments. Organizational arguments are slightly more numerous than ideological ones in the collective ideology, but ideological considerations appear far more frequently than organizational considerations in the familistic ideology.

This table illustrates the weak ideological foundation of communal accommodation. Communal accommodation today is mainly based on organizational and functional considerations, whereas the demand for change is couched mainly in ideological terms. This conclusion was confirmed when we discovered that the great majority of those advancing ideological arguments in favor of communal accommodations were educators, male and female teachers, children's nurses, and instructors. Most of the parents who were not educators, and who supported communal accommodation, regarded it as a necessary administrative evil.

The number of references made to the good of the kibbutz in all responses is equal to the number made to the good of the parents (both 28 precent). Most of the stress is laid on the good of the children (44 percent). Table 16 shows the distribution of these attitudes

Table 16. Distribution of references to the kibbutz, the children, and the parents, on the two sides of the question of sleeping arrangements (percent)

	Collective ideology ($N = 150$)	Familistic ideology ($N = 183$)
Kibbutz	48	5
Parents	22	38
Children	30	57
Total	100	100

in each type of argument. Reference to the kibbutz is much more frequent in the arguments supporting communal accommodation than in those favoring family accommodation. The "conservative" argument is concerned mainly with the good of the kibbutz. The good of the children is mentioned slightly more often than the good of the parents. The argument for change is primarily concerned with the children's good. The good of the parents takes second place. The "neo-conservative" arguments focusing upon the good of the kibbutz are very few.

It should be noted that considerations of the good of the children are conspicuous in the ideology supporting change, not merely as regards the number of times they are mentioned, but also in the vigor and emotional force with which they are presented. References to the good of the parents are more moderate in tone, sometimes expressed reluctantly and almost apologetically. There is a tendency to belittle arguments relating to the parents and even to disguise them by arguing more strongly in favor of the good of the children. However, the parents' own resentment is occasionally discernible behind the facade of arguments based on anxiety for the children.

To sum up the points raised by the quantitative analysis: the arguments supporting communal accommodation are mentioned slightly more often than those supporting family accommodation. Functional-organizational considerations are stressed in the "conservative" argument, while emotional considerations are almost entirely lacking. Ideological considerations are emphasized in the argument for change, and there is also a fair amount of emotional argument. Extra-kibbutz reference is more common among the arguments for change than among the arguments for communal accommodation. The collective argument mainly stresses the good of the kibbutz, whereas the familistic argument stresses the good of the children.

Comparative analysis. It is instructive to examine variations in the intensity of the demand for family accommodation from kibbutz to kibbutz; among those who hold office and those who do not; among men and women; and from one generation to the next.

From general theoretical considerations regarding differentiation according to structural and ideological variables, we derive the following hypotheses about variations from kibbutz to kibbutz: (a) the demand for family accommodation will be greater in communes than in bunds; (b) the demand for family accommodation will be greater in unified communes than in federated communes; the attitude of factional communes will resemble that of unified communes; (c) the demand for family accommodation will be greatest in consumer kibbutzim; second place will be taken by the economy type kibbutzim; the smallest demand for family accommodation will be found in pioneering kibbutzim.

The data indicate that the attitudes can be placed in a sequence with the bund at one end and the factional commune at the other (Table

Table 17. The demand for change in sleeping arrangements: comparison of
types of kibbutzim (percent)

		Communes		
Accommodation favored	Bunds (N = 45)	Federated (N = 104)	Unified (N = 180)	Factional (N = 86)
Communal	64	56	46	23
Family	26	34	44	67
No data	10	10	10	10
Total	100	100	100	100

17). The extreme familistic attitude of the factional commune is rather
surprising: it was assumed that the amount of familism would differ
only slightly from that of the unified commune. The key to this finding
will be found in analysis of dominant values. Differences among the
various types of kibbutzim are not outstanding. In fact, the transition
from kibbutzim of one type to another is gradual.

Comparison on the basis of the value patterns dominant in each
kibbutz is shown in Table 18.

Table 18. The demand for change in sleeping arrangements:
comparison of kibbutz value patterns (percent)

Accommodation favored	Pioneering kibbutzim (N = 80)	Economic-oriented kibbutzim (N = 91)	Consumer-oriented kibbutzim (N = 194)
Communal	61	56	27
Family	27	36	63
No data	12	8	10
Total	100	100	100

Economic kibbutzim are a little more familistic than pioneering
kibbutzim, and are less familistic than consumer kibbutzim. The difference between pioneering and economic kibbutzim is qute small, but
that between economic and consumer kibbutzim is great. It appears
that the consumer pattern greatly encourages the demand for family
accommodation. This finding largely explains the great extent of familism in factional communes, since all the factional communes are
of the consumer type.

We assume that in a collective society, members who are more collectivistic than others will rise to positions of leadership. From this
assumption we may derive the following propositions: (a) support of

communal accommodation will be stronger among office holders than among members who do not hold office; (b) the weight of ideological arguments in favor of communal accommodation will be greater among office holders; (c) office holders will refer to considerations of the kibbutz's interest more often than others.

Table 19 shows the intensity of the demand for change. The holders

Table 19. The demand for change in sleeping arrangements: comparison between holders of public office and other members (percent)

Accommodation favored	Holders of office (N = 87)	Others (N = 353)
Communal	50	41
Family	39	49
No data	11	10
Total	100	100

of office are slightly more "conservative" than the rest, but the differences between holders of office and those who do not hold office is quite small. There is a difference in the arguments brought forth, however. The holders of public office mention ideological reasons in 58 percent of the responses, whereas 59 percent of the responses of other members emphasize organization arguments. Predictably, the holders of office are more aware of considerations of the good of the kibbutz than the rest: 41 percent of their responses refer to the good of the kibbutz as against 28 percent among other members. The good of parents and children is of somewhat less concern among holders of office than among the rest.

Holders of office were found to be only somewhat more conservative, ideologically oriented, and collectivistic than the rest, as regards arguments supporting the "conservative" choice. This conclusion fits our hypotheses, although the differences as regards intensity of demand for change were rather less than expected. From a more detailed examination of the problem we came to the conclusion that office holders cannot be treated as a single category, and that their attitudes are formed principally through interaction with their kibbutz. The office holders' leadership is expressed in the tenacity with which they cling to the dominant opinion in their kibbutz; leadership working against majority opinion was observed only in kibbutzim suffering from a partial blockage of channels of communication.

From the general hypotheses of the "familism" of women members, four secondary hypotheses are derived: (a) demand for change will prevail more among women members than among men; (b) the demand for family accommodation during infancy and at all ages will prevail more among women than among men; (c) the ideological basis for communal accommodation will be weaker among women than among men; (d) reference to the good of the kibbutz will be less frequent among women than among men, while reference to the good of parents and children will be more frequent.

Let us first compare the intensity of the demand for family accommodation (Table 20). The percentage of supporters of communal ac-

Table 20. The demand for change in sleeping arrangements: comparison between men and women (percent)

Accommodation favored	Men (N = 226)	Women (N = 183)
Communal	49	37
Family	40	51
No data	11	12
Total	100	100

commodation among women members is lower than among men. The opposite is true of supporters of family accommodation. The table thus to some extent confirms the hypothesis, but it should be noted that the difference is smaller than expected.

An analysis of the age groups favored for family accommodation shows slight differences between men and women members (Table 21).

Table 21. Age groups favored for family accommodation: comparison between Men and Women (percent)

	Men	Women
Infants	35	30
Young children	45	47
Older children	20	23
Total	100	100

There is no difference in the relative order of importance. The greatest demand centers on young children and then on infants, with the older children coming third. The demand for family accommodation in infancy is slightly stronger among men than among women, but the opposite is true for the younger and older children. This result contradicts the hypothesis of a particularly strong link existing between mother and infant, and we found the explanation for this only after examining the ideological versus the organizational arguments regarding infants. The demand for family accommodation for all ages was found to be slightly more common among women (9 percent) than among men (6 percent).

The weight of ideological considerations proved greater among men than among women (47 versus 40 percent). The male members' answers indicate an almost equal balance between organizational and ideological arguments (53 versus 47 percent), but among women there is a greater discrepancy (60 versus 40 percent). The weakness of ideological arguments in support of communal accommodation is noticeable with all those in favor of communal accommodation, but is more pronounced in the answers of women members than in those of men.

We did not examine statistically which type of argument is stressed most for each age group, but a quasi-quantitative examination of responses regarding infants explains why demands for family accommodation during infancy are relatively few among women. Women members emphasize ideological arguments in favor of family accommodation during infancy more strongly than men. However, they also refer more frequently to organizational arguments against change. The additional burden involved in family accommodation at that age would be borne mainly by them. Organizational considerations thus counteract ideological ones and prevent many female members from deciding in favor of change as regards this age group.

Reference to the general interest of the kibbutz is more common among men (34 percent of men's responses) than among women (23 percent). The opposite is true of reference to the good of the children (35 versus 47 percent), but there is almost no difference between men and women as regards references to the good of the parents (31 versus 30 percent). Men mention all three in almost equal proportions, whereas among women there is a sequence: reference to the children is most frequent, followed by reference to the parents, with reference to the kibbutz coming third.

The differences brought out by the comparative analysis of men and women fit our hypotheses, but are less marked than expected. In order to understand why the attitudes of men and women members are so similar, we conducted a more detailed examination of the intensity of the demand for change. In this analysis, we found that women holding office and those employed in agriculture or in skilled work are less familistic than other women and are more likely to support communal accommodation for all ages. Add to this the fact that relatively few women support family accommodation in infancy, and it will be seen that the peculiar attitude of women to the matter of accommodation derives less from their being mothers and hence more deeply and strongly attached to their children than it does from their problems or lack of problems at work. Dissatisfaction with communal accommodation results mainly from dissatisfaction with work.

The last stage in our comparative analysis is an examination of the distribution of attitudes and arguments in the second generation. From our hypotheses we may assume that members of the second generation will be far more familistic than members of bunds, but less so than members of the first generation.

The data (Table 22) indicate that the attitude of second generation

Table 22. The demand for change in sleeping arrangements: comparison of bunds, second generation, and first generation (percent)

Accommodation favored	Bunds (N = 45)	Second generation (N = 72)	First generation (N = 241)
Communal	64	58	44
Family	26	34	46
No data	10	8	10
Total	100	100	100

members is closer to that of bund members than to that of the first generation. The second generation is slightly more familistic than members of bunds, but much less so than members of the first generation.

In both bunds and the first generation in communes, young children are emphasized far more than infants, whereas among the second generation, infants are more emphasized than young children (Table 23). Older children take third place in the scale. The attitude of the second generation is close to that of the bunds as regards the demand for family accommodation at all ages. Not one of the bund members favored family accommodation in all age groups, nor did one of the members of the second generation overtly favor it.

Unlike members of the first generation and the bunds, members of

Table 23. Age groups favored for family accommodation: comparison of bunds, second generation, and first generation (percent)

	Bunds (N = 15)	Second generation (N = 54)	First generation (N = 130)
Infants	43	50	30
Young children	50	40	44
Older children	7	10	26
Total	100	100	100

the second generation present a large number (15 percent of their responses) of emotional arguments in favor of communal accommodation. More than one member of the second generation supported communal accommodation not from any kind of rational or ideological reason, but because he had pleasant and happy memories of communal accommodation. An examination of the relation between ideological and organizational arguments also proves interesting. The second generation again takes an attitude midway between the first generation and the bunds. The second generation refers to organizational reasons slightly more often than bund members, but less often than members of the first generation. The opposite is true as regards ideological arguments.

A different picture emerges in connection with frames of reference. In the bund, most of the emphasis is placed on considerations of the good of the kibbutz (55 percent of the responses). Parents are mentioned slightly more often than children. The second generation views the problem from its own experience of communal accommodation, and puts most of the emphasis on considerations of the good of the children (50 percent of the responses). Considerations of the good of the kibbutz are mentioned slightly more often than benefit to parents. In the first generation, as in the second, first preference (41 percent) is given to considerations of the good of the children, but this preference is clearer in the second generation.

To summarize these findings: Members of the second generation have adopted an attitude resembling that of the first generation with regard to the demand for family accommodation. Like members of the bunds, they rarely favor family accommodation, rarely refer to older children, and hardly ever favor family accommodation for all ages. Unlike members of the bunds and members of the first generation, the second generation places most emphasis on family accommodation in infancy. In the division between organizational and ideological emphasis, members of the second generation have adopted an attitude midway between that of the first generation and that of members of bunds. Members of the first generation and members of the bunds mention rational ideological considerations in favor of communal accommodation, but members of the second generation also offer emotional arguments. The order of relative importance of the three spheres is identical, but members of the second generation emphasize the good of the children more, and the good of the parents less, than members of the first generation.

Several questions suggest themselves: How does the process of growing up and taking part in kibbutz affairs affect the attitude of the second generation? Is the youths' attitude distinguishable from that of adults, that of bachelors from that of married couples, and that of boys from that of girls?

We may assume that the second generation in a kibbutz is exposed to two opposing influences: the process of institutionalization and the strengthening of the family on the one hand, and socialization in the communal education system on the other. This general assumption leads to secondary assumptions regarding the effects of adolescence on attitudes toward the problem of accommodation. If we assume that communal upbringing ensures a positive attitude toward the kibbutz and restrains the widespread tendency to familism, its effects will be strongest during the period when a young person is under its direct influence. This influence will weaken to some extent upon entry into the working and family life of the kibbutz. This invites two distinct hypotheses: (a) the demand for family accommodation will be more widespread among adults than among adolescents; (b) the demand for family accommodation will be more widespread among married couples than among unmarried adults.

For the purpose of this analysis, we included in our sample of the second generation an auxiliary sample of pupils in the eleventh and twelfth forms of the kibbutz school, who were still under the direct influence of communal upbringing. This sample contains 404 boys and girls from various kibbutzim.[4]

4. Moshe M. Sarell was responsible for organizing the extended study of the second generation (adolescents) and formulating the special hypothesis in this context. A detailed discussion of the hypotheses and of the process of adolescence among kibbutz children will be found in his article (115).

Table 24. The demand for change in sleeping arrangements among the second generation: comparison of adolescents, married adults, and unmarried adults (percent)

Accommodation favored	Adolescents (N = 404)	Unmarried adults (N = 42)	Married adults (N = 28)
Communal	67	66	38
Family	25	24	50
No data	8	10	12
Total	100	100	100

Table 24 shows that there is no difference between these adolescents and the unmarried adults. The difference arises with marriage, not upon leaving school. Adolescents and unmarried adults strongly prefer communal accommodation. Married adults, on the other hand, prefer family accommodation. A comparison of this table with Table 22 shows that the difference between the first and second generations is gradually diminished—the attitude of the married second generation is similar to that of the first generation.

When we compare men and women of the second generation we again assume that there are two opposing influences. The process forcing women members into familism is also at work in the second generation, and it can be assumed that women in the second generation, like those in the first generation, will be more familistic than the men. According to our assumption, the influence of communal upbringing counteracts this tendency. Both sexes are brought up together in the kibbutz. Educational ideology also emphasizes the equality of sexes. We should expect to find differences between the sexes, but not marked ones.

Table 25 compares boys and girls, unmarried men and women, and married men and women. From the numbers favoring communal accommodation we conclude that boys are slightly less familistic than

Table 25. The demand for change in sleeping arrangements: comparison between second generation men and women (percent)

Accommodation favored	Boys (N = 215)	Girls (N = 189)	Single men (N = 28)	Single women (N = 14)	Married men (N = 14)	Married women (N = 14)
Communal	70	63	68	62	43	36
Family	20	30	25	23	50	50
No data	10	7	7	15	7	14
Total	100	100	100	100	100	100

girls, single men are slightly less familistic than single women and married men slightly less familistic than married women. The differences are minimal. This table shows that marriage is the turning point for both men and women. There is almost no difference between boys and single men, and no significant difference between girls and single women. Marriage tends to strengthen support of family accommodation in both sexes. Differences between the sexes are small, and they follow the same pattern.

The internal comparative analysis largely confirms the central assumption that guided our analysis of the attitudes of members of the second generation. The influence of communal upbringing comes out in the limited demand for family accommodation among adolescents and unmarried adults. This influence is also discernible in the limited differentiation between the sexes. The influence of institutionalization can be seen in the change brought about by marriage and in the differences among members of the second generation in the various kibbutzim.

Summary. Let us now sum up the main conclusion regarding the scope, significance, and trends in the demand for family accommodation.

The distribution of attitudes throughout the sample shows that "innovating" and "conservative" forces are equally balanced: the percentage of supporters of communal accommodation equals that of the supporters of family accommodation. In five of the kibbutzim in the sample, the majority were "conservative," in seven the majority were "innovators."

The attitudes of those favoring family accommodation were divided with respect to the age groups proposed for change. The number of supporters of family accommodation for all ages is relatively small. Only a small minority demand family accommodation for older children. Although one might expect the demand for family accommodation would be strongest as regards infants, it appeared that most of the emphasis was placed on the middle age group.

As for the arguments advanced, the collectivist argument is based on the claim that communal accommodation is suited to the organizational and ideological structure of the kibbutz, and that it is an essential educational tool for ensuring intergeneration continuity. The familistic argument, on the other hand, is based on a demand for greater freedom, for the promotion of individual differences, and for stronger ties among family members.

Quantitative analysis of the set of arguments throws additional light on the significance of the trend toward change and fortifies the conclusions drawn from the qualitative analysis: Communal accommodation now appears to be based mainly on organizational and technical considerations, whereas the demand for change mainly raises ideological considerations. Reference to outside factors figures more commonly among the arguments supporting the demand for change than in the argument for the "conservative" outlook. The already existing trend toward change enlists in its aid allegedly scientific theories. Arguments for the good of the kibbutz appear mainly in "conservative" reasoning. As against this, individual-family orientation increases in the arguments used to further the demand for change. Those in favor of family accommodation mainly emphasize the children's benefit. Strong ideological pressure exists in favor of family accommodation in infancy, but as against this, there is strong organizational pressure in favor of communal accommodation at that age. The arguments concerning young children tend mainly to support family accommodation; the demand for family accommodation from the parents' and the children's point of view has to contend with considerations of the good of the kibbutz, but the tendency to "innovate" is increasing. The overwhelming majority of arguments concerning older children favor communal accommodation.

Our hypotheses concerning structural and ideological factors in different kibbutzim were largely confirmed. Significant differences were discovered in the intensity of the demand for change. The relative order of importance of age groups is generally the same. Small but significant differences were discovered concerning the intensity of the demand for family accommodation at all ages.

Comparative analysis refuted our hypotheses concerning office holders. The holders of public office appear to be no less familistic than members who do not hold office.

Our hypotheses as regards the differences between men and women members were largely confirmed. Women members are more familistic than men. The demand for change is stronger among women than among men in most kibbutzim in our sample. Women members holding office, however, and those employed in agriculture or in skilled work, are much less familistic than other women. For women, satisfaction with communal accommodation is closely linked with satisfaction with work and the desire to continue at it.

As regards the second generation, our hypothesis that they stand halfway between the first generation and the bunds was largely confirmed. Institutionalization can be observed in the differences among members of the second generation in various kibbutzim and in the effects of marriage on their attitudes. When the second generation establish families of their own, their attitudes change, and the differential between their attitudes and those of their parents is reduced. The attitudes of married second generation members are similar to those of the first generation.

These were the chief conclusions of the study.

4. The Parental Role in Occupational Placement of the Second Generation

The kibbutz family plays no ostensible role in the process of vocational placement, since placement is a matter that concerns the kibbutz and the member as an individual but not as the son of his parents. Communal childrearing practices are largely designed to neutralize family influence in the socialization process. The practice of providing all kibbutz children with a standardized elementary and secondary education is intended to prevent differences due to schooling; education is provided directly by the collective and does not hinge on family status. In this respect the kibbutz goes further than other societies which have restricted family influence by basing vocational placement on individual competition or which have transferred most placement functions to the public. Presumably, being an extreme case, the kibbutz affords an opportunity to examine the fundamental principles of the collectivist pattern with greater perspective. We shall try to trace the underlying assumptions and problems peculiar to this pattern and the mechanisms conducive to its proper operation. After describing the strictly collectivist pattern we shall try to see how compromise is effected with the demands of the individual and of the family. Finally, the attitude of kibbutz members to the placement demands of the family will be used as an indicator of the general position of the family in the kibbutz.

Before dealing with the special problems of the occupational placement of the second generation let us briefly look at the development of overall placement patterns in the kibbutz from their original configuration in the absolute collective, or bund, to the compromise pattern that is reached with the transition from bund to commune.

At the bund stage the collectivist pattern is decisive. This pattern

NOTE. This essay appeared in Hebrew in *Megamoth*, volume 8 (1957).

rests on a number of interrelated concepts according to which the kibbutz regulates the allocation of functions. Members voluntarily accept the authority of the kibbutz and are unreservedly at the disposal of the work organizer. Satisfaction from work is to be derived from productivity as such, from the very fact of working, whatever the specific task may be. All tasks serve the kibbutz and are, from that point of view, equivalent. In principle any member can perform any function: the presumed equivalence of functions goes hand in hand with a presumed equal capability of all members. The practice of regular rotation is meant to solve any personal problems that might arise from variations in working conditions or in the congeniality of different tasks.

The realities of work organization and economic operations usually require a revision of this absolutely collectivist pattern. Considerable variation soon becomes evident in the relative ability of members to carry out different functions. Many tasks require special aptitudes and inclinations or call for experience, persistence, and vocational training. Considerations of efficiency and rationalization also have their effect. Equalitarianism gradually succumbs to specialization, and the principle of constant rotation of functions ceases to apply, although it is still maintained, to a lesser degree than before, in service branches which do not require a high degree of specialization.

The shift from temporary to permanent placement requires some ideological reformulations as well. In most cases the solution has been to graft the individualist pattern onto the collectivist one. Although according to this new conception the kibbutz still is the main regulator of occupational planning and placement, it is accepted that a member can fully succeed in his work only if it allows him personal expression and if he is permanently associated with it. The member still has to submit to the authority of the kibbutz—the work placement officer may ask him to fulfill tasks which he does not like either for a trial period before his permanent placement or at regular intervals—but fairness now demands that his requests and aptitudes be taken into account in the allocation of his permanent job. According to this pattern fitness of members for their jobs is considered to be in the interest of both the kibbutz and the individual.

The mingling of collectivism with individualism is reflected also in the compromise between rotation and tenure. Before permanently settling in a given job, first of all, a member undergoes a period of selection and adjustment. Time shows whether he is fit for his task and whether he integrates well with the work group. If it turns out that his demands are not dictated by a passing whim, that he truly wants his job and is good at it, he deserves to be permanently instated. Nevertheless, this tenure is no barrier to a change of jobs, should the member so desire. It is also accepted that a member should, for a year or two, take on a different position either in response to a job call-up or as a relief from tension and strain.

This pattern, combining relative stability with moderate rotation, serves several important overt and latent functions. The flexible and gradual approach to job allocation considerably blunts competition. Generally the shifts are temporary and sooner or later most members find their proper niche. Settling down to a job does not mean that the last word has been spoken and does not put a lid on a member's career once and for all. Contact with more than one branch of the kibbutz economy prevents the member's perspective from becoming restricted to a narrow occupational sphere. It makes for more varied experience and larger vision, and to some extent prevents occupational segregation, detrimental to identification with the collective economy as a whole.

As for occupational training, the principle here is that in most branches there is no need for it. Most of the training is acquired during a preparatory period spent on an older kibbutz and in the course of daily work on one's own kibbutz. Experienced senior workers train newcomers, and what is lacking in practical training is made up for by various courses of instruction. Where lengthy training is required candidates are chosen from among the most devoted and successful permanent workers. Vocational training, insofar as it is required, does not precede the taking of a job but usually comes after several years of practical work. Most people leave for vocational training only after they have put down roots within the kibbutz, and frequently after they have set up a family.

The appearance of the second generation poses a test of the collectivist-individualist pattern. The way this pattern operates in the occupational placement of the young highlights its effectiveness but at the same time reveals a number of defects. In the occupational placement of the second generation prime importance attaches to the slowness of the process. Youngsters are given plenty of time to decide on their occupational futures. While still at school, children work in several branches of the kibbutz economy. After completing their studies and becoming kibbutz members they proceed to do their stint of military service. When they come back from the army they are as a rule required to work for a year or two in understaffed divisions for which it is difficult to find workers, for example, the dairy barn or the vegetable garden. Thus many years are spent in a distinctly collective setting until the youngster finally settles in a job. Even then, if he has made a bad bargain or if he changes his mind, he may still ask for a different job. The advantages that this placement system offered the first generation—flexibility, overall view of the entire kibbutz, and selectivity—are still greater for the second.

Nevertheless certain unforeseen drawbacks are also noticeable. The difficulties stem largely from the fact that on the one hand the individualist pattern is stronger and no longer clearly subordinate to the collectivist pattern, while on the other hand the influence of the family has been growing. The collectivist-individualist pattern presumes a considerable range of occupational aspirations; attraction of members of different aptitudes and interests to different branches coupled with the social equality of all functions was thought sufficient to ensure a regular supply of workers for most departments. Collectivist-individualist placement can operate properly only as long as job supply and demand largely coincide, but this balance, as it turns out, is not always assured. Most second generation members are interested in only a few occupations and have rejected certain branches altogether. Many girls, for instance, want to be teachers or nurses; some aspire to agricultural jobs; but most do not want to work in the services, the main occupation of kibbutz women. Among boys the discrepancy between supply and demand is less striking but they, too, show a strong tendency toward technical occupations, especially agricultural mechanics, and a disinclination to work in other fields, mainly the dairy farm and the vegetable garden. Jobs have begun to be evaluated on a scale—it is not steeply graded and absolute, but certain occupations seem to be considered less dignified or popular than others.

A further difficulty is that the second generation starts its working life while the first generation is still in its prime and is still holding down most of the specialized jobs. In a kibbutz the changing of the guards is necessarily gradual. When the kibbutz is expanding, occupational choice is not severely restricted but sometimes the more popular jobs have been filled and for a long time there will be no opening. Reserve cadres for specialized jobs such as agricultural machinery maintenance, teaching, child care, and health services are not infrequently drawn mainly from the first cohorts of the second generation to become kibbutz members, to the disadvantage of their successors.

However, as long as the occupational needs of the kibbutz are implicitly preferred over the fulfillment of personal demands and the job image remains flexible, adaptation and compromise are the rule. This ceases to be so when individual motivation gains the upper hand and the job image becomes rigid. According to the premises of the collectivist-individualist pattern, kibbutz members must choose their occupations from among the jobs offered by the kibbutz. The increase in more or less deviant demands is evidence of individualist considerations. There has been a greater demand for placement in jobs for which sufficient experts are available, and for occupational training over and above what is needed to fill the jobs available. Occupations which remove members permanently from the collective and from physical labor are still shunned, but here and there demands are voiced for training in professions which cannot be easily practiced inside a kibbutz, as are demands for higher education and the development of artistic talents. Personal desires break through the old collectivist pattern and no systematic attempt has yet been made to redraw the line between what is considered legitimate and what is not.

The desire to accede to personal demands and to a lesser extent the requirements of specialization act against the former practice of postponing training. It has been realized that in several occupations it is better for training to come before practical work and that its postponement is disadvantageous. Most vocational training institutions, such as teacher-training colleges, agricultural schools, or nursing schools, are designed for adolescents and only a few are suited to adult students. The admission of persons of a relatively advanced age causes special difficulties even in institutions designed for adults. Members of the second generation are affected by the accepted training patterns outside the kibbutz and not infrequently demand training immediately on coming back from the army since they do not want to become absorbed by kibbutz life before they have a trade. If not training, they want quick permanent job placement; they find it difficult to live for years without clear vocational definition.

The entry of the second generation into the work force raises the further problem of the status of the parents in the placement process. The first generation had dissociated itself from its parents and by entering the kibbutz removed itself from their authority. The position of the second generation is quite different. Kibbutz continuity also implies family continuity, and by now the family has acquired an influence considerably exceeding the narrow bounds allotted to it in the institutional division of labor and by the accepted ideology. Parents have a vital interest in the occupational choice of their children since work, perhaps more than anything else, determines the status and career of a kibbutz member. Parents are conscious of the great importance of the occupational choice for their children's future. They also feel that this may be the last decision their children will make as members of their family, before they set out on their own life within the kibbutz. Voluntarily or involuntarily parents become partners to the decision. Although on the face of it they have no official standing as an interested party and their intervention has no ideological justification, and although as a rule they regard their function as secondary and are reluctant to act, they often try to influence their children. This influence has been noticeable throughout the protracted process of socialization, but it becomes more concentrated and intensive as soon as problems of vocational training and of choosing a place of work begin to loom on the horizon. Sometimes parents collaborate with the official institutions and try to make their children bow to the wishes of the kibbutz; sometimes they act contrary to the kibbutz; sometimes they insist on their own preferences; and sometimes they only help their child to proceed along the path he himself has chosen.

Once the matter comes up for decision—even for temporary decision —attempts are sometimes made to influence the community. Not infrequently parents try to talk to the people in charge or to canvass public opinion in favor of their positions. Sometimes they also appear in public at meetings. In kibbutzim with marked family solidarity the effect of behind-the-scenes influence sometimes takes the form of unwritten interfamily agreements which assure mutual support in matters of vocational training and job allocation. These alliances are not legitimate and are made almost without any words being passed. When the younger generation is at loggerheads with the kibbutz, parents usually side with their children; even if they do not, even if they are opposed to their children's wishes, they find it difficult not to defend them. Open conflict between parents and the kibbutz is rare and points of disagreement are generally settled in one way or another, but sometimes a split is unavoidable and a dispute ensues. Members who for many long years have given much and varied proof of their loyalty to the kibbutz sometimes do not stand the test of unwavering submission when it comes to the training of their children. Matters have in certain instances reached the point where members have absented themselves from the general meeting or threatened to leave the kibbutz altogether.

Thus the collective pattern has to vie with and defend itself against both the individualist and the familistic pattern.

Attitudes toward occupational placement patterns were tested in interviews with a representative sample of kibbutz members. The following three questions were asked: Should the family influence the vocational choice of its children? Should the kibbutz consider the parents' wishes in this matter? Should the kibbutz consider the wishes of the children? The first two questions relate to the position of the parents in the placement process while the third relates to the status of the children. We also asked about the parents' occupational aspirations for their children; the replies to this question were not scored but the reasons given for the choice of occupation helped us to understand the answers to the placement questions.

Let us analyze the questions relating to parents separately and then together. Most subjects who answered the first question, whether in the negative or in the affirmative, added a qualification or definition of the term "influence." A set of fairly well accepted, almost stereotyped, concepts emerged which may be systematically ranked in a scale. Those who favored parental influence distinguished among intervention, influence, guidance, consultation, and creation of an atmosphere; for each of these concepts a distinction has to be made between whether it refers to the children or to the collective. "Intervention" means the exertion of strong open pressure. With reference to the kibbutz: "Kibbutz parents have to watch out for their child when he is in danger of suffering an injustice; they have to fight his battles." With reference to the children: "If the child makes a wrong choice his parents have to intervene and prevent it by all possible means." "Influence" generally means a direct and consistent attempt by the parents to make their views felt: "I shall do all I can to influence my child in this matter"; and with reference to the kibbutz, "Parents are entitled to exert their influence and to take an active part in the discussion." "Guidance" is the exercise of a moderate influence, mainly on the children: "Not to influence but cautiously to lead the child in the right direction"; and with reference to the kibbutz; "Parents do not have the right to urge and demand but they may try to push matters in the desired direction." The term "consultation" suggests a further limitation of the influence parents may exert on their children. With reference to the kibbutz it was stated that parents may "talk to those concerned," "explain and advise," but "they are advisers without voting rights." Some go further and would not allow the parents any initiative in the matter: "The main task of the parents is to give advice but only when the child or the committee expressly asks for it." "Creation of atmosphere" consists mainly of indirect influence, by way of example, rather than of any direct action. According to this view there is not much use in giving advice since what matters is the values the child unwittingly absorbs. From here it is a mere step to negating all influence whatever.

The percentage distribution of attitudes toward parental influence can be tabulated as follows (N = 415).

In favor of:

Intervention	0.4%
Influence	19.0
Guidance	14.4
Consultation	18.3
Creation of atmosphere	0.4
Against parental influence	37.8
No reply	9.7
Total	100

Let us classify these answers in three main categories: affirmative (including intervention and influence), qualified affirmative (including guidance, consultation, and creation of atmosphere), and negative. We then have 19.4 percent affirmative, 33.1 percent qualified affirmative, and 37.8 percent negative. Thus a higher percentage was fully or partly in favor of parental influence than absolutely against it. But outright rejection was slightly more frequent than modified affirmation and much more so than complete affirmation. A not very large minority was absolutely in favor of family influence. Only two respondents in the entire sample were for intervention. It appears therefore that approval of family influence is prevalent, but meets with considerable opposition.

In answering the second question—"Should the kibbutz consider the parents' wishes?"—a decisive majority tended to modify the need for parental consideration. A four-rank scale was established: absolute affirmative: "Yes—definitely"; qualified affirmative: "Consensus should be reached insofar as possible"; qualified negative: "Conflict should be avoided but the parents have no right to claim final consideration"; absolute negative: "It does not concern them." The percentage distribution of responses according to this scale is as follows ($N = 415$).

Favor consideration		49.0%
Absolute affirmative	21.7	
Qualified affirmative	27.3	
Oppose consideration		46.2
Qualified negative	15.8	
Absolute negative	30.4	
No reply		4.8
Total		100

The votes for and against parental consideration were almost balanced, the yeas slightly outnumbering the nays, with more absolutely opposing than absolutely favoring parental consideration.

When the answers to the two questions relating to the parents are read in conjunction with the response about the parents' occupational aspirations for their children, some definition of the parental role vis-à-vis children and kibbutz may in many cases be arrived at.

Let us first consider those opposed to family influence because it is contrary to kibbutz interests. The most widespread argument against parental influence on these grounds was that parents do not represent the educational goals of the kibbutz: "The parents are not always at one with the collective and with kibbutz life," or "parents are the representatives of reactionary forces." Their disappointment with kibbutz life and disillusionment with kibbutz ideals is said to have been transferred to their children: "every mother wants her son to become a professor"; "parents warn their children away from occupations in which they have experienced difficulties." According to this argument, parents are also supposed to be lacking in objectivity: "parents think their children are geniuses and they cannot be relied upon in this matter." Quite a rare argument, but important to our analysis, is the fear of status distinctions, whereby if parents are allowed to exert influence an opening will be provided for hereditary high-status positions.

Side by side with the pattern in which giving priority to collective needs is combined with lack of confidence in the parents, we found a secondary pattern where priority is also given to collective needs but this is coupled with confidence in the parents. Here it is the parents' function to give active support to the educational goals of the kibbutz. "The kibbutz cannot give the required guidance in the direction desired without the parents' support"; "success is assured only when kibbutz and parents act together."

In opposition to parental influence on account of preference being given to the wishes of the children the dominant desire is not to restrict the child's freedom of choice; the child's untrameled inclinations are sacrosanct and his spontaneous development should not be interfered with: "It is the child who decides. One must not force him." This reluctance to give any guidance to one's children and the tendency to give them a free hand often arise from memories of the parents' own revolt against the older generation. "Did we obey our parents? Then why should we ask our children to do what we want?" Sometimes this complete resignation is not the result of any educational approach but of sheer impotence: "Your children won't do what you want them to do anyhow. It is better not to interfere."

Just as in the collectivist pattern we found parents admitted as secondary supporting agents of the kibbutz, here too we see parents admitted as agents supporting their children. It is considered the parents' function to help children to follow the course they have chosen. Parents are supposed to know their children intimately and be able to help them when they are confused and unable to find their own way.

At the other extreme, furthest removed from the purely collectivist pattern, we found a pattern affirming and justifying parental influence. The main argument here hinges on the contention that parents are experienced and know their child well. "Parents have experience of life and of work. Children should obey them." With a slight tinge of guilt one member said: "If I was a good kibbutz member I would no doubt say that it is none of my business. But I am not a good kibbutz member and I believe that children belong to their parents and parents are entitled to demand that they get a suitable occupation."

That opposition to parental influence is based less on considerations of kibbutz interest than on the belief in the right of one's children to exercise free choice is clear from the following tabulation (N = 354).

Opposition to parental influence because of kibbutz interests	17.1%
Parents should serve as supporting agents of the kibbutz	12.7
Opposition to parental influence because of the children's interests	27.2
Parents should serve as supporting agents of the children	33.5
Primary emphasis on parental influence	9.5

When parents are assigned a supporting function, it is again their children rather than the kibbutz that they are expected to support. Only a small minority place primary emphasis on parental influence, and the main ideological justification is not the parents' right to assert their view but their duty to help their children.

Let us now arrange the answers by placement patterns. A collective pattern, based on the supremacy of collective considerations, is discernible in 29.8 percent of the responses. This pattern includes opposition to parental influence because of collective interests and the conviction that the parents should serve as supporting agents of the kibbutz. An individualist pattern, based on opposition to parental influence because of the children's interests, is found in 27.2 percent of the responses. A familistic pattern, based on cooperation between parents and children, is found in 43 percent. Thus a considerable proportion was in favor of a familistic pattern.

We come now to the third question, whether the kibbutz ought to consider the wishes of the children in the matter of occupational placement.

Unqualified affirmative answers partly hark back to the collectivist ideology which looks upon work as a value and a source of satisfaction in itself. But while the collectivist ideology stressed the creative aspect of work, the individualist ideology refers mainly to social status. "Satisfying work is the most important thing in the kibbutz. Everyone is entitled to an occupation he likes—the kibbutz ought to compromise with the children and let them have a job they like."

Most of those who advocated unqualified consideration of the children's wishes placed the main emphasis on freedom of choice and the right of personal expression: "The child should be given his desire—the kibbutz is his home—one must not force anything on him that he does not want." There were some who stressed the special position of the second generation in this regard. Few of those who gave unqualified affirmative answers were aware of the difficulties involved in giving full consideration to individual wishes in a collective, but some distinctly took account of this: "Training is justified even if the kibbutz does not need it and cannot make use of it"; "the kibbutz must make its plans according to existing aspirations and inclinations and adapt itself to them."

Of course, affirmative replies were also subject to various qualifications. With reference to the collective, the following were taken into consideration: the resources of the kibbutz and its ability to pay for the training desired; the potential contribution of the desired occupation to the kibbutz; the appropriateness of the occupation to specific present needs. A second group of qualifications would restrict the duty of the kibbutz to respond to the youngsters' wishes to those cases where interest and inclination have been proved by persistence and success in practical work, and/or there is some evidence of outstanding talent.

At the bottom of the scale we find unqualified negative answers declaring absolute loyalty to the collectivistic pattern. According to this pattern collective needs determine placement policy to the last particular and adolescents have to submit to the kibbutz rules and requirements. "We shall not be able to set up a proper economy and a stable society if we do not place ourselves and our children at the disposal of the kibbutz. The needs of the kibbutz are the main thing."

Let us classify the answers ($N = 415$) in four categories:

Unqualified affirmative: individualist pattern	47.3%
Slightly qualified affirmative: where the individualist pattern comes first and the collectivist pattern second—individualist-collectivist pattern.	21.8
Strictly qualified affirmative: where the collectivist pattern comes first and the individualist pattern second—collectivist-individualist pattern.	17.3
Unqualified negative: purely collectivist pattern.	3.8

("No answer" accounts for 9.8 percent.) Most striking is the great stress placed on the children's right to demand full consideration of their wishes: about half the subjects in the sample gave an unqualified affirmative reply, more than in all other categories taken together. Collectivist considerations were mentioned in 43 percent of all responses, but the collectivist pattern had supremacy in only 21 percent of the total; only 3.8 percent followed a purely collectivist pattern.

The conclusions here are to be treated with some reservation since analysis of the answers shows that they were affected by the proximity of another question on the need for parental consideration. In many instances the response was based on a comparison between the relative rights of parents and children rather than on full consideration of all the factors involved. Often emphatic and unqualified affirmation of the youngsters' rights to have their wishes considered was a protest more against parental influence than against kibbutz authority. The parent-child relationship overshadowed the issue of the children's relations with the kibbutz, and collectivist considerations were put in the background. Full confirmation of this will be found in the comparative analysis below.

Sometimes the subjects suggest the need for objective, impartial evaluation in occupational placement. Reference is made to psycho-technical tests, teachers, and an education commission. Objective evaluation media are no doubt among the major techniques used by all nonascriptive placement systems, all systems based on factors other than ascribed status. Some nonascriptive placement problems can be solved by detailed examination of skills and aptitudes. Careful deliberation based on reliable tests thus replaces the clash of conflicting wills and interests. Stress is shifted from the aspirations of the youngster or his parents to an examination of the youngster's capacities: "The child's attributes rather than his desires should be considered."

The desire for an objective yardstick, characteristic of the nonascriptive placement method, finds its purest expression in the faith placed in psycho-technical tests. From the interviews and from observations conducted during the administration of tests we found that quite a few regard them as the embodiment of scientific method and devoutly believe in their problem-solving powers. Reliance on tests takes the matter out of the hands of all concerned; the decision rests with an independent impartial authority; evaluation of the test is based on reliable criteria and therefore the findings are beyond dispute.

To be sure, there also are objections to overreliance on tests. "I do not believe that it is really possible to evaluate children properly by means of a short and oversimplified questionnaire"; "the idea that the qualities of a person can be properly evaluated by means of a standard questionnaire, without personal contact, arouses distrust and repugnance." Though not expressly mentioned, it is clear that opposition to testing and examination—a major element of kibbutz education generally—and qualms about grading of pupils by level of aptitude alone act as deterrents against overreliance on psycho-technical tests.

Those who favor interposing an objective element but find fault with the tests usually turn to the teachers. Some look upon them as decisive, others as secondary factors acting in conjunction with other factors. What qualifies teachers to play a principal or auxiliary role in this matter is their close and protracted contact with the children. Their evaluation of aptitudes and inclinations is based on long intimate acquaintance rather than on short summary tests. Teachers are familiar with the child's whole life, so that in this respect almost as much weight attaches to their opinion as to that of the parents. In some respects they have an advantage over parents in that they have no definite preferences. Their recommendations are based on a comparative evaluation of achievement. Moreover, teachers generally represent the collectivist scale of values so that they would naturally take the needs of the kibbutz into account. Their recommendations would thus mediate between the needs of the kibbutz on the one hand and the inclinations and aptitudes of the pupils on the other.

The teachers' advantages are evident, and some of the subjects indeed regard their participation as a possible solution. On the other hand there are those who find fault with the teachers too, mainly because of their position in the kibbutz: "The position of teachers in the kibbutz is rather difficult. They bring children up to work but they themselves do not and they are rather remote from the problems of the kibbutz." Others doubt the teachers' objectivity and their ability to evaluate their pupils correctly.

As a result of these drawbacks there were those who came up with an institutional solution: an education commission comprising teachers and parents. Instead of direct parental intervention in discussions concerning their own children, both parents and children are to be represented in an authorized committee. According to this proposal decisions are to be made by the education and labor committees acting jointly.

The labor committee (or the secretariat) would represent the organizational and economic interests of the kibbutz while the education committee would represent personal educational interests. This would lend an official character to the well-considered views of parents and teachers, supported by findings of psychological tests.

In all, seventy of the subjects mentioned the need for some objective method for occupational placement. This number is not great but it should be stressed that the subjects were not expressly asked about this but brought it up spontaneously. Of the seventy, twenty-eight mentioned teachers as a possible solution, fifteen mentioned tests, ten mentioned an education commission, and seventeen were not specific.

Our comparative analysis of the responses can begin with differences among various types of kibbutzim.

From general hypotheses regarding the degree of familism in different types of kibbutzim,[1] the following particular hypotheses may be derived: (a) The demand for parental influence on placement will be less widespread in kibbutzim of the bund type than in kibbutzim of the commune type. (b) The demand for parental influence on placement will be less widespread in federated than in unified communes.

Table 26. Consideration of parents' wishes about occupational placement in different types of kibbutzim (percent)

	Bunds (N = 40)	Federated communes (N = 28)	Unified communes (N = 207)
Favor consideration	27.5	42.0	59.0
Oppose consideration	72.5	58.0	41.0

Table 26 shows that in the bunds there is more opposition to the parents' wishes being taken into account than there is in the communes. In bunds the opposition is greatly in the majority; in the federated communes it has a small majority; while in the unified communes there is a small majority who are in favor. The differences among the various types of kibbutzim, though significant, are not great. In bunds, most of whose members are opposed to parental consideration, a sizable minority is in favor. In the unified communes, most of whose members are in favor of parental consideration, a large minority is against.

1. For background analysis and definition of terms, see Chapter 1.

Table 27. References to interests of parents, children, and kibbutz
in different types of kibbutzim (percent)

	Bunds (N = 39)	Federated communes (N = 91)	Unified communes (N = 196)
Collectivist pattern	15.0	39.4	21.3
Individualist pattern	53.0	19.8	20.8
Familistic pattern	32.0	40.8	57.9

Table 27 shows the distribution of responses of those who, to explain their attitude toward parental influence, referred to the interests of parents, children, and the kibbutz. The collectivist pattern is that based on the supremacy of kibbutz interests; the individualist pattern stresses the independence of the children; the familistic pattern supports cooperation between parents and children. In the familistic pattern are included both those who assign the parents a decisive role and those who assign them merely an auxiliary function. The familistic pattern is most pronounced in the unified communes, less so in the federated communes, and least in evidence in the bunds.

The relationship between the collectivist and individualist patterns in the bunds requires some explanation. Why is the individualist pattern so frequent and the collectivist pattern so rare? The answers indicate that the occupational placement of the second generation is quite remote as an issue and there is no motivation among respondents to give it their full attention. Although asked to answer the questions as parents or future parents, in fact they reply as sons or daughters. Their frame of reference is their relationship with their parents and not with the kibbutz. Their own aspirations are uppermost in their minds, and if they generally put the main stress on their personal desires it cannot be inferred from this that they have no regard for the collective. The requirements of the kibbutz receive no attention because they are overshadowed by the more pertinent issue of protest against parental authority.

Table 28 also shows greater stress on the children's wishes in the bunds than in the communes. The comparison between the relative rights of parents and children appears to have been carried over to this question as well. Prominence of the individualist pattern in the bunds should here be ascribed mainly to preference being given to the wishes of the children over those of the parents and should not be interpreted

Table 28. Consideration of the children's wishes in different types
of kibbutzim (percent)

	Bunds (N = 38)	Federated communes (N = 93)	Unified communes (N = 194)
Collectivist pattern	2.8	8.0	4.2
Collectivist-individualist pattern	5.4	32.0	19.2
Individualist-collectivist pattern	5.4	27.0	24.1
Individualist pattern	86.4	33.0	52.5

to imply disregard of collective needs. In this table we again see that
in the federated communes the interests of the collective are much more
frequently referred to than they are in the unified communes.

With the exception of the surprisingly low number of collectivist references in bunds, our hypothesis is confirmed by this comparison. Bunds
are less familistic than communes, federated communes less familistic
than unified communes. The differences are noticeable and recurrent,
but not pronounced.

Let us now turn to the differences between men and women. Our
general hypothesis leads us to suppose that more women than men
should be in favor of parental influence on placement. Indeed a higher
proportion of women than men do favor considering the parents' wishes
(60 percent of the women; 45 percent of the men). The differences are
noticeable but not great.

Table 29. References to interests of parents, children,
and kibbutz among men and women (percent)

	Men (N = 210)	Women (N = 144)
Collectivist pattern	30.7	21.0
Individualist pattern	28.9	25.5
Familistic pattern	40.4	53.5

In references to the interests of parents, children, and kibbutz, women
again appear to be more familistic, as Table 29 shows. Men make more
reference to the collectivist pattern than women, and women make
more reference to the familistic pattern than men. Further confirmation
of our hypothesis is obtained from responses concerning children's
wishes (Table 30). Men are more highly represented in the collectivist

Table 30. Consideration of children's wishes among men and women
(percent)

	Men (N = 192)	Women (N = 182)
Collectivist pattern	5.7	2.7
Collectivist-individualist pattern	23.7	14.8
Individualist-collectivist pattern	20.8	27.5
Individualist pattern	49.8	55.0

and collectivist-individualist patterns, while more women than men show individualist-collectivist and individualist patterns. The differences are not pronounced but are consistently repeated. The obvious conclusion from all these comparisons is that in the matter of occupational placement women are slightly more familistic than men.

Let us round off the picture by comparing the attitudes of second and first generation kibbutz members and bund members.[2] Our hypotheses are: (a) The demand for parental influence on placement will be put forward more frequently by the first than by the second generation, but the attitude of the second generation will be fairly close to that of the first. (b) The demand for parental influence on placement will be put forward more frequently by the second generation than by the bunds.

Table 31. Consideration of parental wishes in first and second generations and in Bunds (percent)

	Bunds (N = 40)	Second generation (N = 37)	First generation (N = 235)
Favor consideration	27.5	45.9	53.8
Oppose consideration	72.5	54.1	46.2

Table 31 indicates that the second generation does indeed assume an intermediate position between bunds and the first generation. Its attitude is closer to that of the first generation than to that of the bunds.

The distribution of references to various interests is shown in Table 32. Like the first generation, the second deals with the problem from all

2. The attitudes of the first and second generation were compared in five sample kibbutzim whose children have attained membership. The conclusions of this analysis should be treated with caution because it relates only to the second generation in the general sample. The results have to be supplemented by the findings of an auxiliary sample examined in addition to the general sample for a more exact and extensive study of second generation attitudes.

Table 32. Reference to interests of parents, children, and kibbutz in first and second generations and in bunds (percent)

	Bunds (N = 39)	Second generation (N = 30)	First generation (N = 209)
Collectivist pattern	15.0	46.8	30.5
Individualist pattern	53.0	19.8	23.5
Familistic pattern	32.0	33.4	46.0

aspects and refers both to the parents and to the kibbutz. In this respect they differ totally from bund members who did not cover the whole problem but concentrated mainly on opposition to their parents. The individualist pattern is predominant in bunds; in the second generation the collectivist pattern is predominant; and in the first generation the familistic pattern prevails.

In response to the question about children's wishes the individualist emphasis is again pronounced in the bunds (Table 33). The attitude of

Table 33. Consideration of children's wishes in first and second generations and in bunds (percent)

	Bunds (N = 38)	Second generation (N = 30)	First generation (N = 221)
Collectivist pattern	2.8	5.5	2.6
Collectivist-individualist pattern	5.4	33.7	29.5
Individualist-collectivist pattern	5.4	22.4	29.9
Individualist pattern	86.4	38.4	38.0

the second generation is essentially similar to that of the first generation, but reference to the collectivist and collectivist-individualist frameworks is slightly greater in the second than in the first generation.

Thus in most aspects the second generation is closer to the first than to bunds in their attitudes. The second generation is slightly more collectivistic and less familistic than the first generation.

The attitude survey shows that though the familistic ideology is widely represented in the movement it meets with considerable opposition. Those for and against consideration of the parents' views in the matter of occupational placement are about equally divided. Only a small percentage is for outright parental intervention, as against a relatively high percentge utterly opposed to having parental views taken into account at all. Between the two extremes we find a considerable percentage in favor of consultation with and guidance by the parents. A high percentage of respondents thoroughly objects to any parental influence over children.

Those who favor consideration of the family, about half of the sample subjects, generally do not want to give the parents a free hand. Only a minority of them regard parents as an independent and determinant factor. Familistic ideology tends to be moderate and most of its representatives assign the parents an advisory and supporting role. It is based on the idea of cooperation between parents and children rather than direct interaction between parents and kibbutz. The wishes of the children are at the center of the familistic ideology.

The antifamilistic ideology rejects cooperation between parents and children, which is the basis of the familistic ideology, but here too the children's wishes are focal. A large number of respondents attach great importance to the preferences of the children. Thus, simultaneously with the expansion of the familistic pattern, the individualist pattern has also increased. The two ideologies—familistic and individualist—meet in their joint emphasis on the importance of the children's demands.

The prevalence of the collectivist pattern has been considerably reduced. We would mention again that the findings regarding the collectivist pattern cannot be accepted without reservation. The great prominence given to the youngsters' demands means that their wishes are preferred over those of their parents and cannot always be taken to mean that kibbutz authority is ignored.

Comparison of the ideological patterns with accepted behavior patterns gives a more balanced view. The parents play an important role in occupational placement. The extent of their intervention and the say they have in the matter are greater than they are prepared to admit on the ideological plane. On the other hand, observation leads us to attach greater importance to collectivist interests than would appear from the findings. Despite the fierce clash with individualist and familistic tendencies, these interests are decisive in the actual job allocation. They are strongly anchored in the institutional structure of the kibbutz and if their assured position in the ideological system has been undermined they still serve as principal regulators of actual decisions.

The functional analysis has shown that collective nonascriptive placement is based mainly on experience and adjustment. In this context we would again stress the importance of combining job tenure with moderate rotation, and taking into account the sequences of stages of social maturation. The job image must necessarily be open rather than specific and rigid. Personal job choices must pass the test of persistence and success. The collectivist placement system can operate properly only if it is gradual, flexible, and selective.

We also attach considerable importance to the establishment of institutional settings for objective deliberation. It seems that the solution of the problem would lie in the direction of giving representation to all parties concerned at integrated committee and intercommittee discussions. Psychological tests may be used to an increasing extent but only as an aid to wider discussions among teachers, children, and parents in the education committee.

Finally we would mention another factor which has hardly been dealt with and of which the kibbutz movement itself is hardly aware. Smooth allocation of jobs and functions is not possible without an established manpower program, and especially without an induction plan for the more highly specialized jobs. In addition, sufficient information is required concerning the size and composition of each new work force and its members' inclinations and aspirations. Such plans should be drawn up both in the individual kibbutz and by the movement as a whole, since some problems which are insoluble within a single kibbutz can be solved within the framework of the movement. The collectivist pattern is based on compatibility between one's aspirations and aptitudes and between individual preferences and collective requirements. Two-directional coordination is not a matter of course, and cannot be attained inadvertently. Nonascriptive collective placement requires directed mechanisms for overall planning.

5. Mate Selection

Sociologists and psychologists who have studied the second generation in the kibbutzim in Israel have all noted that children born and bred in the same kibbutz do not marry one another as adults. Attempts to account for this phenomenon are usually based on the assumption that it is an exogamous extension of a self-imposed incest taboo generated by the collective system of education. In the kibbutz, children are brought up together in peer groups which substitute, to a large extent, for their families. Children in the same peer group live in close proximity, interact constantly, and share most of their daily experiences from birth to maturity. It is assumed that much like biological siblings, members of the peer group develop an incest taboo that neutralizes their sexual interest in each other, and that this prohibition of sexual relations and marriage within the peer group is somehow extended to all children born and reared in the same kibbutz (19, 45, 130, 131). This explanation, which is based on an analogy to the genesis and extension of the incest taboo in the elementary family, is plausible but tells us very little about the origin of the exogamous tendency or about the mechanisms that maintain and stabilize it. It ignores altogether the structural implications of exogamy and does not deal with its effects on the social system.

Theories of incest and exogamy fall into two major categories: first, those that deal with mate selection patterns in terms of social system functions and emphasize their effect on intragroup or intergroup solidarity; second, those of the psychological-genetic variety that deal with the problem primarily on the motivational level. Very few explanations

NOTE. This essay previously appeared in *American Sociological Review*, volume 29, number 4 (August 1964).

of incest and exogamy attempt to combine the two approaches in a systematic way. The kibbutz presents us with the rare opportunity to observe exogamy in *statu nascendi* and to follow the dynamic process of its initial development and crystallization. Since exogamy in the kibbutz is not an established injunction but an emergent pattern, we are able to examine closely the intricate interplay between social structure and individual volition.

SECOND GENERATION EXOGAMY

Our analysis of second generation exogamy is based on a sociological study of mate selection and marriage patterns of the second generation in three long-established kibbutzim. Let me first sum up the facts revealed by this inquiry.

Among the 125 couples in the sample, there was not one instance in which both mates were reared from birth in the same peer group. In four cases husband and wife were born in the same kibbutz but reared in different peer groups. In addition we found eight couples in which one mate was born and raised in the kibbutz while the other entered the educational institutions of the kibbutz at diverse ages, ranging from three to fifteen. In six of these cases the "outsider" came to the kibbutz and was subjected to collective education just before or after puberty. Only three of these outsiders joined the kibbutz together with their parents; the others came as "external pupils" while their families continued to reside in town. In seven out of the eight couples the respective mates were reared in different peer groups. The single case of intrapeer group marriage occurred between a native and an outsider who was sent to the kibbutz as an external pupil at the age of fifteen. The love affair between these two started after they left school and after an additional period of separation brought about by service in the army and study in town. There were twelve cases of intermarriage between second generation members born and reared in different kibbutzim.

Thus, in-migrants who undergo only part of their socialization in the kibbutz and remain semi-outsiders in it and members of the second generation of other kibbutzim seem to be more acceptable mates than full insiders.

Our data on erotic attachments and sexual relations are scantier and less reliable than our data on marriage. The pattern of distribution of love affairs, however, seems to parallel closely the pattern of distribution of marriages. We have not come across even one love affair or one instance of publicly known sexual relations between members of the same peer group who were co-socialized from birth or through most of their childhood. A small number of love affairs occurred between members of different peer groups; a somewhat larger number occurred between a native and an outsider who entered collective institutions at a later age, and between second generation members of different kibbutzim. The very rare cases of intragroup affairs involve an outsider who came to the kibbutz as an external pupil long after puberty. These affairs began only after completion of secondary school.

The tendency to avoid in-group sexual relations and marriage is, then, strongest between members of the same age group. It is somewhat weaker between members of different age groups and between second generation members of different kibbutzim. Age of entry into the kibbutz educational system is yet another factor: the tendency toward out-group erotic relationships is strongest among those socialized in the kibbutz since earliest infancy. In-migrants who undergo only part of their socialization in the kibbutz are partly outsiders and as such are more desirable than insiders. Our data underline the importance of relations within the peer group, which appear to be at the core of the matter. It should be emphasized, however, that the tendency to avoid an erotic relationship with a second generation kibbutz member is almost as strong as the tendency to avoid an erotic relationship within the peer group. With few exceptions, love affairs and marital unions are extra–second generation.

We did not make a full study of the demographic aspects of our problem, but we did examine the possibility that the exogamous tendency may be a function of such demographic factors as age, sex, and number of available prospective mates in the second generation.[1] Our data indicate that while the limited number of suitable second generation candidates is an important factor, it is certainly not the only or even the major factor operative here. The exogamous tendency appears in all kibbutzim irrespective of the number of available second generation members of a marriageable age. Each of the unmarried members of the second generation in our sample could have chosen from between 20

1. For an attempt to explain incest and exogamy in demographic-ecological terms, see Kreiselman Slater (78).

and 60 second generation members who were within the acceptable age range, yet almost invariably they by-passed this pool of prospective mates and sought erotic gratification and marriage outside it.

A careful analysis of our data led to the conclusion that the tendency toward out-group mate selection in the kibbutz is an attitudinal and behavioral trend and not an institutionalized normative pattern. This tendency differs radically from full-fledged incest taboos and exogamic injunctions, which regulate mate selection by means of explicit norms and negative sanctions.

Scrutiny of the literature on incest and exogamy in different societies reveals a great deal of variation as to explicitness of norms, stringency of prohibitions, and severity of sanctions. The breach may be defined as sinful and punishment relegated to automatic mystical retribution. It may be defined as criminal and subject to penal sanctions. It is viewed in some cases as merely scandalous and disreputable and subject to diffuse public disapproval and derision. It may invoke extreme rage, horror, and revulsion, or merely embarrassment and scorn. This variation should not obscure the fact that infractions of the core taboos and injunctions are hardly ever condoned and almost invariably incur more or less severe negative sanctions.[2]

The second generation tendency toward out-group mate selection in the kibbutz is not backed by any formal or informal prescriptions or proscriptions, and it is not buttressed by any institutionalized sanctions or inducements. The rare cases of affairs and marriages within the second generation attract attention and comment but are not considered in any sense illegitimate or irregular. These unions are fully accepted by parents, friends, and public opinion, without even a shade of censure or unease. Not only is proscription or negative evaluation of such marriages completely absent, but many of the parents prefer them. This difference between a nonnormative trend and a fully institutionalized normative pattern is so fundamental that the two phenomena should not be designated by the same term without due reservations. To underline this basic distinction, I shall put such terms as "incest," "endogamy," and "exogamy" in quotes when I apply them to mate selection trends in the kibbutz.

These findings concerning the prevalence, range, and significance of the "exogamous" tendency among members of the second generation in

2. J. R. Fox (45) tends to ignore the universality of negative sanctioning of the core taboos and injunctions and to overstress the extent of variation.

the kibbutz indicate that this is a self-imposed limitation which cannot be accounted for by either demographic or normative pressures. This brings into even sharper relief the twin questions originally posed: What are the social functions of this tendency? What are its sources and its functions at the level of individual personality?

PATTERNS OF MARRIAGE

The tendency of the second generation toward out-group marriage cannot be studied in isolation. Avoidances should be examined in conjunction with preferences and related to the overall distribution of marital choice categories. The first step toward such an analysis is a detailed examination of the group membership of all the spouses in our sample. Classification of these couples in this respect yields an "endogamy" to "exogamy" continuum, a graded series between two polar extremes. This examination employs the following typology.

1) Intra–second generation marriage: (a) Intra-peer-group marriage—marriage between members of the second generation who were brought up in the same peer group. (b) Inter-peer-group marriage—intermarriage between members of the second generation who were brought up in different peer groups. Such unions are "exogamous" with respect to the peer group but "endogamous" with respect to the second generation.

2) Intra-kibbutz marriage—intermarriage between members of the second generation of a given kibbutz and candidates for membership or members who have joined their kibbutz at later stages. Such unions are "exogamous" from the point of view of the second generation but "endogamous" from the point of view of membership in the kibbutz.

3) Inter-kibbutz marriage—intermarriage between members of the second generation of a given kibbutz and members of other kibbutzim. Contacts between the kibbutzim occur either within the framework of the federation[3] to which they are affiliated or within the framework of the regional organization that unites all the kibbutzim in the region.

4) Intra-movement marriage—intermarriage between members of the second generation of a given kibbutz and members of the youth movements that share the ideology of the kibbutzim and channel their members to settlement in them. There are many institutionalized contacts between the kibbutzim and the youth movements from which they re-

3. To simplify this typology, I have disregarded organizational and ideological divisions within the collective movement, so that intra-federation and inter-federation marriage patterns are not distinguished.

cruit most of their new members. The youth movements send groups of prospective settlers to established kibbutzim for preparatory training; such groups may reside and work in the kibbutz for periods ranging from a few months to two years. Second generation members often serve as instructors and organizers in youth groups and in groups of prospective settlers in town. Such unions are "exogamous" with respect to the kibbutzim concerned but "endogamous" with respect to the collective movement as a whole.

5) Extra-movement marriage—marriage between members of the second generation and outsiders who are not members of the collective movement and do not share its ideology. Such outsiders are either hired professional workers—mostly teachers, but occasionally a resident doctor or engineer—who reside in the kibbutz temporarily but are not members and are not committed to its ideology, or outsiders who have no direct contact and no affinity with the kibbutz ideology and way of life. Members of the second generation meet the latter primarily during the period of compulsory service in the Israeli army.

In our sample of 125 couples the distribution of marriage patterns is as follows.

Intra–second generation:	
Intra-peer group	0%
Inter-peer group	3
Intra-kibbutz	31
Inter-kibbutz	23
Intra-movement	27
Extra-movement	16

These results are tentative and should be viewed with great caution. In many cases it was not easy to determine the group membership of the spouse at the time of marriage, especially among couples who left the kibbutz to join another kibbutz or left the collective movement altogether. There is, in addition, considerable variation among the kibbutzim in our sample, and we are by no means certain that our results are representative of other kibbutzim. Yet the pattern we found does not seem atypical and may well give a good indication of the major trends.

Most marriages are concentrated in the intermediate range of the typology; 81 percent are of the intra-kibbutz, inter-kibbutz, or intra-movement types. Both intra–second generation marriage and extra-movement marriage, the polar extremes, are less prevalent than the intermediate types. Examination of the distribution of the marriage patterns in terms of this typology locates the specific problem in a wider context. Instead of focusing exclusively on the near absence of type 1 we can examine it as part of the total constellation of marital choice categories.

THE SOCIAL FUNCTIONS OF MARRIAGE PATTERNS

The voluminous literature on the functions of marriage patterns in different societies clearly indicates that these patterns have a crucial effect on the social system. (91, 23, 44, 117, 38, 39, 82, 102, 60, 59). Marriage brings about a rearrangement of the social structure by segregating and interlinking subgroups within it. It bears directly on the cohesion and continuity of the social system. What, then, are the functions of extra–second generation marriage from the point of view of any single kibbutz and from the point of view of the movement as a whole?

Close scrutiny of our data reveals that the pattern of marriage outside the second generation has a number of important functions on the local level. The intra-kibbutz pattern is an important mechanism for reinforcing membership ties by kinship ties. The nuclei of settlers and the candidates for membership who join the kibbutz during later stages of its development remain on the margin of the movement for a long time. Direct confrontation with the realities of life in the kibbutz has a corrosive effect on their commitment to stay. Absorption is a prolonged and difficult process, and many drop out at first. Marriage to a son or daughter of an old-timer consolidates the new member's ties to the established kibbutz and reinforces his identification with it. The marital bond and the newly acquired kinship affiliations turn the newcomer, still a semi-outsider, into an insider, and facilitate his adjustment.

Closely related to the function of reinforcing membership ties is the function of recruiting new members. The extra-kibbutz patterns are an important source of additional members. Both sons and daughters are expected to stay on in their kibbutz after marriage and to prevail on their spouses to join them. The kibbutzim in our sample have gained a considerable number of additional members through marriage—the ratio of gain to loss is about three to one. Established kibbutzim suffer from a shortage of manpower, and the flow of new members drawn in by marriage is very welcome.

Thus, membership and kinship are, in a very important sense, complementary. The kibbutz, however, is based on the primacy of membership ties over kinship affiliations and it cannot afford to let kinship gain an upper hand.[4] All established kibbutzim face the problem of the gradual reemergence of wider kinship ties within them. Relatives often form united blocks and conduct a covert struggle for particularistic interests. Occasionally such blocks become quite powerful and exert a considerable influence on communal affairs. Predominance of kinship ties over ties of membership undermines the primacy of collective considerations and engenders internecine strife. The established kibbutzim have devised many mechanisms to limit the influence of kinship groups. One function of the extra–second generation marriage is to check the emergence and consolidation of large and powerful kinship groupings within the kibbutz. When intermarriage occurs between a member of the second generation and a newcomer or an outsider, only one spouse lives in the same community with his family and his siblings' families. Marriage between members of the second generation, on the other hand, would proliferate kinship ties within the kibbutz.

Marriage outside the second generation also helps to bridge the generation gap. The educational system partly segregates the second generation from the rest of the kibbutz. The children's society has its autonomous arrangements and children live within this semiseparate framework uninterruptedly throughout the long process of socialization. They share with their age mates most of the formative experiences of infancy, childhood, and adolescence; internal relations within the peer group are more frequent and more continuous than relations with outsiders. Members of the second generation are highly conscious of their special position in their kibbutz and often tend to keep to themselves. Marriage outside the group mitigates this intense solidarity after maturity. Marrying out propels members of the second generation beyond their group and bolsters their external ties.

Marriage outside the second generation bridges the gap between subgroups within the kibbutz in yet another way: it checks the consolidation of the emergent stratification system. The founders of the kibbutz usually enjoy a privileged position in terms of prestige and power. The kinship ties produced by any considerable number of "endogamous" marriages between their children would reinforce in-group solidarity

4. For a fuller analysis see Chapter 1.

among them and enhance the consolidation of the old-timers into a separate and dominant group. The extra–second generation patterns counteract this tendency to closure and exclusion. Through their children, the established old-timers are linked to less established and more marginal members. Extra–second generation marriage is thus an equalizing mechanism of major importance.

The functions of the prevalent mate selection patterns for the movement as a whole are even more evident. The inter-kibbutz and intra-movement patterns counteract the strong separatist tendencies of the local communities by cutting across the boundaries between them and by strengthening their ties to the youth movements. The function of inter-kibbutzim unions as living links between distinct communities is particularly noticeable in the cases of intercollective "adoption." The Federations have recently developed a system whereby each established kibbutz "adopts" a newly founded kibbutz and pledges to assist it until it is able to manage on its own. Intermarriage links the long-established and newly founded kibbutzim together and gradually reinforces the pseudo-kinship ties entailed in "adoption." Parents and relatives of members of the second generation who have gone over to new kibbutzim maintain frequent and close ties with them and eventually come into contact with other members as well. Since the assistance scheme affects the well-being of their close kin, members of the established kibbutz become personally committed to it and press for a strong alliance between the two communities. Cross-cutting kinship affiliations transform adoption into a comprehensive and lasting partnership.[5]

Of similar importance is the revitalization and renewal of relations with the youth movements. Established kibbutzim tend to settle down and lose much of their revolutionary zeal. The sense of belonging to a revolutionary movement becomes less pervasive and less urgent; growing involvement in local affairs brings about a concomitant limitation of the horizons of identification and participation. There is an increasing tendency toward contraction of commitment and withdrawal from the movement. Estrangement occurs also because of the gradual shift in relations between the established kibbutz and the youth movements. The dependence of the established kibbutz on the youth movements for

5. For a statement and development of the view that the incest taboo and exogamy diffuse attachment and harness it to larger coordinated aggregates, see Slater (125). For an analysis of the way in which estrangement within the group strengthens loyalties to wider unities, see Gluckman (56), chapter 3.

new members diminishes, and at the same time the movement's claims grow manifoldly. The established kibbutzim realize the importance of supporting the youth movements, yet they cannot help feeling hard-pressed and overburdened when confronted with demands to send more youth leaders to the cities and to participate more actively in the training programs. Intra-movement marriage links the youth movements with the kibbutzim and emphasizes the unity of the collective movement that encompasses them all.

Finally, intra-movement and extra-movement marriages bridge the gap between kibbutzim and other sectors of the society. In many notable cases, they provide very valuable personal links with other elite groups. Unions contracted between members of the second generation and military, political, and intellectual leaders or their close kin cement the ties between the kibbutzim and both the pivotal and secondary elites of Israeli society. Extra-movement unions curb separatist tendencies and create solidarities that transcend the local units and reinforce wider unities.

So far, we have analyzed only the positive functions of extra–second generation marriage, disregarding the fact that to a lesser or greater degree these patterns constitute a threat to local continuity. Marriage within the second generation is the pattern most conducive to local continuity. Both spouses are natives of the kibbutz and share a common commitment and attachment to it. Their staying on in the kibbutz after marriage is also safeguarded by the fact that all their close relatives and friends reside there. A new member's ties to the kibbutz are weaker and more vulnerable—he is much more prone to leave and to take his spouse with him.

The threat to local continuity is even more noticeable in the inter-kibbutz and intra-movement patterns. A union between a member of the second generation and a member of another kibbutz or a member of a nucleus of prospective settlers engenders a conflict of loyalties. When members of two established kibbutzim marry, they tend to spend a trial period in each community and settle in the one that is more congenial to both spouses. But marriage with a member of a new kibbutz, or with a member of a nucleus of settlers that is about to found its own kibbutz, creates cross-pressures and counterclaims with no institutionalized solution. Members of the second generation are often attracted by the numerous openings offered to them in the new kibbutz.

They also feel that it is their duty to help the newly founded kibbutz rather than return to the fairly prosperous community established by their parents. In spite of their commitment to their native village and in spite of the pressure put on them by their parents, the conflict is often resolved in favor of the new kibbutz.

Extra-movement marriages are the greatest hazard from the point of view of continuity. Some of the hired professional workers who marry into the kibbutz become attached to it and wish to join as members in their own right. This also happens occasionally with outsiders who have had no affinity and no direct contact with the collective movement prior to marriage. Yet more often than not, extra-movement marriages lead to desertion of the kibbutz and dissociation from the movement. This happens more often when the second generation member is a woman. Both sons and daughters are expected to stay in their native kibbutz, but wives follow their husbands more than husbands follow their wives; linkage of a couple to the kibbutz through a son is therefore less vulnerable than linkage through a daughter (7, 6).

The foregoing analysis of functions and dysfunctions enables us to weigh the effects of the marriage patterns on the social system. Intra–second generation marriage ensures local continuity, yet if it were prevalent, it would deprive the kibbutz of important internal and external integrating mechanisms. It would lead to the consolidation of kinship blocks and to the hardening of the line dividing the old-timers from the newcomers and outsiders. It would separate the kibbutz from the movement and from the society at large. At the other extreme, extra-movement marriage links the kibbutz to the society at large, but this advantage is counterbalanced by heavy losses in terms of cohesion and continuity. The intermediate marriage patterns combine in-group closure with intergroup linkage, and in this respect are more functional than the two polar types. The most prevalent marriage patterns are those that safeguard the cohesion and continuity of the local community, yet at the same time promote the unity and growth of the movement as a whole.

The intermediate patterns provide a functional solution from the point of view of the elementary family as well. Extreme homogamy limits the possibilities of interchanges and complementariness; extreme heterogamy is inherently unstable, since it joins together spouses with conflicting loyalties and incompatible norms and aspirations. The inter-

mediate patterns combine basic homogeneity with manageable differentiation: they enable members of the second generation to marry
newcomers and outsiders without disrupting their matrix of interpersonal relations. It seems, then, that the intermediate patterns perform
important functions for the social system on all levels.

INSTITUTIONAL MECHANISMS

The preceding analysis indicates that the net effect of the present
distribution of marital choices is by and large favorable. This elucidation of functions supplies an indispensable starting point for a casual
analysis, yet in and by itself it does not explain differential incidence.
To account for the adoption of a certain institution it is not sufficient to
show that it is in some sense good for society and serves its long-range
interests (71, 17, 27). Listing the beneficial or detrimental consequences
of an institutional pattern from the observer's point of view does not in
itself account for the actors' attitudes and behavior. Second generation
members are only partly aware of the considerations outlined above,
and even if they do recognize them, that does not mean they actually
choose their mates to suit the best interests of their society. Mate selection is considered a purely personal and private matter and there is a
strict ban on meddling in the process of choice. How, then, do the
functional considerations impinge on the individuals directly concerned?
How does the structure, or the "sake" of the kibbutz interact, as it were,
with individual volition? What are the efficient causes and the immediate determinants of action?

An examination of the social system from the point of view of
differential availability of categories of prospective mates provides an
important connecting link between the functional and causal analyses
of marriage patterns. The fact that the kibbutzim are not closed, self-
sufficient communities but interconnected and interdependent units,
operating within an active and proselytizing movement, is of utmost
importance in this context. The strong separatist tendencies of the local
communities are counterbalanced by external ties. There are first of all
the federative affiliations based on an ideological-political affinity. Sec-
ondly there are the regional schemes that promote cooperation among
settlements situated in the same district, and encompass kibbutzim
affiliated with different federations. Finally, we should take into consid-

eration the manifold ties that connect the kibbutzim with the overall structure of Israeli society.

The external relations of the kibbutz impinge directly on its internal organization. The youth movements supply the kibbutz with reinforcements. The kibbutz accommodates, in addition, transient members of the youth movements who stay for varying periods to get their basic training or to lend a hand during peak seasons. Many kibbutzim have developed special institutions for immigrant youth who stay in the kibbutz for a number of years, combining study and part-time work. In border settlements, units of a special formation of the army combine military duties and work. Even while staying in their native kibbutz, members of the second generation are brought into institutionalized and more or less prolonged contact with groups of new members, candidates for membership, and various kinds of transients, and these out-groups provide a pool of prospective mates. Activity on the regional, federative, and national level further extends the range of participation and provides opportunities to develop durable and meaningful ties outside the confines of the local community (74).

Members of kibbutzim, and especially leaders of the movement, are aware of the dangers of closure and separatism, and have devised ingenious mechanisms for linking different groups and communities affiliated with the movement in common endeavors. Situational exigencies and ideological considerations have led to the expansion of the regional schemes beyond their original, rather limited scope. These schemes curtail local autonomy and have a considerable impact on the economic, social, and cultural life of the participating communities. Large-scale regional enterprises and institutions create a common meeting ground and bring the members of different kibbutzim together. Most important, from the point of view of our special problem, are the regional secondary and vocational schools that draw out and bring together the adolescent youth growing up in these kibbutzim. Several of the inter-kibbutz marriages in our sample originated in friendships formed during study in such an intercollective secondary school.

Many of the inter-kibbutz and intra-movement unions are by-products of a newly developed scheme of federative assistance. A series of serious setbacks in the new settlements and a crisis of recruitment in the youth movements have led the federations to intensify and widen the scope of federative cooperation. After completing their army service, members of the second generation are drafted for an additional year of service in a newly established kibbutz or in a youth movement training group. Recruitment is channeled primarily through "adoption," and most recruits serve in the new settlement adopted by their native kibbutz. Inter-kibbutz second generation teams also participate in maintaining their federation's outposts in outlying, uninhabited, and arid areas. A certain percentage of the annual quota of recruits serve as instructors and organizers of training groups in the youth movements.

Since service to a common cause and prolonged and close contacts breed affairs and lasting attachments, these schemes create ready opportunities for intergroup unions. The widening of the frameworks of cooperation results in a concomitant widening of the range of available mates. The three to three and one-half years of service in the army and in new settlements are concentrated in the beginning of adulthood, so that young people are taken out of the narrow confines of their kibbutz at the time they begin to contemplate marriage.

Influencing mate choice is not an intended aim of these supplementary institutional mechanisms. The established kibbutzim view the inter-marriages brought about by the regional and federative schemes with ambivalence and anxiety. Assistance schemes resulting in permanent settlement of a considerable number of second generation members in the new kibbutzim evoke covert competition and acute tension. To avoid open conflict, some established kibbutzim have reached an agreement with their adopted settlements that as long as the official ties of adoption last, second generation members will not be allowed to settle in the new kibbutz or even volunteer for a second term of service in it. The established kibbutzim press for deferment of the year of service in new kibbutzim until members of the second generation reach a more mature age and are already married and settled down in their native villages. Most inter-kibbutz and intra-movement marriages occur as unintended, unanticipated, and even undesired consequences of organizational arrangements made for other purposes.

At times availability is an outcome of a more conscious and purposeful design to channel mate choice. The demographic policy of the kibbutz is not uninfluenced by considerations of mate selection. Members of the kibbutz are aware of the intra–second generation avoidance. They realize that intra-kibbutz marriage is a safeguard against the desertion of the second generation to other communities and that the best way to ensure local continuity is to provide for their adult children a pool of suitable mates within their native village. They are also partly aware of the stabilizing effect that such marriages have on their new members. The timing of expansion by means of absorbing groups of new members, and the selection of such groups, are not unaffected by these considerations.

The kibbutzim have lately become concerned about the "undesirable" associations developed by members of the second generation during their army service. Service in the army throws the young recruits into direct and intense contact with all segments of Israeli society and provides them with an opportunity to develop attachments outside the aegis of the kibbutz and the collective movement. The kibbutzim try to limit the disruptive effects of these associations by channeling a certain quota of their recruits to the Nahal, that is, to units which undergo their military training in agricultural frontier settlements, because members of the Nahal maintain contact with the movement throughout the period of service. With members of the second generation who serve in other units the kibbutzim attempt to keep in close touch.

The need to counteract extra-movement associations has led the federations to design new inter-kibbutz and intra-movement frameworks of encounter and interaction. An important instance of such indirect yet intentional channeling of mate choice is the ideological seminars and refresher courses, which are planned with matchmaking as one of their unofficial, yet tacitly recognized, aims. This gives rise to much bantering during the seminars, and figures as a major theme in the humorous skits and songs presented at parties. At times the program of instruction and the lectures serve mainly as a convenient cover while the main purpose of the seminar is to provide a congenial atmosphere and ready opportunities for forming attachments. The channeling of mate choice is achieved by means of control over the frameworks of formal and informal interaction. The prevalence of the intermediate patterns stems at least in part, then, from institutional arrangements that make certain categories of mates more readily accessible.

Analysis in terms of differential accessibility supplies an important clue, but not the full answer. Second generation members are more available than any other category of prospective mates. They interact closely and are within easy reach of each other, yet they do not regard each other as erotically desirable. Our initial question is still unanswered. How can we account for this sexual neutralization on the motivational level? What makes newcomers, outsiders, and strangers more desirable? How do these deep-lying tendencies develop during the process of maturation?

MATE SELECTION AND THE PROCESS OF MATURATION

The life of children in the kibbutz is dominated from the outset by a division between the communal sphere represented by the peer group and the private sphere represented by the family. This division determines the ecological patterning and the time rhythm of the child's schedule, and is maintained by the daily shifting from the children's house to the parents' home. The family and the peer group are dominated by different yet complementary principles (5, 72, 40, 106, 107). Relations between parents and small children are very intimate, intense, and full of love. Expressions of love become more restrained and less overt as the children grow up, but the relationship remains warm and affectionate. Throughout the process of socialization the family supplies the child with uncontested love and exclusive personal attention.

The atmosphere in the peer group is more neutral, less affectively toned. A certain routine, diffuse general friendliness and overall solidarity is emphasized, rather than love or intimacy.[6] Everything is shared and each child is entitled to the same amount of attention. The emphasis on commitment to the group discourages dyadic withdrawal; members look askance at intense friendships of any kind, and they occur infrequently (57). Since the child's personal need for exclusive intimate relations is from the outset provided for outside the peer group rather than within it, the formation of erotic attachments in adolescence and adulthood is inhibited. The "exogamous" tendency should be viewed as one manifestation of the basic distinction between peers who are comrades, and intimates who are "outsiders."

Data on educational institutions in the kibbutz enable us to probe a little further into the ways in which the peer groups neutralize and inhibit sexual attraction between their members. Relations between the

6. For analysis of the opposition between dyadic attachment and group solidarity see Bion (13) and Slater (125).

sexes are deeroticized not by means of strict restrictive norms or enforced segregation, but by dealing with sexual problems in a straightforward, objective, and "rational" way, and by minimizing the differentiation and distance between the sexes. Children of different sexes share the same living quarters and physical shame is deemphasized. There is very little differentiation in style of dress and demeanor and hardly any sex-differentiated social activity.[7] Interaction between age mates in the peer group is much tighter and all-pervasive than interaction between siblings. Siblings share activities and experiences only in the family, and their participation is age- and sex-differentiated, but members of the peer groups eat, study, work, and play together as a group most hours of the day and sleep together in the same room or in adjoining rooms at night. We encounter here, then, very close propinquity and very intensive interaction between peers of different sexes.

The deeroticizing mechanisms described above operate throughout the process of socialization, but the norms regulating relations between the sexes, as well as actual behavior, change during different phases of maturation. Attitudes to childhood sexuality are permissive and sexual manifestations in young children are viewed as normal. During this stage children of different sexes sleep in the same room, shower together, play and run around in the nude, and there is a considerable amount of wrestling, tickling, exploring, soothing, and caressing among them. This close contact between the sexes continues until the second or third grade, and then decreases with age. Gradually, a sense of sexual shame emerges, and a growing distance between the sexes. Showers are taken separately. Sleeping arrangements are reshuffled; from the fourth grade on room occupancy is unisexual. All group activities remain bisexual but friendship becomes unisexual.

The onset of puberty brings about a conspicuous increase in sexual shame and the development of considerable hostility between the sexes. Girls take great pains to hide their bodies when undressing and keep to themselves as much as possible. Members of both sexes insist on sitting separately in the classroom and at all assemblies and parties. They declare that they detest each other, and are constantly involved

7. See Spiro (130). It should be noted that the kibbutz described by Spiro is affiliated with a federation that pursues a much more extreme and more rigorous policy of sexual desegregation than the federation in which we conducted our research. Kibbutzim affiliated with the Orthodox religious federation practice considerable segregation of the sexes.

in petty quarrels. The girls regard the boys as immature and uncouth, and treat them with disdain, and the boys retaliate by annoying the girls and poking fun at them. Much of this tension stems from the differential rate of sexual maturation: girls reach puberty and manifest a renewed interest in sex a few years earlier than boys. This interest is directed to older students and to other young unmarried males in their kibbutz and not to their peers. The boys react to this development with resentment and aggression. This hostility continues until the age of fourteen or fifteen and then recedes, as the boys catch up with the girls and the relations between them cease to be charged with tension. The intensity of physical shame decreases. Girls and boys conceal their nude bodies from each other but this is now done without much fuss in a calm and matter-of-fact manner. The unity of the peer group is restored and relations between the sexes become easy, unconstrained, and friendly. During most of their adolescence age mates interact with each other as asexual peers rather than as potential sex objects.

Attitudes toward adolescent sexuality are more restrictive than attitudes toward childhood sexuality. The educational ideology upheld by both teachers and parents maintains that adolescents should refrain from sexual relations until they finish secondary school. It is felt that preoccupation with sexual matters prevents full concentration on school activities and has a disruptive effect on the peer group and on the student society. The energies of the adolescents are channeled to work, to study, and to hectic participation in extracurricular group and intergroup activities. All social participation is group- rather than couple-centered (141, 15). Seductiveness, coquetry, and flirtatiousness are strongly discouraged. Sex does not loom very large in the lives of these adolescents. Shifting relations and indiscriminate experimentation are not common, nor do many couples go steady (67). There are few infractions of the injunction against sexual intercourse. Couples who become engrossed in each other and neglect their duties are admonished by their educators and peers to restrain themselves and to "return to the fold."

During this stage interaction cutting across divisions between peer groups increases considerably. Intergroup cooperation is highly organized and much more intensive than in the primary school. The committees elected by the students have jurisdiction over all matters other than purely academic ones. Interaction between members of different peer groups occurs also in youth movement activities and in the numerous cultural-interest and discussion groups. In most established and well-to-do kibbutzim there are, in addition, a student choir, a student orchestra, and a student paper, which require close cooperation among many students. Activity in age-heterogeneous groups leads to a student solidarity that complements and reinforces peer-group solidarity. Students of the senior classes have a strong "generational" consciousness and view themselves as the representatives of the second generation in their kibbutz (89, 33, 12).

Another relevant feature of adolescent life is a change in the balance between the communal and family spheres. Young children are deeply dependent on their parents. They gradually outgrow this intense involvement and become attached to their age mates. Adolescents become firmly embedded in their peer group and in the students' society and drift away from their families. Their relations with their parents remain friendly and affectionate, but no longer very intense or intimate. The solidarities cultivated by communal education gain an upper hand and partly supersede family solidarity.

After graduation from secondary school, members of the second generation may engage in sexual relations with impunity and are given a free hand with respect to choice of mate. There is no objection to premarital sexual relations as long as they are not treated in a frivolous and offhand way. The prevalent view of sexuality and marriage stresses personal autonomy and genuine intimacy, and it is felt that both sexual relations and marriage should be anchored in spontaneous love. The search for a mate draws members of the second generation away from their peers and away from all other members of the second generation. As noted before, the overwhelming majority of love affairs and marital unions are extra–second generation and, as far as we can judge, relations between adult members of the second generation are friendly and familiar but devoid of any signs of erotic tension. Members of the second generation view their relations with each other as "sexless" and erotically indifferent.[8]

8. Two different psychological hypotheses have been proposed concerning this neutralization of sexual attraction. Spiro bases his analysis on Freudian premises and assumes that sexual attraction between cosocialized children of opposite sex is inhibited and suppressed but persists subconsciously (130). Fox constructs a neo-Westermarckian model and assumes that intense heterosexual bodily contact before puberty extinguishes desire (45). Since our research does not supply data on subconscious motivation, we cannot resolve the problem of suppressed versus extin-

How do members of the second generation account for their tendency to out-marriage? How does the transition from adolescence to adulthood lead to the emergence of "exogamy?" One of the most frequent reasons given by second generation members for their lack of sexual interest in each other is overfamiliarity. They firmly believe that overfamiliarity breeds sexual disinterest and that it is one of the main sources of "exogamy." Our second generation respondents stressed that they knew each other "inside-out," or more figuratively, "We are like an open book to each other. We have read the story in the book over and over again and know all about it." That this is an important issue with them we learn also from the reasons they give for their interest in newcomers, outsiders, and strangers. They refer to the curiosity, excitement, and anticipation that unfamiliar people evoke in them and to the exhilarating sense of discovery and triumph they get when they establish a relationship with one of them. They describe the unfolding of an affair as an exchange of confidences and emphasize the importance of relating and comparing different life histories. The affair with the outsider is experienced as an overcoming of distance between persons and as a growth of a newly won and unfamiliar sense of intimacy. The most perceptive and introspective among our respondents regard their affairs with unfamiliar persons also as a means of self-discovery. The effort to bridge the gap and reach mutual understanding requires self-scrutiny and brings about a heightened sense of self-awareness. The search for self-awareness and genuine intimacy as distinct from mere familiarity is an insistent and recurrent theme in many interviews.

Closely related to the issue of overfamiliarity is the issue of privacy. The concern with privacy is very intense. Adolescent couples are very secretive about their relationships. The typical partners give few overt indications of their relationship. They do not appear together in public as a couple nor do they seek each other out informally between classes or at work. All meetings are clandestine. It would be unthinkable to show any physical sign of affection in the presence of other people. This exaggerated secrecy disappears after adolescence, but the concern with privacy remains very strong. As one of our respondents put it "In the

guished sexual attraction. Both hypotheses have only limited explanatory value: as they stand, neither can fully account for the genesis of second generation "exogamy." They explain the neutralization of sexual desire between members of the same peer group but not the generalization of attitudes engendered within the peer group to the second generation as a whole.

children's society everything is 'ours.' This affair is mine. It is something of my own that I do not want to share with others. I try to keep
it to myself as much as I can." Communal living and constant sharing
of daily experiences with peers seems to breed a strong urge to seclude
one's personal life and protect it from external intrusion. Maintenance
of secrecy is also a mechanism for dealing with stringent group control
against dyadic withdrawal (125). The threat to group cohesion is less
evident if the relationship remains subdued and covert.

One of the major advantages of the extra–second generation over the
intra–second generation union is that it is more amenable to segregation
and seclusion. Members of the second generation are part of a highly
interconnected network of interpersonal relations. Being the firstborn
of their kibbutz they are at the center of public attention. An amorous
attachment between members of the second generation attracts immediate notice and incessant comment. The courtship will be conducted
with the whole community looking on. It is much easier to keep secrecy
or at least to maintain a semblance of privacy when the partner is a
newcomer or an outsider who has few or no contacts with the kibbutz.
Members of the second generation take great pains to guard knowledge
of their extra–second generation affairs from public notice.

The aspirations and expectations of second generation members concerning their mates often reflect the external influence of the ideals of
romantic love derived from novels, poems, plays, and films (8, 139).
The quest for individuation and genuine intimacy, however, should not
be attributed to illicit external influences. These concerns are anchored
in the image of love and family life upheld by the kibbutz and are
therefore legitimate. Preoccupation with overfamiliarity and lack of
privacy stems from the internal dynamics of the system, and reflects the
dilemma caused by the interplay between communal and private
spheres of the kibbutz.

The social and psychological dynamics engendering this quest for
individuation are further clarified by a consideration of the relation
between "exogamy" and the demand for local continuity. Loyalty to
the kibbutz is defined in localized terms, and members of the second
generation are pledged to stay in their native kibbutz for the rest of
their lives. This duty gives rise to serious problems that become particularly acute during the transition from adolescence to adulthood. The
kibbutz is part of a revolutionary movement that puts a premium on

discontinuity and creative innovation. Since it still depends on reinforcements from the youth movements, it encourages young people to
dissociate themselves from their parents and continues to glorify rebellion. At the same time, it expects its own second generation to stay on
in their native villages and continue their parents' lifework there. In-
heriting a revolution engenders an inevitable dilemma. The second
generation is called upon to continue and conserve in a movement committed to discontinuity. Most members of the second generation accept
responsibility to their heritage and stay on in the kibbutz, but their attitude toward continuity is very ambivalent.

The duty to stay on in the native village engenders a deep fear of
closure because it implies blocked mobility and a curtailment of life
chances. It imposes a drastic limitation on free choice of domicile, of
career, of associates and of friends. The cultivation of external contacts
and the period of service outside the kibbutz mitigate local closure but
at the same time accentuate the problems involved in local continuity.
Resettlement in the kibbutz after prolonged service outside it entails a
difficult reorientation and readjustment. Many second generation members are loath to sever their external ties and to forgo the more variegated opportunities offered by life outside their kibbutz. They feel cut
off and hemmed in. They realize that the course of their lives is set
from the outset and that their future is predetermined by membership
in their home kibbutz. The tendency to marry out is an attempt to
counteract this limitation. The large majority of extra–second generation mates have been brought up outside the kibbutz; they come from
a different milieu and represent the outside world. "Exogamy" enables
second generation members to extend their contacts beyond the narrow
confines of the circle of people with whom they have been associated
since they were born. It expresses their craving for new experiences and
new contacts. Most important, perhaps, it affords them opportunities
to explore on their own, to initiate and experiment. In short, out-group
marriage enables the second generation to escape the in-group closure
imposed on them by their education and by their commitment to continuity.

The relation between "exogamy" and the commitment to continuity
is especially significant in the context of relations between the first and
second generations. Parents and children are at cross purposes on this
issue. Parents have a strong vested interest in "endogamy." Their major

concern is to ensure that the new family will stay on in the kibbutz. From the point of view of familial and local continuity, marriage within the second generation is the safest solution, and it is, in fact, a first preference with many parents. They view with enthusiasm and anticipation any sign of attachment between their children and give them their full blessing. The tendency of their children to marry out is a source of constant anxiety, and they watch the children with unease until they settle down. Parents are not supposed to have any say whatsoever in the matter, yet they cannot refrain from comments and covert pressure. They openly oppose the decision of their children to move to another kibbutz and do their utmost to win them back. Their opposition to marriage outside the collective movement is particularly strong and stubborn in cases where such unions threaten to lead to desertion of the kibbutz and estrangement from the movement.

The "exogamous" tendencies of the children should be examined in conjunction with the "endogamous" preferences of their parents. In the confrontation between the generations parents represent the tendency toward in-marriage, while children represent the tendency toward out-marriage. Viewed in this context, "exogamy" is, among other things, an attempt to cut loose from the parents and redefine relations with the first generation. Our material reveals many undertones of resentment and opposition to the parents' generation. Exogamy is often defended in terms of the right of the second generation to self-determination and free choice, irrespective of the wishes of the parents and the kibbutz. The second generation has a strong urge to break out and explore the more variegated possibilities of the surrounding world. Exogamy is an attempt to dissociate from the first generation as a whole and from parents. It expresses a quest for a separate and partly independent identity (84, 90).

This interpretation of "exogamy" throws additional light on the functions of the intermediate marriage patterns. These patterns are compromise solutions that enable members of the second generation to meet halfway the pressures on them and to work out the dilemma of continuity versus discontinuity.[9] Our study indicates that in the majority of cases the conflict is resolved in favor of continuity. Most members of the second generation either stay in their native kibbutz or join another

9. For a general discussion of the problem of identity and loyalty to a historical heritage see Erikson (36).

one. Joining a young frontier kibbutz and starting anew there is essentially a reenactment of the revolutionary deed of the parent generation. Although it breaks local continuity, it affirms the revolutionary tradition. The individual quest for separate identity is an aspect of the revolutionary ideology and as such is not without normative support. Only a minority of the second generation marry outside the movement and dissociate themselves from it. Total estrangement is uncommon.

Our material did not allow full examination of the relation between choice of marital partner and degree of identification with the kibbutz and the movement. Unions outside the movement, however, are more prevalent in less integrated kibbutzim, in which a rebellious second generation rejects many of the tenets of the collectivist ideology, than in kibbutzim in which the second generation is more loyal to the kibbutz and its values. Only 6 percent of marriages in the most integrated kibbutz are extra-movement, compared with 27 percent in the least integrated one. In many cases a decision to marry outside the movement is not an accidental outcome of circumstances, but a culminating step in a long developmental process of dissociation; it reinforces a pre-existing estrangement (84). By combining "exogamy" and "endogamy," the second generation reconciles dissociation with identification and maintains a flexible balance between rebellion and loyalty.

Mate selection is thus a solution to the basic dilemma of individuation. The intermediate patterns make it possible for members of the second generation to maintain continuity without being totally hemmed in and encapsulated. The compromise between in- and out-marriage enables them to cut loose without losing their roots, to remain within the fold yet achieve distinctiveness.

CONCLUSION

The thesis that marriage brings about a realignment of the social structure, and that it has a direct bearing on the cohesion and continuity of the social system, has been fully demonstrated with respect to kinship-dominated primitive and traditional societies. The social functions of mate selection are less evident when we turn to nonfamilistic societies. The decline in the strategic importance of kin lines, which reduces the impact of mate selection on the overall institutional structure, also reduces the need for stringent regulation of mate choice. Young people are given more leeway in their choice of marital partners, and the channeling of selection becomes more indirect and covert. Spontaneous love is regarded as the most important basis of marriage, and mate selection is defined as purely personal matter. Relegation of mate selection to the private sphere obscures its social functions. Small wonder that most theories of mate selection in modern societies deal with it as a process of interpersonal negotiation and minimize its repercussions on the social structure. Great emphasis is put on the "fit" and compatibility between personalities in terms of either complementary or similar character traits, (148, 113, 68).

The present study demonstrates the inadequacy of a purely interpersonal spproach to the analysis of mate selection. The kibbutz is a nonfamilistic revolutionary society. Kinship affiliations are irrelevant in most institutional spheres and there is no institutionalized normative regulation of mate choice. Yet marriage patterns have a direct impact on the cohesion and continuity of the social system; they mesh closely with the overall institutional structure and serve as crucial integrating mechanisms (59, 125).

Analysis of the intermediate marriage patterns reveals that their main function is to maintain a delicate and flexible balance between in-group closure and intergroup connectedness. Endogamy is essentially a segregating boundary-maintaining mechanism, safeguarding the internal uniformity and cohesion of the group and ensuring its continuity as a distinctive unit. Exogamy is an interlinking associative mechanism, connecting groups and cementing them together as segmental units within wider unities. Ascendancy of endogamy leads to withdrawal from out-group commitments and to separatism. Ascendancy of exogamy leads to overdiffusion of attachments and to attenuation and withering of narrower loyalties. It engenders discord and conflicting commitments and threatens continuity. The intermediate patterns reconcile the drawing inward with the thrust outward. The centrifugal tendencies in exogamy are held in check by the centripetal drag of endogamy. A combination of exogamy and endogamy militates against insulation yet safeguards distinctiveness.

While I have emphasized the social functions of the patterns of mate selection, I have also examined the ways in which the marriage patterns meet the needs and interests of the individuals directly concerned. Developmental analysis has revealed that the interpersonal "fit" approach is inadequate even with respect to individual motivation. One of the most important conclusions of this study is that mate selection is a way of resolving the conflict between rebellion and loyalty. The quest for a partner is influenced by the way in which collective identification is counterpointed by individual identity. The development of a lasting commitment to a spouse is intertwined with the process of defining and delimiting one's commitments to the collective.[10] Marriage involves an interplay between the life-stage transition of the individual and social processes. Individual choice has far-reaching repercussions on the social system and conversely, social system determinants channel and direct individual choice (75).

And last, but perhaps most important, this study has dealt with the more general theoretical problem of the relation between functional and causal analyses. Starting from the assumption that elucidation of functions cannot in and by itself account for the distribution of the marriage patterns, we have sought the efficient, operative causes and direct determinants of action and spelled out the institutional mechanisms and devices that channel and influence mate choice. An important connecting link between the two modes of analysis is purposeful action based on awareness of function. The anticipation of future outcome contributes to the movement toward a goal so that this goal is, to some extent at least, a cause of its causes (34, 41, 66). The kibbutz is a planned society. So far as some of the institutional patterns affecting mate selection directly or indirectly are introduced with reference to their intended consequences, analysis of function leads to analysis of cause.

Another important connecting link between functional and causal analyses is the degree of individual identification with society and its values. Recognition that an institutional pattern serves the best interests of society would not, in itself, guarantee that it would be adopted and adhered to. Identification with the kibbutz partially merges personal and collective goals. Hence the considerable congruence between individual needs and aspirations and long-range societal interests, which leads to the development of a personal commitment to continuity.

But this is only part of the explanation. Marriage is not regulated by

10. In terms of Erikson's analysis of critical life stage tasks, our case study indicates that the process of establishing intimacy is closely intertwined with the process of identity formation (35, 36).

consciously held norms. Moreover, most functions of the marriage patterns are latent. Recognition of the issues involved is partial, vague, and unequally distributed within the system. Even leaders and educators, who are more clearly conscious of the effects of mate selection on the social system than those directly concerned, recognize only some of the implications of the problem. Purposeful and conscious indirect control of mate selection is of only secondary importance. Channeling of mate choice occurs primarily as an unintended, unanticipated, or even undesired consequence of institutional arrangements made for other purposes. The incidence of marriage patterns is determined mainly by the framework and setting of interaction as well as the interpersonal relations engendered by the social structure and the system of socialization. The processes that influence mate choice stem from the internal dynamics of the system and reflect the tensions and conflicting interests, the pressures and counterpressures inherent in it. Thus, elucidation of functions and examination of causes are partly overlapping yet partly independent modes of analysis.

6. Aging in a Revolutionary Society

The kibbutz has solved many of the basic and most persistent problems of aging. Aging members enjoy full economic security. Communal services take care of them in case of ill health or infirmity. Retirement from work is gradual and does not entail an abrupt and complete break from work routines. Aging members are not cut off from community life. Social participation serves as an alternative avenue of activity and provides respected substitute functions; in many cases it compensates the aging member for his gradual loss of competence and status in the occupational sphere. What is most important, grown-up children are expected to live in the community founded by their parents who are thus able to maintain close and constant relations with their children without losing their independence. Elderly and older people are thus spared much of the insecurity and isolation, the futile inactivity and dependence entailed in aging.

Yet in spite of these safeguards and advantages, aging on the kibbutz is by no means an entirely smooth process. On the contrary, it often requires a difficult and even painful reorientation. In this essay the focus of our analysis will be on the main ideological and structural sources of strain, and on an examination of the institutional mechanisms by which kibbutzim cope with problems of the aged.

SOURCES OF STRAIN

The ambivalent position of old age in a future-oriented and youth-centered society (76) is one of the main sources of the strain of aging

NOTE. This essay previously appeared in *American Journal of Sociology*, volume 67, number 3 (November 1961), copyright 1961 by the University of Chicago. Reprinted by permission of the University of Chicago Press.

in kibbutzim. The movement's founders had dissociated themselves from traditional Jewish life and had rebelled against the authority of their elders. Most members were trained in radical nonconformist youth movements whose values and patterns of behavior had a decisive and indelible influence on the emerging patterns of communal life. The original revolutionary ideology was reinforced by the personal experience of rebellion. All this glorified youth as full of potentialities, free, and creative, and emphasized discontinuity.

The appearance of the second generation naturally brought to an end the disrupting of intergenerational ties. Children are expected now to settle in the kibbutz founded by their parents and to continue their life work there; the family is no longer considered an external and alien influence. The continuity of the kibbutz depends on intergenerational continuity, and the second generation is called upon to be responsible for maintaining and developing the heritage of the first.

The new ideology of continuity is just beginning to take root. It is, as yet, of only secondary importance because the collective movement, constantly seeking reinforcement from the youth movements, relies on youth-centered appeal and continues to preach rebellion and discontinuity. Since this spirit predominates, aging is looked on as a process of steady decline, a gradual fall from grace.

The central position accorded to work and the exceptionally high evaluation of productivity lead to the same effect. The founders of kibbutzim underwent a process of voluntary deurbanization and proletarization which reversed the traditional Jewish hierarchy of occupational prestige. Retraining for hard physical labor and settlement on the land were imperative for survival in the difficult conditions of settlement. Strenuous work, a dire economic necessity, has become much more than that: it has been endowed with deep meaning and dignity and invested with a quasi-religious seriousness, as an important instrument for the realization of social and national ideals as well as an ultimate value in itself. The idealized figure of a farmer-pioneer has become one of the main symbols of personal redemption and of national revival.

Work and productivity, in all kibbutzim, has become a compelling drive (128). Absence from work, even for a legitimate reason, engenders feelings of discomfort and a sense of guilt; an individual who shirks his work responsibilities is severely criticized. The position of a lazy or incompetent worker is precarious, regardless of his other accomplishments and achievements. The position of any member in the kibbutz is determined primarily by his devotion to his work and the excellence of his performance. Those engaged in physical labor in agriculture enjoy highest prestige.

Retirement from work is gradual. Aging members are not suddenly relieved of their major social function but undergo a steady and cumulative decline in occupational status. Inevitably, as they lose their capacity for hard work and find it increasingly difficult to excel in their tasks, they gradually become part-time workers and are transferred to lighter tasks, sometimes in a less arduous, nonagricultural occupation. If an aging member happens to hold a managerial position, he relinquishes it in due time, for most branches of the economy require a full-time manager. Old people often wander from one work assignment to another, doing odd jobs here and there.

Aging members thus gradually cease to be self-supporting, grow more dependent on communal institutions, and require more services. Even though most have earned their keep in many years of hard and devoted work, they cannot face declining productivity without misgivings: the constant emphasis on productivity and self-maintenance discourages any too easy adjustment to growing dependence. Moreover, unlike dependence on a state pension or on an old-age insurance scheme, dependence on the kibbutz is not neutral and anonymous. The aging member sometimes experiences it as a direct personal dependence on his fellow members. No wonder, then, that many elderly members refuse to make use of their right to part-time work and continue to work full-time as long as they possibly can.

The need for hard productive labor and the ideological emphasis on it in agriculture put elderly members at a considerable disadvantage. Moreover, the constantly changing rationalized and mechanized economy of kibbutzim puts a premium on up-to-date specialized training, with which long experience gained during many years of practical work often cannot compete. Insofar as long experience engenders rigid adherence to routine and hampers adjustment to new techniques, it is a liability. Elderly people are thus severely handicapped. Younger people, stronger and more flexible, are often better trained and more up to date.

Paradoxically, the emphasis on equality, another important value, further harasses elderly members. Social status in the kibbutz is a function of ability, not of age: young people enjoy social equality with their elders, and there are few symbols of deference. Aging members have no claim to vested positions; their contributions in the past do not entitle them to special consideration.

The fear of losing one's position in the occupational sphere is a major source of insecurity of the aged and a cause of much anxiety and discontent. Analyses of self-images of aging members and of the stereotypes employed to describe old age clearly indicate that retirement is crucial in heightening the awareness of the onset of old age. Many members define the reduction of their hours of work as the beginning of the end (127, 105).

Gradual retirement spares the workers the shock of an abrupt and total loss of their major social function, and enables them to adjust to retirement stage by stage. Moreover it enables the community to utilize the productive capacities of all members fully and spares aging members a long period of involuntary idleness. It should be stressed, however, that full retirement at a fixed age has one important advantage over gradual retirement.[1] Complete retirement constitutes a clear-cut break; gradual retirement spares the worker a major crisis, but at the same time subjects him to a long and difficult process of continuous reorientation and readjustment.

The rivalry between old and young can be fully analyzed only when viewed against the wider ramifications of the relationship between successive generations. The second generation is expected to stay in the kibbutz founded by their parents. This pattern of familial continuity enables the parents to maintain close contact with their children, but it engenders considerable strain in the occupational sphere. Occupational opportunities are rather limited: members of the second generation have to compete directly with the first generation for the available jobs.[2] As members of the kibbutz they are in free competition with the older generation, a competition in which the most suitable candidate usually wins—and the better worker is more often than not the younger.

Fear of blocking the channels of advancement often leads to a policy of early replacement of older members by younger ones, even if the aging workers are more suitable and more qualified for the job.

1. On the influence of full retirement at a fixed age on morale see Friedmann and Havighurst (47). Most researchers emphasize the grave difficulties entailed in adjustment to total retirement. There is, however, some evidence that these difficulties are overstressed; see Tibbits (137) and Streib (132).
2. On a similar problem in primitive societies see Gluckman (56), pp. 56–57.

The anomalous age distribution and incomplete generational structure of kibbutzim are of utmost importance in this matter. The founders of a kibbutz are usually young people, of the same or similar age, and unattached. At this initial stage there are no aging parents and no young children in the kibbutz. When additional groups and individuals join the founders at different stages of community development, the age distribution becomes more varied. A number of elderly parents of new members will be found in most established kibbutzim. These parents live in the kibbutz and enjoy the status of "member's parent" but do not, as a rule, become full members: they are marginal, and the generation structure remains for a considerable time truncated and incomplete. It is only when the original founders themselves become grandfathers and grow old that the kibbutz develops into a full-scale three-generational structure.

The uneven and discontinuous age distribution and the incomplete generational structure have many repercussions on the process of occupational allocation. Children born in the kibbutz begin to come of age while all members of the first generation are still in possession of their full working capacities and hold most jobs which require specialized skill and experience. The process of taking over is a prolonged one: in kibbutzim which have ceased to expand and have not evolved special mechanisms to speed up the taking-over process, the restriction of occupational opportunities is felt very keenly. Any attempt of the aged to hold on to their positions limits the occupational choices open to the second generation. The young people resent being hemmed in; they become restless, and in some cases leave their parents' kibbutz in search of better openings. Thus, severe and protracted blocking of avenues of occupational mobility endangers intergenerational family continuity.

Our material indicates the growing importance of parent-children relationships in the process of aging. To elderly members, the gradual withdrawal from the occupational sphere enhances the importance of the family. Curtailment of their outside activities bring about a concomitant decline in the number and intensity of outside contacts, and they may seek solace and emotional security in their relationships with their children. Grandchildren thus become a major preoccupation, especially with aging women.

Elderly people render their children many small but important services. Although children are looked after mainly by communal institutions the need for aid is not completely satisfied. Children come to their parents' quarters after work hours, and the parents look after them during the afternoon and take them to the children's houses at night and put them to bed. But if they are very tired after a day's work, the parents may find it difficult to cope with their children without some rest. Parents who have a number of young children will find the afternoon noisy and hectic, and here grandparents may be a great help. They take their grandchildren for walks. They help with older children after the birth of a new baby. They take over the care of children when their parents go on vacation. Whenever either parent is absent from the kibbutz attending refresher courses for specialized training or seminars for advanced studies, the grandparents replace the parent and compensate the children for the temporary separation. They help regularly, but especially during emergencies.

Grandparents' needs are provided for by communal institutions. But they, too, often need help, especially when they are incapacitated or very old. Children visit their parents regularly and help with nursing during illness. They bring food from the communal kitchen to their parents' apartment whenever the parents are unable or disinclined to eat in the communal dining hall, and they carry the parents' clothes to and from the communal laundry. These small domestic and personal services grow very important when the parents are old or infirm; they are indispensable when there is only one widowed and very old parent left.

It should be stressed that the services children render to their parents are on the whole not very irksome or time-consuming, being auxiliary functions. The old parents' primary needs are provided for by the kibbutz so that they retain to the very last a semi-independence. In the support and care of aged relatives the children only supplement kibbutz institutions. Their limited responsibilities and duties do not, in most cases, interfere with their normal routines. This curtailment and limitation of obligations seems to reinforce rather than weaken family relationships. As a rule, the sense of responsibility toward old parents is not undermined; quite the contrary, the children are able to help spontaneously and generously. The relationship is free of the feeling of resentment and of the sense of guilt engendered by too heavy responsibilities (140, 112).

The ties between aging parents and children are, thus, firmly based

on reciprocal services, on a constant give-and-take of small but significant and continuous services. During the first and middle stages of
aging, services flow mainly from parents to children, who receive more
help than they give. It is only during the last stages of aging that the
asymmetrical exchange is reversed in favor of the parents, but it seldom
becomes completely one-sided. Only in cases of long-term infirmity do
aged parents impose a severe strain on their families.

The importance of the interrelation between parents and children
can be clearly demonstrated by examining the problems of aging among
unmarried and childless members, on the one hand, and among parents
whose children have left the kibbutz on the other. Needless to say, we
do not find here the extreme isolation and bitter loneliness found elsewhere (140). Old people remain full members of a cohesive community
and continue to participate in its life. Their diminishing participation
in the occupational sphere may be partly counterbalanced by enhanced
participation in communal affairs. They are surrounded by friends and
neighbors. Yet in spite of all these benefits and substitute functions,
most of those who have no children living in the same kibbutz feel
very lonely and discouraged, especially if they have no other relatives
in the kibbutz.

Increasing age enhances the importance of geographical proximity
and daily face-to-face contact.[3] The aged find it increasingly difficult
to get about and visit their relatives who live elsewhere; they need daily
care and company. The social and health services and their friends and
neighbors take on some of the functions of children, but this substitute
aid cannot completely fill the gap. Old parents have no qualms about
accepting personal services from their children since the relationship is
based on reciprocity and deep affection, but they feel unhappy if they
have to trouble a nurse more often than do other old people. Accepting
aid from neighbors occasionally, they regard it as not quite right to depend on them for regular services, and they are not completely at ease
even with very close and old friends.

Some of the childless old members attach themselves to the family

3. Litwak (85) advances the hypothesis that close relations with kin can be
maintained in spite of distance or of breaks in face-to-face contact. However, his
sample did not include people over forty-five years of age, and he himself noted
that older people might vary significantly in this respect. His analysis of patterns
of geographical mobility of extended families indicates a tendency to move closer
together in the later stages.

of a friend or neighbor, as additional or substitute grandparents. This creates a basis of common interest and cooperation and enables them to accept the help offered not as a favor but as part of a mutually satisfactory relationship. In some cases the problems are solved by bonds of enduring friendship and mutual aid between two old and childless people. These alternatives offset some difficulties but they do not entirely replace the family.

There is a marked contrast between the interests of old members in the occupational sphere and their interests as members of families. As workers they would like to slow up replacement of old workers by younger ones. But as parents they want their children to achieve their occupational aspirations without delay and press for assignment to desirable and important jobs as soon as possible. Thus parents pay the price for family continuity by undergoing difficulties in the occupational sphere, for family continuity can be maintained only by early replacement.

A smooth process of aging entails both disengagement and reengagement. It depends primarily on a smooth retirement from work, and a successful reorientation to civic and domestic relationships and to leisure activities (92, 65). The elderly, having more free time, are often at a loss how to use it and need advice. Life in kibbutzim is work-centered: for many work was an all-absorbing and often deeply satisfying activity; they had little time, and perhaps no great need, to develop hobbies. Retirement creates a void not easily filled, and the main problem is to find a new balance between work and social participation on the one hand, and study and recreation on the other.

We must take into consideration the overemphasis on planning which is typical of recently founded revolutionary societies. Consciously or unconsciously, the members assume that all human problems can be solved by comprehensive social reorganization. Sooner or later they learn that social planning cannot cure all ills. Very often certain ends must be sacrificed in the interest of others, and in the course of solving a problem new ones often are engendered. Schemes which favor one subgroup may cause serious difficulties to other subgroups. Emphasis on one institutional sphere may entail strains in adjoining spheres. Gains in one area may be offset by minor or major losses in others. Members of kibbutzim are surprised and deeply disappointed when it becomes obvious that total social planning leaves many problems unsolved and even causes new and unforeseen strains; they are easily discouraged and prone to be impatient. Even those who, in the process of aging, seem well ordered and well balanced very often feel defeated. In many cases we found a considerable discrepancy between our evaluation of the degree of adjustment achieved by an elderly member and his own self-evaluation. We found that many of the aged tended to underrate advantages and overrate disadvantages: many took the amenities provided by the community for granted and magnified their difficulties.

The overemphasis on planning has yet another important consequence: the aged tend to rely on organizational changes rather than on ideological reorientation and personal resocialization. They do not fully realize the need for a deliberate cultivation of flexibility in role (64)—hence a certain rigidity and failure to undertake long-range preparation for inevitable change.

The importance of structural position is clearly expressed in the differences between aging men and aging women in kibbutzim. We were led by our data to expect that women would find it more difficult to adjust to aging than men. Climatic conditions, hard labor, and the negative attitude toward beauty care contribute to a comparatively early onset of aging. Most older women drift away from agriculture and child care to service institutions, such as the communal kitchen and laundry, where work is often hectic and full of tension, or monotonous, boring and of low prestige. Women, we find, are less inclined than men to participate in communal affairs, and few manage to find a suitable substitute role in this sphere. Most seek comfort in their relations with their kin and usually cling more to their familial roles than do men. However, since activities in the family are limited, these cannot in most cases fully compensate women for withdrawal from other spheres. Women tend to engage in leisure pursuits more than men, but there is as yet little systematic cultivation of them in the collectives. Thus women in the kibbutzim apparently have less chance to achieve a balanced and well-ordered old age than men,[4] and we therefore expected them to be more critical of the collective.

This hypothesis was examined in our inquiry in a subsample of two

4. Men have a more difficult adjustment to aging than women in working-class families. See Townsend (140), chapter VI. There is little comparative material on retirement of women and its effect on their adjustment to aging.

long-established kibbutzim. The sample included half of all the members above fifty years of age: the average age of the women was fifty-seven, that of the men was fifty-eight. The respondents were asked to evaluate the position of aging members in the collective. Table 34 in-

Table 34. Attitudes of aging members and aging parents of members toward their positions in kibbutzim

	Number	Appreciative	Critical	Very critical
Aging members	81	25%	44%	31%
Men	42	31	45	24
Women	39	18	44	38
Parents of members	33	67	24	9

dicates the difference between the statements of men and women. As is shown here, fewer women than men have an unqualified favorable evaluation of the position of aging people in the kibbutz, and more women are very critical of the collective. When asked to compare the position of aging men and aging women, about 70 percent of the women and 62 percent of the men felt that women have a more difficult time than men; only 6 percent of the women and 10 percent of the men stated the reverse.

The connection between the system of values and the strains entailed in aging is conclusively demonstrated by comparing members' parents (who are only quasi-members) with elderly people who are founders of the collective and full members in it. Members' parents do not serve on committees; they are partly isolated and do not participate as much as full members in kibbutz social life. Moreover, many do not fully identify themselves with the kibbutz and find it difficult to get used to its way of life. On the face of it, one would expect quasi-members to be less adjusted than full members who have more substitute functions and are better integrated in the collective. Analysis soon revealed, however, that members' parents are on the whole much happier and more contented than the others. Many, indeed, describe their life in the kibbutz in glowing terms. By contrast, aging members are much more aware of the disadvantages. Their praise of the kibbutz is guarded and qualified, and they will always point out the need for further planning and reorganization. Table 34 also shows these differences. (Members' parents in the sample are older than aging members: the average age is about sixty-four. They numbered fourteen men and nineteen women.)

Members' parents, it is seen, who are in a less advantageous position in the kibbutz, express a markedly more favorable evaluation of the position of aging people in the kibbutz than the better situated and more privileged aging members. This seemingly paradoxical finding can be accounted for only if we take into consideration the ideological and structural position of the two groups. Members' parents are not imbued with the prevalent faith in youth, work, and productivity, and— being marginal—they are less susceptible to the pressure of public opinion. Having come to the kibbutz near or after retirement age they are grateful for the possibility to work part-time and do not regard this as a come-down. As they do not set their hopes high, they are easily satisfied and enjoy many of the amenities of aging in the collective without suffering from the concomitant strains. The aging members, who are an integral part of the system and adhere to the dominant values, find it much more difficult to avoid the inherent pressures and strains.

REDEFINITION OF POLICY

The kibbutzim tended at first to disregard the spreading discontent among their aged and to ignore the symptoms of strain. Those who voiced resentment and pressed for change were usually regarded as incorrigible malcontents. The increasing number of aging members in the long-established kibbutzim and their persistent criticism have gradually brought about a growing awareness of their problems.

The fact that kibbutzim are not rigidly doctrinaire and that their structure has remained fairly flexible and dynamic is of crucial importance. The collective movement has recently started to develop supplementary institutional mechanisms which cope, to some extent, with the inherent difficulties of aging. Some of these mechanisms develop as spontaneous adaptations to a changing situation; others evolve as indirect and unintended consequences of planning in other fields. In addition, proposals and specific plans crop up which deal directly with the rights and duties of the aging.

As indicated, tension develops mostly in the occupational sphere. Consequently, efforts at reorganization are directed mainly toward careful reassessment of the policy of gradual retirement. One of the main problems is the absence of generally accepted and explicit norms of retirement. There is no clear definition of the age of retirement or of the right to progressive reduction of work hours; each kibbutz deals with retirement in its own way, and considerable individual variation is the rule even within a single kibbutz. Their rights and duties being undefined, the aging are hesitant to apply for partial retirement even when they need it very badly. To solve this problem the Federation of Kevutzot and Kibbutzim developed flexible standards to guide the collectives.

The systematic increase of suitable employment opportunities (26, 28,) is yet another subject of the planned redefinition of policy. The federation has set about reorganizing the existing work branches and recently engaged a research institute to undertake a thorough job analysis of all work branches. This research sets out to identify the skills, knowledge, and abilities required in each job, and to sort out those that, after certain modifications, can be successfully filled by the aging.

An increase of possibilities of employment and a considerable improvement of the position of aging members has been achieved by dividing some of the work branches into subunits and entrusting the elderly with responsibility in some of them. Older people resent being gradually deprived of initiative and authority and find it difficult to work under the supervision of a much younger worker. The pattern of subdivision retains for them a measure of responsibility and independence, while the partial segregation of old and young workers limits potential conflict. Not all branches are amenable to such a subdivision, but many efforts are made to give the aged as much independence as possible. Quite a number of old members work on their own. The bedridden and the house-bound get work which they can perform whenever they feel like it. Placement is slowly becoming more selective and personal.

The development of new work branches in kibbutzim and the employment of the aged in jobs outside the community have considerably widened the opportunities for old people. Many kibbutzim have developed light industries and crafts which employ mainly aging members. Moreover, a considerable number of the aged find suitable employment in local and countrywide organizations. They work outside the community and return home every day or every weekend. They keep part of their salary for their personal needs but most of it goes to the kibbutz. A certain number of elderly members in established kibbutzim volunteer to serve as social and agricultural instructors in the "adopted" newly established kibbutzim. The young and inexperienced members of the adopted kibbutzim profit from the experience and knowledge of the older persons, and treat them with respect. The instructors, for their part, serve as a living link between the two communities and feel they are making a real contribution toward the development of the movement; it gives them a new lease on life.

Continuation of employment and successful adaptation to a new job often depend on available possibilities of training. The Federation of Kevutzot and Kibbutzim has a program of refresher courses and retraining seminars. Many aging members had discarded a nonmanual occupation before joining the kibbutz. If, when they are no longer able to continue their work in agriculture, they want to return to their former occupation, they are able to do so provided they get systematic retraining. A considerable number of aging members are sent for comparatively long periods of study. Quite a number of them retrain as teachers, librarians, and accountants.

The kibbutzim realize that enhanced social participation is a necessary antidote to the loss of status entailed in gradual retirement and may compensate the aging for the limitation of their occupational opportunities. They consequently conduct a constant fight against the not uncommon tendency to retreat and retire from public life. The kibbutzim nominate aging members to all important committees and exert pressure on them to accept; they are, in fact, overrepresented on most committees. The kibbutzim also nominate aging members to temporary terms of office in the federations and in many other central countrywide organizations. These are mostly elite positions which provide wide scope for activity and initiative. Most of the leaders of the federations and most of its representatives in outside bodies, such as the government, the parliament, and the trade unions, are, in fact, elderly.

The kibbutzim promote both systematic group leisure activities and personal hobbies. They organize study groups and art classes which especially attract aging women. The main emphasis is on cultural activities and not on light recreation. Gardening, photography, cultivation of arts and crafts, philately, and reading are the most popular hobbies. Development in this sphere is on the whole slow and inadequate.

The reassessment of policy toward aging has brought about a certain redefinition of the division of tasks between the family and communal institutions. As noted above, combined care by communal institutions and by relatives works well, except in cases of long infirmity and early onset of senility. There is, besides, the problem of old people without children or near relatives in the kibbutz. The kibbutzim have tried to solve these problems in different but complementary ways: to develop additional communal services which will supplement the family and delay as long as possible the need for transfer to a hospital or nursing home, and to build up suitable institutions for cases of severe mental and physical deterioration. The kibbutzim place the main emphasis on enlargement of communal services and resort to the institutional solution mainly in cases needing personal care which cannot be dealt with within the framework of the community.

The kibbutzim have started to provide domiciliary services such as special nursing and home care for their aged. Some kibbutzim engage a special nurse or social worker who is in charge of old people in the community. Her main task is to help the families whenever the burden becomes too heavy and to provide substitute aid to old people who have no close relatives in the kibbutz. Even some assistance from the nurse will very often relieve the strain and enable relatives to carry on with their duties. Domiciliary services defer the necessity of maximum nursing care.

There is some experimentation with new types of dwelling for the aged as well. Some kibbutzim set up older parents in an independent small apartment directly adjoining that of their children. Other kibbutzim favor an arrangement of segregation by age. Planners feel that they can provide various services more economically and more effectively when the aged are concentrated in one area, easily accessible to the center. In addition, these planners assert that concentration of people with similar life experiences and perspectives enhances their social interaction (114).

The collective movement is now seriously considering the development of an interkibbutz old-age insurance scheme which will pay each member a regular pension on retirement. The pensions are to go the kibbutz and contribute toward the maintenance of aging members. The scheme will enable retired workers to continue to be at least partially self-supporting and will enhance their feeling of security and independence (77). It is hoped that the kibbutzim will be able to put aside

part of this money for the development of comprehensive old-age services.

Underlying the institutional reorganization is an ideological reorientation. There is a growing awareness that the basic difficulties inherent
in aging in the kibbutzim are directly related to the overemphasis on
youth, on work, and on productivity. There are some signs of the
emergence of a more balanced view of life as well as a more realistic
conception of the potentialities and limitations of planning.

7. Differentiation and Elite Formation

The study of social differentiation in Kibbutzim provides an opportunity to observe differentiation as it appears within a primary group based on spontaneous solidarity and on an intense identification with equalitarian values. The establishment of a comprehensive social structure and the development of subsystems within that structure entail a process of routinization. Formalization and differentiation are the two main aspects of this process. The original basic homogeneity is disrupted by the division of labor, the articulation of an authority structure, the crystallization of various solidary subgroups, and the establishment and growth of families. In this essay we will discuss the relation between elite formation and the consolidation of other solidary subgroups.

The allocation of jobs in kibbutzim was originally based on the assumption that, except for a few tasks which required highly specialized training and considerable experience, every member would be able to perform any given task. The kibbutzim insisted on frequent job changes, and especially so in the managerial and leadership positions. In time, the necessity for specialization and the exigencies of running a comparatively big enterprise resulted in a partial retreat from the original assumption. Considerations of efficiency have overruled the principle of job rotation in many spheres of social and economic life in the kibbutzim. The tendency toward a more articulated and more stable division of labor is discernible in the assignment of jobs as well as in election to public office. There is evidence of the emergence of a stable and distinct elite.

The crystallization of solidary subgroups is another aspect of the process of differentiation. The groups of settlers who join the original

NOTE. This essay previously appeared in *Scripta Hierosolymitana,* volume 3 (1955).

founders of each community at different stages of its development very often remain distinguishable from the founders. Sometimes these subgroups assimilate and become completely integrated. Most of them, however, retain their identity and constitute semiseparate subgroups within the framework of the kibbutz.

Processes of elite formation and of crystallization of solidary subgroups appear in varying degrees in all kibbutzim. Hardly any attempt has as yet been made to examine the extent of differentiation and to account for it in terms of a general theory of stratification.

The first research in this direction was done by E. Rosenfeld (110).[1] Her main conclusions are as follows.

1) In spite of the absence of economic differentiation, she found two clearly crystallized social strata in kibbutzim. The differences in rank between the emerging strata are based on the objectively defined attributes of managerial positions in work or administration and on seniority. Leaders and managers are recruited from the subgroup of old-timers; these veteran managers and leaders make up the upper stratum. The lower stratum is heterogeneous, and is composed of old-timers and newcomers and of responsible, permanent workers as well as temporary ones. The significant distinction, in terms of the balance of rewards and the role played in the process of change, obtains between the upper stratum on the one hand and the whole rank and file on the other.

2) Rosenfeld employs the typology of rewards proposed by K. Davies and W. Moore, namely (a) sustenance and comfort; (b) humor and diversion; (c) self-respect and ego expansion. No special rights as to sustenance and comfort are attached to managerial-leadership positions, but upper-stratum members are privileged to some extent as to humor and diversion, and highly privileged as to self-respect and ego expansion.

3) Differences in living conditions and reward balance in each stratum create two types of vested interests with regard to institutional change. Those more directly exposed to disfunctional consequences of the collective systems have a stake in pressure for change, while those experiencing more directly its functional aspects want to preserve the system in its entirety. Members of the underprivileged lower stratum demand a higher standard of living and more independence from communal institutions. The privileged upper stratum is "conservative" and opposes these demands.

---

1. Similar conclusions are arrived at by S. Landshut (79). A simplified treatment of the same problems is to be found in H. A. Auerbach (1).

The importance of Rosenfeld's study lies not so much in its conclusions as such, as in the basic hypothesis of correlation between the balance of rewards, extent of differentiation, and trends of institutional change. This hypothesis was the basis of further examination of the process of differentiation in kibbutzim.

ELITE FORMATION

The extent of consolidation of a leader-manager elite and its relation to other subgroups were examined in explorative research in six kibbutzim. A careful study of this problem entailed: (a) a working definition of the leader-manager elite; (b) the setting up of a systematic framework for the examination of the degree of consolidation of subgroups; (c) change of the typology of rewards; and (d) analyses of the emergence of the elite in terms of balance of rewards.

We included in the leader-manager elite[2] all members engaged in work organization and overall administration, and in direction of the community. These are: (a) Holders of key public offices (treasurer, secretaries for internal and external affairs, work-allocator, and so forth). (b) Managers of the main branches of production (for example, dairy, sheepfold, vegetable garden, citrus groves, green fodder, dry farming, or industries, if any). (c) Managers of services (communal kitchen–dining hall, laundry, clothing storeroom, children's houses, and so forth). (d) All members of the council (usually including most of those in *a*). (e) All members of the central economic committee (usually including some of *b*). (f) Chairmen of other important committees (health, housing, recreation, education, and so forth).

Key public offices and managerial positions are full-time jobs. Chairmen and members of all committees carry out their public functions in their spare time. Nomination to any of these jobs and offices is subject to the approval of one of the main committees or to the ratification of the general assembly.

Examination of the institutional framework and of the members' evaluation of the relative importance of the various management-leadership offices led to a classification of elite positions into two sub-

2. In this research we concentrated chiefly on the elite of leaders and managers. A full analysis of the elite in kibbutzim would entail examination of the technical-professional elite and the ideological-cultural elite in each kibbutz on the one hand, and on the other, an examination of the elite of the collective movements and representatives of kibbutzim in the countrywide elite.

categories. In the subcategory of primary elite positions we included the key office holders, all members of the council, and all members of the central economic committee. In the secondary elite we included the branch managers and the chairmen of the important committees. The range of activity in secondary elite positions is limited. It is the holders of primary elite positions who coordinate and direct the community as a whole. Their influence is pervasive and continuous.

The extent of consolidation of the elite and of the subgroups was assessed by examination of the following aspects: representation; turnover and mobility patterns; formal and informal leadership; exclusiveness in interpersonal relations; attitudes toward basic ideological issues.

The analysis of representation, of the rate of turnover, and of mobility patterns applies to a period of seven years. Analyses of informal leadership, of the network of interpersonal relations, and of ideology deal with members who were actually in office at the time of our study as well as with members who were found to be alternative candidates for nomination and were only temporarily out of elite positions.

Representation. The main subcategories examined as to their representation in the elite were those based on (a) former membership in a youth movement group or in an agricultural training group; (b) seniority of stay in the settlement; and (c) country of origin. In all the kibbutzim included in our sample, representation is not proportionate, and in some of them we found one subcategory with considerably more representatives in the elite than had any of the others. The tendency toward monopolization is more marked in primary elite positions than in secondary ones.

In none of the kibbutzim did we find a monopolization of most of the elite positions. Nomination is based on a policy of gaining the widest possible participation and representation of the members in the kibbutz's public life on the one hand, and on considerations of the need for continuity and efficiency on the other. Some time may pass before individual newcomers or a minority ethnic group cease to be peripheral and begin to participate in communal affairs. There are some signs of the blocking of channels of recruitment. There are subgroups that remain passive and almost unrepresented. It should be stressed, however, that the elite is as a rule heterogeneous and that most major subcategories and subgroups are represented in it to some extent.

Length of stay in the kibbutz proved to be an important determinant of degree of representation, but it was not the only one. Country of origin and former membership in a youth movement or training group often counterbalance and attenuate the influence of seniority. Both have marked effects on representation. A strong tendency toward monopolization appeared only in kibbutzim where the categories overlap. Reinforcing determinants of differentiation were found to be correlated with highly disproportionate representation. Cross-cutting categories and basic homogeneity as to degree of indoctrination and as to way of life counterbalance monopolization.

Turnover and mobility patterns. Consolidation of the elite as a closed and stable group depends on a considerable slowing down of the turnover in elite positions. The upper-stratum hypothesis assumes permanent membership in the elite. Examination of the rates of rotation and a follow-up of mobility patterns during the seven years covered by our study modify this assumption in many respects.

A trend toward longer tenure appears in leadership and managerial offices as well as in other jobs. In each of the kibbutzim in our sample we found a number of office holders who are almost permanent members of the elite. Some occupy one of the central positions most of the time. Others pass from one elite position to another almost without interruption. Some of the key offices rotate among a limited number of experts who take turns holding them. Nor is it uncommon for members in key positions to hold a number of positions at the same time. On the other hand, it should be stressed that the rate of turnover in elite positions is considerably more rapid than it is in any other sphere. The number of members who are considered indispensable, and consequently occupy one elite position or another most of the time, is small—no more than a few members in each kibbutz. There is no uniform rate of turnover in all elite positions and there are considerable and significant differences among the subcategories of key offices. Figures adduced below substantiate these conclusions and indicate the main trends of development in this respect.[3]

Tenure of office in the council (which is the main executive body) is

3. The figures quoted here pertain to the terms of tenure in one of the kibbutzim in our sample. We chose this kibbutz because we reached a more exact method of examining turnover while analyzing it. Terms of tenure in other kibbutzim are not very different from those cited here.

comparatively short. Most members of the council hold office for one year, some for two years. A longer term is rare. Only a few of the members in office at the time of our project had been in the council previously during the seven-year period covered by our examination. The average continuous term of duty is about 1.4 years. The discontinuous term of duty is 1.6 years.

Tenure of office in the main economic committee is longer than in the council. The average continuous term of office there is 1.9 years. A number of the members of this committee had held office in it once or even twice during the previous seven years. The discontinuous average term of office is thus longer than the continuous one: 2.5 years.

The full-time public offices are the most important elite positions. The average continuous tenure was found to be 1.7 years. The secretary for internal affairs does not hold his job for more than one year as a rule. The treasurer has the maximum tenure in this category: 3 years. The average discontinuous tenure in these positions is 2.3 years.

The average continuous tenure in all the primary elite positions mentioned above is 1.9 years. The average discontinuous tenure in this category is 2.6 years.

The highest average continuous tenure was found in the management of the branches of production: 2.9 years. Average discontinuous tenure is 3.3 years. Maximum continuous tenure is 6.2 years.

Tenure in consumption and services is much shorter. The average continuous tenure is 1.9 years. Average discontinuous tenure is 2.2 years. Maximum tenure is 3.6 years.

Chairmen of committees have an average continuous term of 1.9 years. The average discontinuous tenure is about the same.

The average continuous term in the secondary elite positions, when they are considered as a whole, is 2.6 years. The average discontinuous tenure is 3.1 years.

Members of committees other than the council and the economic committee, who were not included in the elite, have an average continuous tenure of 1.6 years and a discontinuous one of 2.2 years.

Tenure in primary elite positions is thus shorter than in secondary elite positions. Movement in and out of high office and in and out of a given range of offices is considerable.

The trend toward bureaucratization is partly counterbalanced by institutional devices which check the formation of a leading group with permanent power. Assignment to office by election, limited tenure, and the division of responsibilities among many semiindependent committees encourage widespread participation and prevent the consolidation of a rigid authority structure.

Examination of mobility patterns indicates the importance of the committees in this respect. Thirty or 40 percent of all community members serve on one of the committees. It is in these committees that newcomers get their initial experience in management and gradually attain recognition. Even when the committees are fairly inactive and have little influence on community affairs, they serve as channels of mobility. Key positions are entrusted to members who make their mark. Movement from secondary to important committees is considerable. The committees are stepping-stones in advancement to elite positions.

Examination of jobs and public offices held by members of the elite during the preceding seven years revealed recurring patterns: (a) Alternating periods of productive manual work and full-time public office. Periodic abstention from public office and return to productive work is not so prevalent as it once was, but still occurs quite often. (b) Transfer to semiprofessional jobs such as that of accountant, teacher, and mechanic. (c) Recurring temporary terms of office in elite positions outside the settlement. Members of kibbutzim are very often nominated to temporary terms of office in countrywide organizations that deal with common political, administrative, and cultural matters; in youth movements; in the political parties; in the army; and in government institutions. Holders of elite positions outside the community are recruited mainly from the active and influential office holders in each community.

Examination of the changeover in voluntary public committee work reveals frequent and recurring movement from secondary to important positions and vice versa, as well as retreat to temporary inactivity. Members who have once occupied important elite positions are not allowed to remain inactive for long. They generally return to public office after a period of inactivity, but not necessarily to one of the main positions.

The examination of rates of rotation and of mobility patterns leads to the conclusion that turnover in elite positions is still considerable. The constant increase in membership in kibbutzim, economic expansion, the scarcity of competent, experienced managers among newcomers, and the growing emphasis on efficiency inevitably lead to a

slowing down of the rates of replacement. The trend toward bureaucratization of management and leadership is partly counterbalanced by
the following factors: routinization of tasks; intensive vocational training; recruitment to elite positions outside the community; and difficulties of recruitment.

Kibbutzim have by now evolved established ways of dealing with
many problems. Rules of procedure, binding laws and regulations, and
definite routines are to be found in many spheres of activity. Some of
the tasks which in the first phases of communal development required a
great deal of personal skill and initiative have by now become matters
of routine. Quite a number of members have gained experience in the
course of their work and have come to specialize in certain spheres of
social and economic organization. Many members have attended special
intensive courses in their respective fields of interest, while others have
been sent to longer established kibbutzim for training and experience.
The number of candidates for some of the jobs and public offices increases gradually, and the nomination committee is able to change the
personnel of some of the committees and to replace some of the office
holders without seriously undermining efficiency.

Another important factor is the assignment of members of kibbutzim
to elite positions in the wider institutional framework. Kibbutzim
occupy an elite position in the community at large and have all sorts
of vested interests in outside bodies. They are highly represented in
many countrywide organizations and institutions. As mentioned above,
candidates for elite positions outside the community are chosen mainly
from those holding elite positions within the community. Recruitment
to elite positions in outside bodies speeds up turnover and prevents the
blocking of channels of mobility within each community.

The difficulties of recruitment are of crucial importance in this context. In all the kibbutzim in our sample we found both assumed and
sincere reluctance to accept the responsibility of certain major positions. Only in rare cases does a member accept nomination without protest. It has become an almost regular procedure for candidates to claim
that they are unsuited to the position, or are unable to accept it. Some
of these refusals should not be taken too seriously and are just a way
of proving that one does not covet authority. Ceremonial refusal is
quickly overcome and has little effect on recruitment. In many cases,
however, refusals are sincere and candidates cannot be easily prevailed

upon to accept the position offered. Some of the positions are by no means easy to fill, and members accept them only on condition that their tenure be limited. Office holders insist on their right to return to their former occupations and refuse to remain in public office longer than one term at a time. Obstinate refusals are very rare and the nomination committee generally manages to persuade the candidates to take on responsibility. In some cases, however, it is necessary to bring informal pressure to bear and the candidate accepts nomination only after long discussion and a plenary decision. Refusal or reluctance to assume office varies according to the office in question. It is much more difficult to recruit members for management positions in consumption and services, for service on social committees, or for some of the key central offices than it is for production management or membership on economic committees.

Tendencies to temporary withdrawal and refusals to hold office for more than a term at a time speed up turnover and counterbalance bureaucratization.

Elite and informal leadership. The distinctive characteristics of the elite were further clarified by examination of the relations between elite and informal leadership. In the category of informal leaders we included all the influential members who did not hold any official elite position at the time of our study. The distinction between formal and informal leadership is not clear-cut in a kibbutz. Elite positions are not highly formalized and office holders have direct and constant contact with most of the members. Moreover, the distinction is temporary in most cases. The multiplicity of offices, the emphasis on widespread participation, and the tendency toward withdrawal from office result in speedy recruitment of any member who is felt to wield some influence on his fellow members for some reason or other. Members who have acquired a reputation as efficient mangers or as influential leaders are not allowed to stay away from office for long. Sooner or later they are called upon to accept responsibility and are assigned to one of the elite offices. Informal leaders who for a comparatively long period were not assigned to office were found only in kibbutzim with very disproportionate representation. The leaders of underrepresented subgroups in these kibbutzim wield considerable influence in their own subgroup, but do not hold any elite position. The extended nonparticipation of informal leaders in the elite indicates a strong tendency toward monopolization.

A clear-cut and long-term distinction between formal and informal leadership is rare, but even in kibbutzim which try to avoid blocking the channels of mobility there is no complete overlapping of the two categories. Some types of influential leaders are more highly represented in the elite than others. The growing emphasis on economic problems and on efficiency, for example, has entailed a larger representation of managers and experts in the elite. Quite a number of members who had been prominent leaders in their youth movements or training groups did not occupy elite positions in the community at the time of our study. Some of them had taken up work in various branches of production or in teaching, and were active in the social committees (health, recreation, education, and so forth). Others had turned to activity in the countrywide movement and spent varying periods outside their communities. Very few of the elite office holders appeared on the list of members who were considered to be the most faithful adherents of kibbutz ideals. Most of those who fulfill the function of giving friendly advice or sympathy in cases of personal strain or difficulty are not office holders.

Another type of unrepresented or underrepresented leader is the opinion leader, whose main unofficial function is to appraise the working of communal institutions. Opinion leaders usually express their approval or disapproval in informal conversation, less often in the general assembly. Their pervasive influence is based on their special position in the community. Opinion leaders are, as a rule, permanent and successful workers in highly respected occupations like agriculture, child care, and medical service. The approval and esteem they gain as able workers in important occupations reinforce their interpersonal influence. The disapproval of malcontents, who are marginal, does not carry much weight with fellow members. Most opinion leaders are in opposition to the office holders, but they do not unite or make a concerted attempt to replace them. Most of them avoid assignment to public office. They seem independent and impartial because they do not covet positions of authority. Their reputation remains intact because they do not have to stand the severe test of bearing the responsibility of key positions. Opinion leaders direct, form, and express public opinion and wield considerable influence.

Interpersonal relations. Closure in informal association is one of the main indexes of the crystallization of status groupings. A close scrutiny of participants in both spontaneous and planned informal gatherings, and an analysis of patterns of visiting on weekdays and holidays, clearly indicate a high degree of closure in interpersonal relations among the subgroups. The more intimate attachments of each individual and each family are confined in many cases either within the bounds of the subgroups or within the confines of a subcategory comprising a number of subgroups.

In all the kibbutzim in our sample we found a small clique comprising some of the office holders and a number of informal leaders. Members of this small informal group meet quite often and discuss community affairs. In most cases it is an amorphous and unstable group. Membership in the clique is definitely not a family affair. The family friends of the members of this group do not, for the most part, belong to the group itself. It is perhaps significant that the casual as well as the planned meetings of the clique are as a rule held in one of the public buildings or in the room of one of the bachelors and not in the family rooms. Informal relations in the clique tend to be distinct from family relations.

The clique is a small group. Only a few elite members are included in it. Consideration of the elite as a whole clearly indicates that there is no break in social relations between the elite and the rank and file. Most members of the elite do not visit each other frequently after working hours. There is a considerable amount of tension between some of them, especially the veterans among them. Quite a number try to avoid close contact with other elite members. Most elite office holders establish their more intimate friendships with members of their own subgroups who are not members of the elite. The line dividing the elite from other members is not an important one from the point of view of interpersonal relations. Diffuse informal relations tend, on the whole, to be segregated and insulated from the more formal and functionally specific relations entailed in elite positions. The elite is not a separate and exclusive status group.

Ideology and the process of change. The relation between ideology and the dual social division was examined by an opinion study dealing with the basic issues of communal life. The main emphasis of our inquiry was put on attitudes toward proposals which would redefine the relations of the individual and the family toward communal institutions, and which would raise the standard of living.

Differences of opinion cut across the division between the elite and the rank and file in all the kibbutzim in our sample. The "innovators," who argue for less dependence on communal institutions and a higher standard of living, are by no means confined to the rank and file. The proportion of "conservatives," that is, those who remain true to the initial ideals of the revolutionary phase of the movement, is as a rule higher in the elite than in the rank and file, but quite a number of elite office holders are innovators. In two kibbutzim innovators have gained ascendancy and are in the majority.

Differences of opinion cut across the distinctions among the subgroups as well, but the subgroups seem to be ideologically more homogeneous than elite. In two kibbutzim the most conservative subgroups are composed of newcomers who have very little representation in the elite. Most members of these subgroups are young, single, and highly indoctrinated with the rather stoic, self-denying ideals of the collective movement. They strongly disapprove of the tendency of most old-timers to press for less privation, more privacy, and more independence. In four kibbutzim, however the old-timers are more conservative than the newcomers; these newcomers had very little ideological training prior to their joining the kibbutz. Country of origin, seniority, age, sex, and family status have a marked effect on opinions on basic ideological issues, but the main variable seems to be the nature of ideological training and the degree of indoctrination in youth movements and training groups.

Of special interest in this context are the opinions expressed by elite office holders from the underrepresented subgroups. Representatives of the conservative subgroups are, on the whole, staunch adherents of the conservative trend and protest against the leniency of other elite office holders. In kibbutzim in which the underrepresented subgroup was composed mainly of innovators, we found two different contellations. In two of these kibbutzim most of the recognized leaders of the underrepresented subgroup accept the views of the majority of the overrepresented subgroups and try to inculcate the values of the conservatives in their own subgroups. They identify themselves with the old-timers and are hardly aware of the disparity between the subgroups.

In the two remaining kibbutzim the situation is quite different. Most of the recognized leaders of the underrepresented subgroups there hold the same views as the majority of the members of their own subgroup. They identify themselves with their subgroup and represent its views in the elite. They are acutely conscious of differences between the subgroups.

The differences in the degree to which the mobile members of underrepresented subgroups identified themselves with their membership group were found to be correlated to the degree of monopolization of elite positions by the overrepresented subgroup and to the degree of closure in interpersonal relations. In kibbutzim where the overrepresented group was also the reference group of the leaders of underrepresented subgroups, we found open channels of mobility and less closure in the relations among members of different subgroups. The leaders of underrepresented subgroups participate freely in all informal activities and have fairly close contacts with other elite office holders. The awareness of differentiation and identification with a membership group were found to be correlated to monopolization and to the gap in social relations. An analysis of diversity of opinion and identification only in terms of the dual division between the elite and other members failed completely. Any attempt to deal with change without taking into consideration the degree of indoctrination and degree of participation yields a grossly oversimplified and distorted picture.

ALLOCATION OF REWARDS

The attempt to account for the specific characteristics of the elite in kibbutzim brings us to the problem of rewards.

Typology. In our analysis of the allocation of rewards we shall not use the Davies and Moore typology, which is vague, incomplete, and unrelated to basic-system functions. The categories are moreover on different levels of analysis. We will distinguish among: (1) means-object put at the disposal of the actor which he may use as he pleases; (2) objects of direct gratification either purely expressive or expressive-evaluative in emphasis; (3) relational rewards—rewards derived from institutionally regulated attitudes of actors toward one another.

Relational rewards are further classified in terms of the two-pattern variables of affectivity-neutrality and specificity-diffuseness, yielding four basic types of relational rewards. The neutral relational rewards are: (1) approval of specific achievement, and (2) diffuse ascriptive esteem. The affective relational rewards are: (3) specific affective response, and (4) diffuse affective acceptance.

In our treatment of the problem of rewards we followed Parsons (99, 100, 101), but found it necessary to modify his typology and his definition of the terms to some extent. Our analysis differs from that of Parsons in two important respects. Parsons does not take into account the significance of means-objects as rewards to the actor. He makes a clear-cut distinction between facilities which are primarily instrumental and rewards which are primarly expressive, and includes all means-objects in the category of facilities. It seems to us that a line should be drawn between facilities which are allocated to the actor for the performance of his role, and means-objects which are put at his disposal and which he may use as he chooses. The budget put at the disposal of a department director for the carrying out of the tasks relating to his office is a facility, while the salary paid him for his work is a reward. The specific authority which is allocated to office holders for the execution of their tasks is a facility. Diffuse authority which is not restricted to the execution of tasks and which the office holder may use for furthering personal ends should be considered a reward. Means-objects motivate and sanction adequate performance. Means-objects which are put at the disposal of the actor and which he may use as he pleases are included in the category of rewards.

Another distinction, implicit in Parsons' analysis and made explicit in our typology, is between relational and nonrelational rewards. The relational rewards are derived from positive attitudes of others. They imply mutually oriented attitudes. Both means-objects and objects of direct gratification are inherently partly independent of the interaction process. Parsons overemphasizes the conspicuous-expressive aspect of style of life and treats nonrelational rewards as symbolic manifestations of attitudes. He seems to imply that one enjoys a steak or a concert mainly because they symbolize and express social status. But objections may have expressive significance which is not derived from, and is at least partly independent of, the attitudes of other actors.

The typology delineated here is analytical and the meaning of concrete rewards depends on their significance in any situation of action.

Our examination of the allocation of rewards is based on discussion of the problem of recruitment to elite positions. We made use of reports on the working of nomination committees and put special emphasis on the reasons given for reluctance to assume office and for resignation from office. We asked office holders to describe their sources of satisfaction and the difficulties inherent in their jobs. Considerable light was thrown on our problem by analysis of disputes and conflicts among elite members, or between them and ordinary members.

Nonrelational rewards. The distinctive features of the system of rewards in kibbutzim are the almost complete absence of means rewards and the essentially nonstratified distribution of direct gratifications. There is no payment for service. The standard of living is basically homogeneous. Any differences in standard of living among individual members are based on such factors as age, sex, family status, state of health, and seniority. The gradual allocation of better housing and of more furniture and equipment according to these factors brings about some differentiation. A marked gap between the highest and the lowest standards and a low rate of equalization in housing facilities and personal amenities result in considerable, though not permanent, inequality. However, the differences in standard of living are unrelated to a hierarchy of positions or to a degree of achievement.

A major disadvantage entailed in holding elite positions is the loss of leisure. Sessions of committees take place after work hours. Office holders very often work from early morning till late at night. Elite members have less free time than the rank and file.

There are a few minor advantages attached to holding office. Office holders have easier access to kibbutz institutions and may get somewhat better service. Elite members whose work entails frequent travel to town have the opportunity to buy little presents for their families. They have a little more cash, more opportunities for recreation, and more freedom of movement. These advantages are of no small importance in the strict equalitarian organization of the kibbutz. Elite members, however, are not the only ones who enjoy these privileges. Most senior members have easy access to communal institutions and have no difficulty in getting what is due them. Anybody who works outside the community gets a small additional allowance for personal expenses; drivers get the same sum as office holders. Because the special advantages are not exclusively attached to elite positions, they cannot serve as indicators of social position and as symbols of status.

Authority is another source of both means and direct gratification. Members of kibbutzim are dependent on kibbutz institutions for the satisfaction of their needs. Legitimate power means partial independence. Office holders have the right to direct others. They have their say and wield considerable influence in their sphere of competence. Office holders who actually direct the policy of the whole community have wide-ranging authority.

Analysis of our material brings out quite clearly that authority is a fairly important reward. Very few admitted it openly, but immunity from overdependence and legitimate power of direction seem to be sources of direct gratification. Office holders are not very outspoken about it, but it crops up on many occasions.

The significance of authority as a source of rewards should not, however, be exaggerated. It is not of primary importance in the reward scheme. Basically, authority is defined in kibbutzim as a facility, and not as a reward. Authority is specific and limited. There is a strict prohibition against exercise of authority outside the prescribed bounds of one's own sphere of competence and against utilizing it for personal ends. There is no rigid authority structure and very few direct and effective sanctions. The office holders depend on voluntary cooperation. They have difficulties in work relations in their own sphere of activity and in coordinating affairs with other managers. The office holders can do very little about these difficulties. If lack of cooperation becomes serious, they can only refer the problem to one of the committees or to the general assembly. Authority is limited in both range and efficacy. Furthermore, as will be shown in the analyses of relational rewards, the evaluation of authority is ambivalent and high authority does not necessarily lead to high prestige.

Relational rewards. The strict limitation of the allocation of non-relational rewards enhances the importance of relational rewards.

Voluntary public service is one of the main values of the collective movement. Holders of elite position who volunteer for service and work hard on behalf of the community win the respect of their fellow members. The esteem accorded to them is, however, not unambiguous.

In evaluating different positions the main emphasis used to be on productive labor—mainly agriculture. The exigencies of running a complex and specialized enterprise have resulted in a shift in the relative importance of the bases of evaluation. The old aversion toward authority positions in management and administration is much weaker. Most members evaluate elite positions highly, although the bias against them has not disappeared completely, and is still operative to some extent. So tenacious are the tenets of equalitarian ethics that there is considerable reluctance to discuss elite status except in an oblique and indirect fashion. Very rarely did we get a wholehearted, ungrudging, and unreserved high evaluation of elite positions as such. Elite members are somewhat apologetic and on the defensive when asked to evaluate the relative importance of elite positions. Analysis of our material makes it quite clear that the scale of differential evaluation is not unequivocal, and that esteem gained by holding a position is therefore not free from ambiguity.

Another factor is of crucial importance in this context. The social standing of members is determined not so much by the value attached to a position as such, as by the assessment of personal qualities and the degree of conformity to norms—and, more recently, with the growing importance attached to economic success, by the evaluation of achievement. In many cases the main emphasis has shifted to approval according to standards of efficiency. Elite positions provide ample opportunity for proving one's abilities by the successful fulfillment of roles. Office holders are in the center of public attention and success in their office is rewarded by general recognition. Competent office holders are accorded approval and rise in the hierarchy. The reward gained is in some cases considerable. The emphasis on approval, and not on ascriptive esteem, is, however, a source of strain. The temporary and shifting placement according to specific achievement results in basic insecurity. Many office holders feel they have to be continually proving themselves, that their activities are constantly being scrutinized and criticized. Sharp criticism is one of the main reasons given for withdrawal from office.

The absence of symbols of status and excellence and the prevalence of the equalitarian pattern of behavior should also be mentioned. There are very few easily perceptible indexes of either esteem or approval. Successful holders of important positions are praised in informal conversation. The reputation they have gained by serving their community is very often commented upon and some of them are treated with genuine respect. There is, however, no institutionalized public expression of deference. There are no ritualized salutations, no honorific titles, no order of precedence at any public meeting. Deferential behavior is almost completely ruled out. There are no exemptions from burdensome tasks and no special immunities. Elite members serve in the communal kitchen and dining hall on Saturdays and holidays just like all the other members. Differences are minimized, and members who have higher status make a special point of behaving simply and as inconspicuously as possible. Invidious distinctions are suppressed, since patterns of behavior are focused on the denial of differences.

Affective rewards. The attempt to develop a comprehensive social structure on the basis of primary group relations results in a shifting of emphasis to affective rewards. Hence the importance attached to response in reciprocal relations and acceptance by fellow members. General sympathy, solidarity, and identification with the community are the core of the reward system. Elite office holders are responsible for the main spheres of communal organization. Directly or indirectly they influence the overall direction of the community. Their central position helps them to preserve a wider perspective. They can grasp the community as a whole and identify themselves with it. Those who are recruited to elite positions outside the community develop solidary relations with the countrywide elite. Acceptance in the elite of the more comprehensive community may become a source of affective rewards. The weakening and contraction of solidary relations within the community is the main problem which besets the office holders in this sphere.

Preoccupation with public affairs involves the inevitable sacrifice of more intimate relations. Office holders have very little time left for their families and close friends. Public office held by one member of the family confers on other members of his family neither a perceptibly higher standard of living nor a marked rise in social standing. There is some transfer of the esteem gained by the elite member to his relatives. The immediate family shares, to some extent, the social standing attained by one of its members, but the emphasis on personal qualities and personal contribution precludes the consolidation of the family as an undifferentiated status group. Individuals are not identified with their families and are assessed mainly according to their own individual merits. Thus there is little compensation for the temporary estrangement from the family which results from holding public office.

The estrangement from family and friends is sometimes accompanied by isolation in the community. Loss of acceptance is caused mainly by a certain discrepancy between the norms which define approved behavior in interpersonal relations and the functional consideration of efficiency. Office holders have to act in an authoritative way. They have to decide between conflicting claims and to disregard personal considerations. The decisions they reach are often disapproved of by many members, so that they can hardly avoid friction and disputes. Success very often means conflict and estrangement. Many of the most competent office holders, who are accorded high esteem and approval, are not liked. Only a few of them appear on the list of the most popular and well-liked members; most have a high social position but are somewhat isolated. The gain in esteem and approval may very well be counterbalanced by the loss of acceptance.

The loss of diffuse solidarity is serious and is acutely felt because most social relations are limited to the one inclusive community. There is no secluded sphere of family relations. Daily activities involve constant interaction and complex coordination. It is difficult to draw a line between different spheres of interaction and to avoid tension. Diffuse friendly relations have special significance in this context.

The growth of the settlement and its economic expansion introduce a notable change in this respect. The growing differentiation among spheres of activity and the increase in the number of members and subgroups entail some segregation. Heterogeneity was found to be more important than the number of members and the mere size of the settlement. Crystallization of subgroups is of crucial significance here. These subgroups may become competing foci of intensive primary relations and may replace the inclusive community as the main reference group. Office holders very often consider themselves, and are considered to be, representatives of subgroups. They protect themselves from criticism by limiting their relations with members of other subgroups. The cohesive subgroup thus becomes the main source of security. The intense solidarity of the subgroup may counterbalance the loss of acceptance incurred by the holding of office in elite positions. Tension is isolated by limiting the range of face-to-face contact and by the segregation of diffuse and more intimate social relations from specific work relations.

Reward balance in different elite positions. Up to this point we have dealt with the balance of rewards of the elite as a whole, but the balance of rewards in elite positions is not uniform. There are perceptible and significant variations in the rewards allocated to different types of elite positions.

The reward balance of managers of production branches is more positive than that of managers in consumption and services. Branches of production are highly evaluated and are put at the top of the esteem scale. Management in this sphere is not divorced from manual labor. The authority exercised by production managers is based on expert knowledge and experience. Success in the performance of their roles is clearly expressed by higher production and higher income. It is readily recognized and easily estimated. Members who do not work in the same branch and are not experts know very little about it. The number of members who know enough to criticize is therefore quite limited. In some of the production branches, especially those which enjoy the highest esteem, we found solidary work groups characterized by "we consciousness," intensive informal relations among members, and specific patterns of behavior. Members of the work group very often appear in the assembly as a united body. They have common interests with respect to the allocation of capital investment, machines, and manpower, and support the demands which the manager makes on their behalf. The need to present a united front in out-group relations often outweigh inner tensions. The backing of a cohesive work group is an important factor of stability in the recruitment of managers of production.

The evaluation of consumption and services is, generally speaking, lower than that of production. Managers in these spheres have close contact with most of the members and serve them under conditions of relative scarcity of goods. Norms of distribution are not always clear. The decision as to the specific needs of the individual often rests with the manager. Vagueness of norms and the difficulty of dealing with special cases are sources of friction and numerous disputes. Faulty performance affects each member directly and is therefore easily discernible. There is comparatively little specialization in this sphere and every member considers himself competent to criticize the managers; there are very few criteria of success. Work groups are not as solidary as those in production.

The full-time central elite positions are very highly evaluated. Some of these positions, however, entail a considerable amount of tension and ambivalence. Office holders in these positions are not engaged in productive manual labor. They are held responsible for the proper functioning of all communal institutions. They are at the center of public opinion and any serious complaint is as a rule directed against them. The authority structure is not very clearly articulated. Overall coordination depends on the ability of office holders to mediate among conflicting claims and to reach working agreements. Refusal among managers to follow directives of the overall management seems to be more prevalent than noncooperation within the work group. There are no clear standards of performance and no distinctive and easily recognizable index of success.

Finally, there are more sources of tension in social committees than in purely economic ones. Two main difficulties are inherent in the chairmanship of social committees, namely: roles are relatively unstructured, and friction ensues from decisions on personal problems. Isolation of tension is difficult because of the constant contact with a comparatively large number of members.

The analysis of reward balance in elite positions has made it quite clear that the elite is not an undifferentiated unit from the point of view of allocation of rewards, and that elite positions are not devoid of tension. It seems significant that the incidence of withdrawal from office, and to some extent the length of tenure as well, are correlated to the variation in reward balance and to the degree of tension in different types of elite positions. As mentioned, there is much more reluctance to assume office and to continue holding it for a long time in the management and organization of consumption and services, in social committees, and in key central offices than in the management of production branches and economic committees. Short tenure in positions which require both marked ability and experience (such as the central key positions) is directly related to the degree of ambivalence, insecurity, and estrangement. The diversity of reward balance in different elite positions and the concomitant tension explain why there is so slight a tendency toward the consolidation of a united and exclusive group of active and influential members permanently in power.

CONCLUSIONS

The main conclusions of our explorative research are as follows,

1) Attempts to analyze our material in terms of a division between elite and nonelite failed completely.

2) The integration of subgroups on the basis of seniority in the community, country of origin, and former membership in a youth movement or training group is stronger than integration on the basis of functional position in the elite. The elite is not a closed and solidary status group.

3) Reinforcing criteria of differentiation and overlapping categories enhance marked differentiation and closure of the subgroups. Cross-cutting categories and small differences as to way of life enhance widespread participation.

4) The absence of a marked tendency toward the consolidation of a united and closed elite is related to the diversity of reward balance in different elite positions and to the considerable strain entailed in some of these positions.

5) The increase of esteem accorded to key positions, the growing segregation in different spheres of interaction, and growing representation in the countrywide elite entail a considerable reward gain and enhance the integration of the elite.

6) The analysis of the relation between differentiation and the trends of institutional change should be based on examination of the degree of indoctrination, the extent of monopolization of elite positions, the range of informal participation, and the balance of rewards in all institutionalized roles.

The conclusions summarized here are tentative. Our sample is not representative, and it may well be that one conclusion or another does not apply to all kibbutzim. The main emphasis in this summary is on the examination of our basic hypotheses and on the setting up of a systematic framework for further research.

8. Secular Asceticism: Patterns of Ideological Change

Historically asceticism has been associated with the religious view of life. The ascetic does not wish to be distracted from religious meditation by excessive effort or interest spent on secular activity. Abstinence from sensual pleasure is a sacrifice to the Divine Will and a means of self-education, making the believer worthy of God's grace. Asceticism finds its fullest justification in those religions which reject the life of this world. The world and its pleasures are viewed as impure and sinful; it is man's duty to abstain from them as much as possible. The stringency of the ascetic rule is generally directly related to the extremism with which worldly existence is rejected.

The various Protestant sects form an exception to this rule. They have developed a conception combining self-restraint with acceptance of this world.[1] Seclusion in monasteries is strongly rejected and secular activity is affirmed. The believer is called upon to work strenuously and selflessly for the realization of God's kingdom on earth by scrupulously and strictly fulfilling his earthly duties. Whereas the religious asceticism that stems from a rejection of this world is passive and leads to retreat from society, the religious asceticism which accepts the world is active and militant. Its antihedonistic orientation does not stem from a negation of pleasure merely because of its secular nature, but from the larger duty to direct all efforts toward the achievement of the religious goal, which incorporates both a secular and a religious element.

The ascetic conception based on a rejection of this world is clear-cut

NOTE. This essay, written with Zippora Stup, appeared in Hebrew in *Sefer Bussel*, edited by S. Wurm (Tel Aviv, 1960).

1. See Weber (142). In this study the term "secular asceticism" refers to self-restraint in material consumption.

203

and unyielding. All secular activity is frowned upon, and so is the enjoyment of its results. The ascetic conception which is based on acceptance of this world, on the other hand, is more problematic since it calls at one and the same time for participation and limitation. It urges intense activity in this world, while circumscribing the right to enjoy its benefits. Studies on the relationship between Protestantism and capitalism have shown that the early capitalistic entrepreneurs regarded their occupational role as a religious calling that demanded, and rewarded, diligent work, thrift and productive investment, and peristent resistance to consumer satisfactions. The association of secular activity with self-denial was made possible because the economic role was perceived as a religious function; for it was its religious legitimation that invested this asceticism with meaning and guarded it against hedonistic tendencies. As the religious commitment diminished, ascetic values lost their force and aspirations to raise the standard of living became dominant.

Many parallels may be drawn between Protestant and kibbutz asceticism. Both concepts stem from a complete acceptance of this world, and both call for action and accomplishment. There is, however, one decisive difference: kibbutz asceticism is not based on any religious sanction. The ideology espoused by the kibbutz movement is completely secular.

While much research has been done on the different types of religious asceticism, secular asceticism has remained totally unexplored. Consequently, many questions remain unanswered. What are its sources of legitimation? What protects it from hedonistic tendencies? What are the focal points of its strength and weakness, and what has been the course of its development? In this essay I shall try to answer these questions by presenting an analysis of the secular asceticism that is part of kibbutz ideology, and by describing the changes it has undergone in the course of its development.

At one time, frugality and abstinence were an important element in the values system of the kibbutz. They constituted an essential value in themselves as well as through their close interrelation with other central elements of the original kibbutz ideology, being directly derived from such fundamental tenets as emphasis on goal, collectivism, and a future-oriented perspective. No essential significance was attached to hedonistic consumer satisfactions, the main things in life being one's commitment and the accomplishment of the tasks and goals set by this commitment. This in turn implied a negation of self-contained individuality; the individual was supposed to attain his personal goals by working together with those who shared his commitment for the reform of the entire community. A future-oriented perspective was the direct corollary of this goal emphasis and of the collectivist ideal. The individual could transcend the narrow, restricted boundaries of his personal existence by joining the community and transposing his concern from the present to the future. His gaze was thus diverted from everyday matters—the search for immediate, transient satisfactions—and riveted to the wider horizon of the future which held out the prospect of lasting achievements. The kibbutz member had therefore to equip himself with patience, forbearance, and self-discipline, and put off minor gratifications for the sake of the fuller, more perfect satisfaction of final accomplishment.

The three basic tenets and goals of kibbutz ideology are: national renaissance, total social reform, and self-realization. In some form or another, restraints are called for, jointly and severally, in the pursuit of all three goals—the national-ideological, the social, and the individual.

The relationship between the kibbutz and the national renaissance movement was the starting point of ideological asceticism. Here ideology coincided with hard facts. The main function of the kibbutz was to create a material base for the existence of the Jewish people by modifying and amplifying its occupational structure and establishing a self-supporting economy. This had to be done under highly unprofitable conditions. Farm settlements were set up on nonarable land without basic capital or skilled labor. The kibbutzim first had to reclaim the land, train their members to manual labor and a rural way of life, and from their meager income set aside the necessary basic capital for the consolidation and gradual expansion of their farm. Theirs, moreover, were frontier settlements which for many hard years were forced to defend themselves against marauders. The success of the enterprise depended on the willingness of the members to cut down on consumption expenditure and to invest any surplus in the development of the farm. The purpose of hard work was not to raise the standard of living or to accumulate profits but to expand production, a goal which was not confined to the individual kibbutz.

According to kibbutz ideology every kibbutz was supposed to contribute, through constant expansion and development, to the economic consolidation of the Jewish community as a whole. The kibbutz movement conceived of itself as the vanguard of the people and felt under pressure to promote economic progress for the general good. Thus emerged what we may refer to as an ideology of materialistic idealism. All physical and mental resources were to be harnessed and directed toward the development and consolidation of a productive economy, but not for profit-making or for pleasure. The incentive to economic activity was not the prospect of material wealth and consumption but a firm commitment to a system of values. Working for the economic progress of the kibbutz thus became, to some extent, a kind of secular worship or religious service. Work was valued both for its material results and for its own sake. Devoting oneself to work while curbing one's personal needs and desires became the symbolic ritual expression of one's dedication to the ideal. This kind of asceticism, imbued as it was with symbolic significance,[2] was bound to have economic consequences.

Kibbutz ideology aspired to change the occupational structure of Jewish society by voluntary deurbanization and proletarization. The shift from city to country entailed, to some extent, economic hardship. It was impossible to become a farmer without being prepared to face long years of thrift and frugality. But leaving town also had romantic overtones of a return to nature, where life would be simple and pure, free of all pretense and artificiality. This naive and passionate idealization of rural life also contributed much to the ascetic ideology.

In the process of proletarization the rather ambivalent relationship between asceticism and socialism becomes apparent. Since one of its main aims is to raise the standard of living of the working man, socialism does not, in principle, reject the aspiration to a higher standard of life. But while material improvement is not invalidated as one of several final ends to be achieved, it is inadmissible as an immediate goal. Over-eagerness to attain material rewards is regarded as a diversion from the struggle for the full realization of socialist aims. It is bound to lead to concessions and to hasty bargains and compromises resulting in minor benefits. The stress is shifted from total reform to marginal demands.

2. Here the parallel between kibbutz and Protestant asceticism is particularly close (142).

Instead of seeking the good of their class, workers begin to look after their own interests; instead of striving for class mobility, they become concerned with their personal careers. There is also a symbolic significance in the acceptance of voluntary poverty. A high standard of living is typical of the monied classes. Identification with the class struggle requires a symbolic rejection of the enemy camp. A working class style of life is a sign of solidarity and of class awareness. This is true of socialist movements everywhere, but it applies with still greater force to the particular brand of socialism that developed in the kibbutzim. The working class to which this movement catered had no prior spontaneous existence, but had first to be created by a process of voluntary proletarization. Acceptance of the bitter poverty which was the laborer's lot in those days was a decisive test of solidarity.

A life of poverty also served as a badge of distinction for the select group of those who were actively involved in the realization of the goal. Socialism, in its kibbutz version, relied neither on economic and political bargaining nor on coercion, but on an elite intent on immediately implementing its program by establishing socialist cells and exerting its influence through personal example. In order to be assured of success, this elite had to pursue its tasks with unswerving devotion, without deviating from its course or seeking any personal gain. Voluntary poverty was regarded as a badge of affiliation with this elite, the tangible evidence of its moral force and influence.

The main incentive to asceticism was the extreme compliance of the early kibbutzim with the socialist ideals of equality and cooperation. Rewards were distributed according to such factors as age, health, and seniority. This equality did away with any distinctions by role or performance. The attainment of preferential consumer rewards was no incentive to role acceptance and performance. With consumption no longer serving as a major source of motivation, extreme normative regimentation was required. The pattern for regulating and balancing needs was laid down by the community. Most needs were met in kind in such quantity, rate, quality, and manner as was determined by the community, so that the individual had little scope for exchange or manipulation. Consumption practically ceased to be a legitimate personal outlet.

Such restriction and normative regulation of consumption as are required by the values system and institutional structure of the kibbutz are possible only so long as the needs of its membership are few, simple, and fairly standardized. As consumer demands increase they also tend to become more diversified, and threaten to throw the collective consumption pattern out of gear, since a wide and varied range of consumer demands obviously makes it more difficult for the community to enforce a standard distribution pattern. Increased emphasis on special personal requirements breeds a demand for greater freedom of action and choice, with the imminent danger that consumption will become regulated by individual rather than communal needs.

A steady rise in the standard of living may also generate tension between members' personal claims and the equalitarian precepts of the community. A kibbutz can maintain a uniform standard of living and rate of progress only so long as amenities are simple and relatively cheap. It takes a long time to supply every member with expensive equipment and comfortable housing, and in the meantime there is a considerable and protracted gap in living conditions between the first, the second, and the third person in line. The last in the queue may have to wait for many years to receive his allocation. Although the resulting inequalities are due to the way in which the agreed-upon rules of distribution work, and do not have a lasting affect, they are not easy to accept and can become a source of resentment and envy.

Abandonment of the ascetic ideal jeopardizes the principle of collective consumption in another respect too. As consumption becomes more important, the rigid pattern of curbing expenditures breaks down, giving rise to ever new demands. The growing desire for immediate satisfaction makes it more difficult for members to adjust to restrictions and delays in the supply of acknowledged needs. The sense of inequality becomes more acute; kibbutz institutions are subjected to pressure and can no longer perform their function properly.

Feeling willfully deprived, kibbutz members thus tend to turn to outside sources, semilegitimate or nonlegitimate, to make up for what the kibbutz has failed to provide. This, however, merely serves to intensify the process of differentiation. Quite frequently kibbutzim are forced to reestablish equality by supplying costly equipment to those who could not benefit from private outside sources. In this way the consumption level of the kibbutz in fact comes to be measured by external standards. The ultimate disintegration of the ascetic ideal thus also deals a death blow to the principle of collective consumption.

So much for the relationship between asceticism and national-socialist ideology. Before going further we should, however, note that kibbutz asceticism does not operate solely on the communal level but that its roots strike down to the value system that regulates the individual's self-image and attitude to life. In living a life of frugality and austerity he is considered not to be ceding any of his personal independence or making a sacrifice for the general good, but to be fulfilling one of the essential conditions that make life worth living. The pursuit of material satisfactions is looked upon as a distraction from the essential to the incidental, from the permanent to the transient. Through the propensity to consume, an individual's energies are wasted on trivia and he is diverted from total devotion to the ideal. Austerity implies freedom bought through self-discipline, a release from transient desires and external superficialities. The simple life is the true life. The man who has chosen it casts off all pretense and eschews all that is affected, artificial, and showy. Thus, the ascetic ideal is nourished by a deep contempt of creature comforts and material possessions. The doctrine of the common good enables men to bear the badge of poverty gladly and freely and breeds an elite that harks back to the age of chivalry, with its ideal of the poor but noble knight who does his duty and accepts the way of life he has chosen out of a sense of perfect commitment.

The pioneering ideology in its purest form is bound up with the ascetic ideal which is intimately related to each of its basic values. Asceticism is inherent in the underlying philosophy of the kibbutz, and is also necessary on the practical plane in order to put this philosophy into effect. An ascetic way of life is the hallmark of the true kibbutz pioneer.

This pattern, however, has not generally been preserved in its pure form. In the course of the years decisive changes, internal and external, have taken place which have had a profound effect on the ascetic elements in kibbutz ideology. Israeli society has become more and more institutionalized, and so have the kibbutzim. Changes in the social set-up outside the kibbutz have accelerated parallel processes within. Thus by examining the modifications that have taken place in kibbutz ideology, we shall be able to glean some insight into the wider ramifications of the process of change.

Ascetic values began to succumb precisely at those points where the original ideology was at its weakest, highlighting its internal inconsistencies. In order to be able to describe the gradual transformation that has taken place we must first define more closely what kibbutz asceticism stood for and what distinguished it from other ascetic ideologies. This type of asceticism was neither antimaterialistic nor antisecular, and was devoid of any spiritual transcendentalism. Its central values were goal-oriented and designed for practical application. Now, any fusion of idealism with materialism is essentially strained and insecure. With the establishment of a complex social and economic organization, the materialistic element was bound to gain in strength and impinge upon the ideological element. As materialistic considerations began to supervene, the kibbutz was no longer able to resist consumer temptations, a process to which it gave in all the faster because there were no sanctions to stem the tide.

The ideals of monastic self-denial and mortification were always foreign to kibbutz ideology, which neither emphasized the purifying power of abstinence nor sanctified pain, sorrow, and suffering. Consumer abstinence was not an end in itself, but a means of releasing resources for other purposes. There was no consistently held antihedonistic ideology in which self-denial in itself could become a spiritual discipline.

The peculiar character of kibbutz collectivism must also be taken into account. It was not inspired by opposition to individualism. In giving priority to the community collectivists never intended to slight the individual. The underlying assumption is that individual and communal interests are in perfect harmony with each other. Even when the individual dedicates his life to the common good, he does not give up his independence to the extent of becoming totally engulfed by the community. His social activity offers ample opportunities for personal expression. He merely gives up small, transient pleasures for the much more lasting, meaningful satisfaction of knowing that he is working for the common cause. It is therefore considered quite legitimate to apply the test of personal satisfaction to life in any given kibbutz or to the movement as a whole.

A nonascetic trend is discernible in another element of the original ideology. We have already hinted at the ambiguity of the relationship between socialism and asceticism. Raising the standard of living of the working man is one of the primary goals of the socialist movement. Opposed to the existing world order on grounds of both justice and efficiency, it holds out a promise of material prosperity for all if its principles are put into practice and society is reorganized accordingly.

The kibbutz is supposed to be a model socialist microcosm. Since it has to compete with the surrounding nonsocialist economy, it must prove itself capable of providing superior conditions for its workers. It is, therefore, hardly surprising that its members should also judge it by its capacity to fulfill their consumer demands.

We have seen the close connection between asceticism and collective consumption, and noted that when excessive emphasis is placed on consumption, the principle of collectivism can no longer be properly applied to it. The development of the consumer aspect cannot be properly understood without qualifying this conclusion in one major respect. When the bulk of the surplus resources is constantly ploughed back into the economy, ultimately a glaring discrepancy develops between the state of the community and that of the individual, who toils and labors year in, year out, only to be told regularly that difficult and straitened circumstances necessitate further economies and retrenchment. If ideological values are no longer held in the same esteem as before, the customary frugality may provoke resentment and resistance. A disparity arises between accepted practice and official ideology, between the members' overt and latent desires. This dichotomy has dialectical consequences: the continued postponement of fundamental satisfactions inadvertently enhances their value. Consumer satisfactions are no longer disparaged. On the contrary, every advantage or presumed advantage that may be gained in this field assumes an exaggerated importance.

The extremely restricted consumption budget poses a difficult problem. Frequently a kibbutz is forced to cut back on essentials. It takes a long time for items already approved to be distributed among the members, and long delays are no rarity. The restricted means enforce uniformity and standardization with so little variety that there is practically no individual choice. The narrow budget scarcely makes it possible to cater to special personal needs, and members' personal allowances are far from adequate. Thus, both private and public consumption spending is severely limited.

Conditions in many kibbutz consumer institutions are such that the members' personal demands cannot be met courteously and efficiently. The not infrequent cases of negligence and disorder are largely due to the insufficient funds and manpower allocated for the purpose. The consequences are more serious than strained tempers and inadequate amenities: many kibbutz members begin to harbor serious doubts as to whether the kibbutz is able to provide them a decent living. To prevent further loss of confidence, the people in charge of consumer institutions do all they can to improve matters, to obtain additional funds, better consumer mechanisms, better working conditions. It becomes necessary to divert sufficient means and manpower to this area in order to preserve collective consumption.

The attenuation of the ascetic ideal is thus a process of internal evolution which is partly sanctioned by the original ideology. The weaknesses of the ascetic ideology do not become apparent as long as the individual identifies fully with the communal enterprise and feels that his life is rendered so meaningful as to compensate for the minor discomforts of thrift and frugality. Yet this sense of total commitment is likely to give way under the strain of daily reality. Any ideal, when put into practice, tends to become distorted, and principles are pushed aside by practical considerations. The vision of a glorious future becomes translated into minor daily rebuffs, complaints, and compromises. Realization of a revolutionary program to some extent also spells disappointment—a disappointment that is the fate of all revolutionaries once they find that the ideas for which they have fought are not truly shared by everybody around them. The magic of the common enterprise may easily vanish once the gap between ideal and reality becomes apparent, highlighting the discrepancy between individual existence and the social setting.

The establishment of the State of Israel was the decisive turning point in this process of disillusionment. Before that there were indications of the impaired validity of the ascetic ideal, but the final achievement of one of the goals of the national movement lent emotional support and official legitimation to their gradual abandonment. The tremendous effort involved in the achievement of independence was succeeded by a period of dissolution and relaxation. The fact that only part of the ideal had been realized was ignored, and a sense of success prevailed. The individual felt he now no longer had to postpone his satisfactions or give up his personal comforts.

The establishment of the state was of paramount importance for the kibbutz from another point of view as well. Through the organization of an institutionalized body politic, various social processes were brought to a head which largely undermined the acknowledged leadership of the collective settlements. The voluntary idealistic structure was replaced by the rule of the state, operating by force of law and through the manipulation of the resources and rewards available to it. Fewer tasks were assigned to the kibbutz movement, and the contradictions between kibbutz values and society at large emerged with greater force. Previously the elite status of the kibbutz had been generally acknowledged and affirmed. The external confirmation of its elite role and the internal confidence with which it assumed this role served as a source of rewarding and dutiful pride to its members. This enabled them to carry out their tasks and withstand the trials of austerity without complaint, free of a sense of deprivation. Once their self-confidence became undermined and their leadership status was no longer generally acknowledged, this delicate balance of duty and reward was upset. Doubt and status anxiety began to gnaw away at the tacit acceptance of asceticism. As kibbutz members were deprived of the sense of leadership and pioneering they started to clamor for immediate satisfactions. A consumer-oriented ideology began to develop which gradually parted from the original asceticism.

So much for the past development of secular asceticism in the kibbutz, its reliance on ascetic elements inherent in pioneering collectivism, and the ideological and social processes that led to its collapse and the emergence of a consumer-oriented ideology. Now let us examine the present situation.

ATTITUDES

To examine the present-day attitude of kibbutz members toward ascetic ideals we put the following question to a representative sample: "Is there any justification, as a matter of principle, for leading a simple life and limiting consumption? If so, what is it? Explain."[3] Since we were interested in tracing the ideological development we deliberately phrased the question so as to relate to values and principles. The ascetic ideology was presented in terms of two concepts which refer to its two most essential elements. The concept of limited consumption embodies the call to abstinence, frugality, and thrift, while the concept of the

3. This question was included in an open questionnaire used to interview a representative sample of members of twelve kibbutzim. For a full description of the methods used, see the appendix.

simple life sums up the reflection of asceticism in everyday life patterns. This distinction was the main key in analyzing the development of compromise patterns adapting the original values to the new reality and mediating between the ascetic and consumer-oriented ideologies.

Classification of the responses to our questions showed four distinct patterns: the ascetic pattern; the life style pattern; the situation pattern; and the consumption pattern.

The ascetic pattern implies full acceptance of all ascetic values, while the consumption pattern implies their total rejection. Between these extremes there are two compromise patterns.

In the life style pattern the duty to limit consumption is not recognized, but the need to live a simple life is affirmed. "Simplicity is fully justified; the self-imposed restrictions on consumption are not." "When you limit your consumption you deprive yourself of things which you need, but the simple life can be beautiful." What this group wants is a simple, modest style of life, with well-cared-for clothes that are neither affected nor showy; comfortable, functional, but unpretentious homes; spacious, good-looking public buildings without excessive grandeur or luxury. Occasionally, to be sure, all ascetic values are abandoned and only the formal stylistic aspect remains: "simple, even if expensive." It should, however, be noted that in most cases style is not divorced from an underlying asceticism, generally expressed in contempt for ostentation and conspicuous waste.

The second compromise pattern is the situation one, where attitudes are determined by existing circumstances. Asceticism is no longer a matter of principle, an end in itself, but a means to an end. It is accepted as a necessary evil that has to be borne in emergencies or under the pressure of circumstances, but not as a purpose in life. It is a pragmatic necessity but not an ideal. "One should not make an ideal of it, but should spend according to one's ability." The reason for imposing restrictions is purely economic. Here asceticism becomes a temporary necessity, strictly limited in time, whatever the duration.

A careful distinction must be made between those who think that circumstances justify asceticism for a short time and those who would justify it for a long period. Similarly, much depends on the frame of reference to which it is applied. There are some who think that austerity must be practiced for a long time until both the State of Israel and the kibbutz movement are put on a sound economic basis. This wider frame of reference is associated with the realization that for a long time to come both the state and the kibbutz movement will remain economically dependent and as long as this is so, restraint is indicated. Austerity is regarded as an oppressive nuisance, but there is a willingness to submit to the dictates of necessity until the final goal has been fully achieved. As far as the extent of their commitment is concerned, those who follow the long-term situation pattern are not much different from the ideological ascetics. There is, however, a marked difference between them and the group that justifies restraint exclusively on a short-term basis. Here there is only a minimum commitment to asceticism, divorced from any of the broader national or kibbutz goals. Once the kibbutz has attained the initial stage of consolidation, all restraints can be cast off. "It is only necessary at the beginning, when the kibbutz first settles on the land." Some think that consumption should be curbed only in times of serious emergency. "Self-restraint is necessary only during an economic depression."

The situation pattern thus appears to be far from unequivocal. While those who think that circumstances warrant a long period of asceticism are closer to the conservative extreme,[4] those who think that austerity is warranted only for short periods at a time are not far removed from the outright reformers. It is only a short step from their attitude to a total rejection of ascetic values. In fact, some expressed themselves quite strongly on this point: "A simple life? Why on earth? One's aim should be a maximum of comfort." "You cannot go back to the period of the early pioneers; we deserve a decent standard of living—why suffer?"

The ascetic and the consumer patterns are equally represented in the sample, showing up in 32 and 33 percent of the responses respectively (N = 415). The life style and the situation patterns are also equally divided—both 17 percent—and together are about equal to either of the two extremes. Thus the conservative pattern accounts for about one third of the response, as do the two compromise patterns, with the reform-minded consumption-oriented group constituting the remaining

4. "Conservatism" and "reform" are used with reference to the internal development of the kibbutz movement. Those who uphold the ascetic ideal want to preserve the existing order of things, and those who advocated a consumer orientation are in favor of change. Obviously, in a wider social context the ascetics are the reformers who are out to protect the revolutionary gains while the reformers are the ones who want to revert to the accepted pattern. For further elaboration on conservatism and reform in revolutionary movements, see Pareto (98).

third. It should be noted that only 1 percent of the sample failed to respond or equivocated in its answer. On the contrary, the response was extremely lively and there were few evasions and prevarications. It seems we touched upon a major ideological issue whose importance is fully recognized and acknowledged.

Of the 17 percent classified as the situation pattern, 2 percent would justify long-term austerity; 8 percent short-term; and 7 percent did not specify. Thus a considerable percentage failed to qualify its response. Among those who clearly defined their attitude, those who thought that a short period was enough were in the majority.

ANALYSIS OF MOTIVATIONS

Let us examine the reasons and assumptions underlying the ideology that preaches austerity and simplicity, and as against this, those that make for its gradual attenuation and lead to the emergence of a con-sumer-oriented ideology. Here we distinguish between the ascetic and the consumer motivations. Three of the attitude patterns found have an essentially ascetic motivation: the strictly ascetic pattern which advo-cates both austerity and simplicity; the life style pattern which confines iself to simplicity; and the situation pattern which upholds the need for austerity. An antiascetic motivation is to be noted mainly in the con-sumption pattern which rejects both restraint and simplicity, but is partly apparent also in the situation pattern which rejects the simple life and in the life style pattern which rejects austerity and restraint.

The ascetic ideology. It will be recalled that the ascetic ideology is based on three distinct value systems: the national, the socialist, and the personal. Classification of the motivations given, by meaning and frame of reference, shows that there are five types of ascetic sanctions: ethical, socialist, national, rural, and kibbutz. The rural and kibbutz sanctions, which at one time were incorporated within the main ideologi-cal systems, have been partly detached and become semi-autonomous.

Apart from this classification by meaning and frame of reference, the motivations were subclassified according to whether they were value-oriented, goal-oriented, or formalistic in nature. In the first category the motivation is directly related to ideological values. Austerity and sim-plicity are regarded as independent and supreme values in their own right, or as part of a wider system of values from which they are directly derived. In contrast to this, the goal-oriented motivation is situational in that asceticism is not regarded as an independent value but as a means to an end that is not directly connected with it. Then there is the formalistic motivation where symbolic significance is attached to a particular style of life. Here a distinction should be made between those for whom it is merely an outward label and those who regard it as essential, for while sometimes an insistence on simplicity stems from ideological conviction, in other instances it denotes merely adherence to external appearances considered to be typical of kibbutz life. The significance of these distinctions and their relevance to our analysis will become clear in the course of our discussion.

The ethical motivation rests mainly on independent, personal values that are upheld for their own sake. In the kibbutzim included in our sample not much was left of the former contempt for creature comforts and minor pleasures. We found little of the old self-confidence, dedication, and sense of liberation that had inspired the original ascetic attitude. The fundamental doctrines received only vague and partial expression although their essence still came through in the response. As stated, concentration on ideal values is the basis of this attitude. Austerity and simplicity are regarded as the means for liberating man from his transient desires and directing his being toward the attainment of true and lasting values. In the words of our respondents: "Simplicity is elevating—it enables human beings to turn their attention to permanent values"; "if you give up the simple life you get dissipated by trivialities."

The socialist motivation derives the need for asceticism from the association of the kibbutz with socialism and the labor movement. The main stress lies on working class solidarity and a fitting style of life, rather than on ideological value considerations. "After all, we are workers, not middle class people. Luxury is the hallmark of the bourgeois." Very few respondents made reference to such basic values of socialism as equality and cooperation.

The national motivation is fundamentally goal-directed. Simplicity is considered necessary because it helps in the attainment of the national goal. A concentration of effort on national duties calls for as many resources as possible to be diverted to expanding production, manpower training, and the intake of immigrants, and requires that spending be curtailed. According to the original conservative ideology kibbutz members were supposed to serve as a model to the nation as a whole in their dedication to the task of national revival. Their willingness to stint themselves was regarded as a decisive test and indication of their elite pioneering status. Only a handful of respondents gave prominence to the national motive. And even they did not think that kibbutz members should make a greater sacrifice than the public at large.

The rural motivation is based on two assumptions. First, it is maintained that agriculture does not yield high and steady profits, so that farmers must live a frugal life. Second, the rural style of life is considered to be simple and natural. "A sparing life is the farmer's lot all over the world." The rural motive was only rarely combined with the national motive and associated with the need for greater efficiency and productivity. It was much more frequently related to farming as such.

The kibbutz motivation has the narrowest frame of reference of all, since the kibbutz represents only a very small social group. On the other hand it should be borne in mind that it embodies social, national, and personal goals so that when it is used as a frame of reference all these ideologies are tacitly acknowledged.

On the intrakibbutz level we were concerned mainly with the extent to which members are aware of the connection between asceticism and regulated consumption. As we have seen, asceticism forms an integral part of kibbutz ideology. The materialistic idealism that is characteristic of the kibbutz movement calls for the diversion of all possible resources to production and a far-reaching curtailment of consumer spending. The extreme fashion in which the ideals of equality and cooperation are upheld also tends to diminish the importance of consumption.

The proponents of asceticism were not unaware of its close connection with the ideological and ethical structure of the kibbutz. As we shall see, the kibbutz motivation was in fact the primary one. However, despite the frequency with which the kibbutz was cited in support of the ascetic ideal, there was usually only an oblique realization of the interaction of asceticism with the specific aspects of kibbutz life. Thus there were those who related simplicity to a concentration on goals. Others pointed out that the main hazard in consumer spending was its natural lack of limits—a greater danger to the kibbutz than to other forms of society. A rise in the standard of living was also regarded as a potential threat to interpersonal relationships. And finally, the craving for luxury was said to threaten the self-sufficiency of the kibbutz.

Asceticism was justified by reference to the kibbutz way of life in 44 percent of the responses (N = 319). Personal ethics accounts for 25 percent of the responses, rural style of life for 16 percent. Reference to wider frameworks, socialism and the nation, was rare (7 and 8 percent respectively).

Now let us classify these motives according to their emphasis on values, goal, or style of life (N = 319):

Values		41%
Independent	19	
Derivative	22	
Goal		26
Life Style		33
Expressive	29	
Designatory	4	
Total		100

Excluding the designatory life style emphasis, we may note an ascending continuum in emphasis from independent values to expressive style. The values-oriented category is dominant, followed by the life styles category, with the goal-directed category ranking last.

The implications of these findings will become fully apparent from a cross classification by both motive and emphasis, showing the emphasis pattern of each type of motivation (Table 35). Table 35 shows that

Table 35. Percentage distribution of responses reflecting the ascetic ideology, by motivation and by emphasis (N = 319)

	Personal ethics	Socialist	National	Rural	Kibbutz	Total
Values	20	3	—	7	11	41
Goal	—	—	8	—	18	26
Life style	5	4	—	9	15	33
Total	25	7	8	16	44	100

values emphasis is dominant only among those motivated by personal ethics; goal emphasis appears only in the national and kibbutz motivations; and life style considerations are dominant in the kibbutz and rural motivations. Insofar as asceticism is related to values, these are above all personal, with concern for the kibbutz being second in line and rural values coming third. Socialist values seem to count for little and the national effort is not referred to at all. The motivation of those who have the nation in mind is purely goal-oriented, while the scanty appeal to socialist ideals is made on largely formal grounds, resting mainly on the symbolic significance of a proletarian style of life. The kibbutz motivation is largely goal-directed and devoid of deeper ideological significance, asceticism being regarded as a means for attaining the ends of the kibbutz, serving its purposes or symbolizing its ideals.

Up to now we have dealt with motivations independently of the attitudes to which they refer. As will be remembered, three attitude patterns were established: ascetic, life style, and situation. Table 36

Table 36. Percentage distribution of responses reflecting the ascetic ideology, by pattern and by motivation

	N	Personal	Socialist	National	Rural	Kibbutz	Total
Ascetic pattern	193	26	8	7	15	44	100
Life style pattern	90	32	9	1	18	40	100
Situation pattern	36	6	—	18	12	64	100

relates these patterns to the various motivations. The ascetic and the life style patterns show great similarity in the type and relative importance of their underlying motivations. The differences are minor: the kibbutz motivation is somewhat less pronounced in the life style pattern, where slightly more weight is given to personal ethics. The situation pattern stands in strong contrast to these two, resting mainly on concern for the kibbutz, which is followed at some distance by national and rural considerations; personal motives are few and socialist ones nonexistent. Here the chief consideration is the economic development of the kibbutz, while the state of agriculture and of the national economy serves as subsidiary justification.

In the number of motives cited in support of each, the three patterns are found to be arranged in descending order, from the ascetic through the life style down to the situation pattern, in favor of which only few arguments were adduced. Although the ascetic pattern received less than twice as many votes as the life style pattern, it was supported by more than double the number of arguments. Again, although the situation and life style patterns received the same number of votes, there were 90 arguments adduced in favor of the one as against 36 in favor of the other. Altogether the conservatives were more expansive in their reasoning and had more ready arguments to offer. Decreased ideological awareness went hand in hand with the attenuation of the original values.

Let us now examine the three attitude patterns in relation to their motivational emphasis (Table 37). We shall first compare the ascetic

Table 37. Percentage distribution of responses reflecting the ascetic ideology, by attitude pattern and by motivational emphasis

	Values emphasis	Goal emphasis	Life style emphasis	Total	N
Ascetic pattern	48	26	26	100	133
Life style pattern	39	15	46	100	90
Situation pattern	18	82	—	100	36

and life style patterns. The figures clearly show the shift that has taken place here. In the ascetic pattern ideological value considerations predominate, and the end-gaining and life style emphases are given equal weight. In the life style pattern the formalistic emphasis is predominant, followed by ideological considerations, with goal-oriented motives lagging far behind. Our component analysis is confirmed in another respect: as demonstrated by Table 37, the life style pattern is not determined solely by formalistic considerations, but is supported by an almost equal number of value-linked arguments, not much less so than the ascetic pattern. The life style pattern is founded to about the same extent on ideology as on the search for a fitting style of life, and though the goal-directed element is subdued it has hardly disappeared. The situation pattern presents a completely different picture. Here, as is to be expected, goal-directed considerations reign supreme, with a small minority of ideological motivations directly related to economics: the role of physical labor, independence, savings, economic progress. Life style considerations are nonexistent.

The Consumer Ideology. The arguments adduced in favor of consumption do not add up to an independent ideology equivalent to the ascetic one. Here a strong antinormative trend makes itself felt, placing personal pleasures and creature comforts in juxtaposition and opposition to ideological principles and norms. The need to protest against the dogmatism of the opposite view reduces the ability of the consumer-oriented group to evolve valid alternative values of its own. Many respondents resorted to arbitrary, unmotivated statements; few were able to produce a well-reasoned line of argument. The same ideologies which have inspired the ascetic view are used in support of the claim for increased consumption, the only difference being one of interpretation. Nevertheless, occasional traces of ethical protest may be found, where consumption is regarded as a rightful and important means of expression. I shall present the motives underlying this view classified into the same categories as were used for the motives cited in support of the conservative view so as to bring out the connection between the two.

The personal motivation for the consumer ideology derives from the individual's right to the fulfillment of his personal needs. A hedonistic orientation was noticeable in many of the personal arguments. There was also evidence of protest against the constant postponement of immediate needs for the sake of some exalted aim. Another important element was the desire to live a normal life, like anybody else, without higher aspirations and pretensions and a sense of noblesse oblige.

Individual aspirations to entrenchment and the satisfaction of personal desires find collective support in socialist ideology. Socialism, which at one time was the source of inspiration of secular asceticism, has become one of the main cards of the consumer ideology. According to this conception, the function of socialism is to fight for better conditions for the working classes, and its object is to attain as high a standard of living as possible. Practically no symbolic significance is attached to the standard of living, preoccupation with which is regarded by the supporters of the ascetic ideology as a bourgeois stigma. A middle class style of life is not rejected. On the contrary, an adequate standard of living is regarded as a legitimate, unobjectionable working class demand.

Since the relationship between socialism and asceticism is far from unambiguous, the socialist argument of the antiascetics has some real merit. As consumer interests are, however, clearly opposed to the national interests, it is much more difficult to justify consumption spending on national grounds. Hence the arguments adduced under this heading tend to be evasive, apologetic, and less than frank. The presumed national benefits that might accrue from a higher standard of living in the kibbutz are the improved prospects for taking in new immigrants. The kibbutz, it is claimed, can do its share in immigrant absorption only if it can assure the newcomers the same conditions they can hope for elsewhere in the country. But more than on behalf of the new immigrants, the consumption-oriented group speaks in its own behalf. There is a pronounced desire to emulate the outside world and accept external standards, accompanied by the fear of otherwise becoming an object of contempt and derision.

In analyzing the ascetic ideology we noted the effects of a waning elite consciousness, in that kibbutz members were not inclined to accept more stringent commitments than obtained in other parts of the community, and some went so far as to make their willingness to knuckle under to a regime of austerity contingent upon a corresponding decrease in the national standard of living. In the consumer-oriented arguments a further step has been made in that direction: a definite claim is put forward for material rewards, in emulation of standards outside the kibbutz.

The rural way of life, which played such an important role in the ascetic ideology, appears here in a shrunken and modified version. It is referred to only in a negative way, in the context of the rivalry between town and country. It is contended that the country might go under if its living standards are not raised. As in the national motivation, the wish to resemble the outside world predominates. Thus, while the ascetically minded group dwelled on the special features of the countryside, which it wanted to preserve and emphasize, the consumption-oriented group is interested in removing all distinctions.

The kibbutz motivation for the consumption ideology rests mainly on considerations of keeping and increasing the membership of the kibbutz. Some refuted any connection whatsoever between asceticism and the kibbutz: "The kibbutz came into being to cater to the needs of its members, not to restrict and curtail them."

We found 126 arguments in favor of consumption priorities, most of them—91—adduced by supporters of the consumption pattern, and a minority—16 and 19 respectively—by supporters of the life style and situation patterns. In view of the paucity of such motivations in the latter two patterns, we refrained from a detailed motivational analysis by pattern, but confined ourselves to a general comparison with the ascetic ideology. Table 38 compares the distribution by type of motivation. In the consumption ideology there are far fewer kibbutz, somewhat fewer rural, and substantially more personal, socialist, and national justifications.

It was to be expected that more personal and fewer kibbutz arguments should be advanced for consumer priorities. It is also under-

Table 38. Percentage distribution of motivations for ascetic and consumer ideologies

	Personal	Socialist	National	Rural	Kibbutz	Total
Ascetic ideology (N = 329)	25	7	8	16	44	100
Consumer ideology (N = 126)	37	16	14	10	23	100

standable that less reference should be made to farming aspects. But the sizeable weight of socialist and national considerations requires some explanation. While the consumer ideology is based mainly on individual rights, it seeks additional—if only partial—justification on the collective plane. In socialism it finds a secure values legitimation. The aspiration to a higher standard of living is turned into a recognized ideal espoused by a large social movement. Further support is found on the national level, mainly in the claim that the kibbutz is entitled to its due share in a fair distribution of means and rewards. By thus making appeal to socialist and national principles, the rights the individual arrogates to himself, without apparent justification, are turned into a legitimate prerogative. Instead of giving up the good fight, the consumer ideology takes up the cudgels anew, this time against social and national discrimination. In the ascetic ideology, socialism and nationalism represented a source of commitment to values and goals. Now their significance is totally altered: they are looked upon as a source of emancipation, freeing the individual from his obligations to the community so that he can turn to his private affairs.

Let us now examine the value, goal, and life style emphases of the motivations underlying the two ideologies (Table 39). There are notable

Table 39. Percentage distribution of emphases in ascetic and consumer ideologies

	Value	Goal	Life style	Total
Ascetic ideology (N = 329)	41	26	33	100
Consumer ideology (N = 126)	80	16	4	100

differences. In the ascetic ideology the dominant value emphasis is fairly well balanced with the emphasis on life style which ranks second, and the goal emphasis which ranks third, so that the gap between them is small. In the consumer ideology, on the other hand, hardly any reference is made to the style of life; goal attainment is given minor emphasis; values reign supreme—but values of a totally different kind. It is hardly surprising that these values should not inspire an urge to goal-fulfillment or encourage the adoption of a distinctive style of life.

COMPARATIVE ANALYSIS

Comparison of different types of kibbutzim. The foregoing motivational analysis was mainly designed to elucidate the response patterns of the attitude survey, which will serve as the main index for the following comparisons.

The attitude toward asceticism is the principal key to understanding the ideological change that has taken place in the collective movement. For this purpose it is of particular importance to compare kibbutzim of different ideological types. In this classification three main categories were used: the pioneering pattern, based on dedication to the national cause and on total social reform; the economic pattern, based on aspirations to economic efficiency, progress, and consolidation; the consumer pattern, based on aspirations to a higher standard of living. While the pioneering pattern stands on its own at one end of the scale, the economic pattern may appear in combination with either of the other two. In the economic-pioneering pattern both economic development and the promotion of pioneering ideals are aimed at, and in the economic-consumer pattern, economic development is related to a rise in the general standard of living. The consumer pattern, again, has two variants: the consumer-economic pattern, where the desire for a higher standard of living is to some extent qualified by economic considerations, and the simple consumer pattern, at the opposite end of the scale. The sample kibbutzim were classified both by institutional and by ideological criteria. In the following analysis, however, we have confined ourselves to the three main categories.

By definition the ideological patterns are closely related to the attitudes toward asceticism. In the pioneering ideology, which is based on value commitment and collective identification, asceticism is a firmly accepted value. In the more instrumental economic pattern the main object is expansion and development of the kibbutz economy. In the consumer pattern, on the other hand, the demand for a higher standard of living is if not fully at least partly sanctioned. From this we arrive at the following hypotheses: (a) The ascetic pattern will be most prevalent in the pioneering kibbutzim, less so in the economic-oriented kibbutzim, and least of all in the consumption-oriented kibbutzim. (b) The consumer pattern will be most prevalent in the consumption-oriented kibbutzim, less so in the economic-oriented kibbutzim, and least of all in the pioneering kibbutzim.

It is not easy to predict the distribution of the compromise ascetic attitude patterns, but from our analysis the following hypotheses may be deduced: (c) The life style pattern, which essentially represents a neoconservative attitude in that it tries to adapt the original values to present-day realities, will be most prevalent in the economic-oriented kibbutzim and relatively rare in the pioneering and consumption-minded kibbutzim. In the pioneering kibbutzim it is not likely to be common since here the conservative ideology has just begun to be transformed and adapted. In the consumption-oriented kibbutzim, on the other hand, an outright consumer ideology will presumably be taking the upper hand. (d) The long-term situation pattern will be most prevalent in pioneering and economic-minded kibbutzim, and the short-term situation pattern most prevalent in consumer-oriented kibbutzim.

Let us now test these hypotheses in the light of our findings. In Table 40 it is immediately evident that the hypothesis relating to the pio-

Table 40. Attitude patterns in different types of kibbutzim

	Pioneering kibbutzim (N = 70)	Economic-oriented kibbutzim (N = 160)	Consumer-oriented kibbutzim (N = 185)
Ascetic	31	37	28
Life style	14	23	12
Situation			
Long-term	1	4	—
Short-term	10	5	9
Unspecified	5	6	7
Total	16	15	16
Consumer	39	25	40
Unknown	—	—	4
Total	100	100	100

neering kibbutzim must be totally rejected. A surprising similarity in attitudes was found between the pioneering and consumer-oriented kibbutzim. Practically the only difference was that in the consumer-oriented kibbutzim some members refused to take a position on the matter, which was not the case in either of the other two categories. At the same time our assumptions regarding the relationship between the economic- and the consumer-oriented kibbutzim were largely corroborated. An ascetic attitude was more commonly adopted in the economic-oriented kibbutzim than in the consumer-oriented ones. The hypothesis regarding the life style pattern was fully confirmed. This pattern was more prevalent in the economic- than in the consumer-oriented kibbutzim. The long-term situation pattern is more prevalent in the economic-oriented than in the pioneering kibbutzim and totally nonexistent in the consumer-minded kibbutzim. The short-term situation pattern is most frequently found in the pioneering kibbutzim, less so in the consumer-oriented kibbutzim, and least of all in the economic-oriented kibbutzim.

While our hypotheses regarding the economic- and consumer-oriented kibbutzim were largely confirmed, the pioneering kibbutzim were much more consumer-minded than we had expected. The distribution of attitude patterns found here requires some explanation.

We were able to gain some insight into this problem by taking into account the age of the kibbutzim. With the aid of the seniority variable, we were able to relate the internal development of each kibbutz to the development of the kibbutz movement and of Israeli society as a whole. We had initially assumed that the ideology of the pioneering kibbutzim, all of which are fairly young, was essentially the same as the original pioneering ideology, so that such a major element as asceticism could hardly be lacking. In making this assumption we were disregarding the value transformation that has taken place in the kibbutz movement and in the country at large since this ideology was first conceived. Members of the older kibbutzim received their indoctrination at a time when asceticism formed an integral part of kibbutz ideology and was also generally accepted throughout society. Members of the younger kibbutzim, however, received their indoctrination and founded their settlements at a time when ascetic values had lost much of their standing. On isolating the seniority variable we see that as one gets away from the earlier ascetic period, asceticism plays a steadily decreasing role in the values system of the kibbutz.

We took 1948—the year the State of Israel was established—as the dividing line for our definition of age, because it marks the official termination of the Jewish colonization period. Even before that date ascetic values had begun to erode, but the ultimate achievement of one of the goals of Zionism marked a decisive turning point. This date was used to distinguish both between old and new kibbutzim and between old and new members. The kibbutzim founded before 1948 include senior members as well as new members who joined after 1948, while the population of the post-1948 kibbutzim consists exclusively of new members. We have, therefore, three categories: new members of old kibbutzim, new members of new kibbutzim, old members of old kibbutzim. Knowing that the post-1948 kibbutzim are predominantly of the pioneering type, while the kibbutzim founded prior to 1948 fall into two groups—economic-oriented and consumer-oriented—we obtain the following five categories: new members in pioneering kibbutzim; old members in economic kibbutzim; new members in economic kibbutzim; old members in consumer kibbutzim; new members in consumer kibbutzim.

Table 41 compares the distribution of attitude patterns in these five

Table 41. Attitude patterns in kibbutzim classified by age and type (percent)

	Ascetic	Life style	Situation	Consumer	Total
New members in pioneering kibbutzim (N = 70)	31	14	16	39	100
Old members in economic kibbutzim (N = 131)	46	21	12	21	100
New members in economic kibbutzim (N = 29)	21	21	20	38	100
Old members in consumer kibbutzim (N = 73)	42	12	10	36	100
New members in consumer kibbutzim (N = 69)	12	10	29	49	100

categories. This table clearly shows that the attitude pattern is affected more by seniority than by the ideological type of the kibbutz. In the economic-oriented kibbutzim the ascetic pattern is much more common among the old than among the new members, while for the consumer pattern the opposite is the case. Again the situation pattern is more prevalent among the younger members. The ideological effect is apparent only in the life style pattern, where old and new members are equally represented. In the consumer-type kibbutzim the differences are still more pronounced, except in the life style pattern. The ascetic pattern is much more common among older members and the consumption pattern less so, while many more young members than old follow the situation pattern. In the economic kibbutzim the older members are slightly more ascetic and less consumer-minded than in the consumer kibbutzim, but the differences are slight. The most interesting finding is the considerable difference in the life style pattern: the older members in the economic kibbutzim are apparently more prone to translate the original ideology into terms of a special style of life than are older members in the consumer-oriented kibbutzim.

A comparison of the percentages in Table 41 for the new members in the three types of kibbutzim shows that here the ideological factor is paramount. In the pioneering kibbutzim, new members are more inclined to accept the ascetic pattern than in the other two types of kibbutzim. Those in the economic kibbutzim are more ascetically inclined than those in the consumer kibbutzim. The consumption pattern predominates in the consumer-oriented kibbutzim and is equally represented in the economic and pioneering kibbutzim. The neoconservative life style pattern is most prevalent in the economic-oriented kibbutzim, and least of all in the consumer-oriented kibbutzim, while the situation pattern is most highly represented in the consumer-oriented kibbutzim and least frequently in the pioneering kibbutzim.

Thus the attitudes of the younger kibbutz population vary considerably according to the type of kibbutz. Among the new members of the pioneering kibbutzim the ascetic and the consumer patterns are almost equally balanced, as are the life style and situation patterns. Among new members of economic kibbutzim, on the other hand, the consumer pattern has a clear majority over the other three patterns which are equally balanced. In the consumer-oriented kibbutzim the consumption pattern has the decisive majority, followed by the situation pattern, with the ascetic and life style patterns constituting an insignificant minority.

This brings us back to the hypotheses which were contradicted by our initial findings, before the ideological and seniority factors had been isolated from each other. On examination of the effect of the ideological factor within the same seniority group the hypotheses are strongly corroborated. The new members of the pioneering kibbutzim were found to be the most conservative and the new members of the consumer-oriented kibbutzim the most reform-minded, the new members of the economic-oriented kibbutzim occupying an intermediate position between the two. Our conjectures regarding life style compromise pattern were also confirmed. This pattern was found mainly among the new members of the economic kibbutzim. A clear continuum was also obtained in the situation pattern.

Comparative analysis has shown that the seniority variable is primary and the ideology variable is secondary. Yet ideology remains effective in determining the differences among new members of the pioneering, economic-oriented and consumer-oriented kibbutzim. Hence, once the seniority variable has been eliminated, our original assumptions regarding the effect of the ideological variable are found to apply.

It should be recalled that our starting point for the preceding analysis was the attitude distribution found in the pioneering kibbutzim. These are new members of new kibbutzim. To what extent the more detailed analysis has helped to clarify the picture will be evident from a comparison between them and the old and new members of the older kibbutzim (Table 42). The main element in this comparison is the

Table 42. Attitude patterns in kibbutzim classified by age and by age of members (percent)

	Ascetic	Life style	Situation	Consumer	Total
Old members of old kibbutzim (N = 204)	45	18	11	26	100
New members of new kibbutzim (N = 70)	31	14	16	39	100
New members of old kibbutzim (N = 98)	14	13	27	46	100

attitude of new members of new kibbutzim—those of the pioneering type. Had ideology been the only variable affecting their attitude, they should have been at the conservative end of the scale. On the other hand, had their attitude been affected solely by seniority, they should have been at the consumer end of the scale, since they had the least direct contact with the original ascetic ideology. However, in view of the interaction of both these variables, they take up a middle position between the old members and the new members of the older kibbutzim, and are neither the most ascetic nor the most consumption-minded. In fact, they lean somewhat more to the side of the older, more ascetic members.

Main office holders. The attitudes of members occupying a central position in the kibbutz by virtue of the offices they hold deserve special attention, since they are likely to wield a considerable influence over the course of affairs. From the way the kibbutz leadership is recruited and from a job analysis of the positions concerned, it could be assumed that the more collectively minded members are the most likely to attain leadership positions. In the selection process preference is naturally given to the more community-oriented members, for as a rule office holders are chosen on the basis of previous community work. Even where an office holder was originally not more community-minded than the rest, he is likely to become so in the course of his work. Given the social structure of the kibbutz, it is easier for the office holders to perform their tasks satisfactorily if all members have the common interest at heart and are willing to practice individual restraint. Their success largely depends on the members' willingness to minimize demands and put off immediate gratifications. Collectivism and a resultant trend toward asceticism therefore are a direct outcome of the structure of the existing channels of mobility and leadership positions. It may thus be postulated that the ascetic and neoconservative life style patterns will be more prevalent and the consumption pattern less prevalent among office holders than among other kibbutz members.

As Table 43 indicates, however, the hypothesis that office holders

Table 43. Attitude patterns among office holders and other kibbutz members (percent)

	Ascetic	Life style	Situa-tion	Con-sumption	Total
Office holders (N = 76)	30	16	19	35	100
Other members (N = 394)	32	16	16	36	100

are more conservative than the rest was not confirmed by our results. Their attitudes proved to be substantially the same.

We arrived at a satisfactory explanation of these unexpected results only when we realized that the attitudes of the office holders are split according to the type of office they hold. They may, thus, be divided into three groups: officers operating in the social sphere—kibbutz secretaries and coordinators of the membership committees; officers operating in the economic sphere—treasurers, coordinators of the principal economic operations; and officers operating in the service sphere—the caterer, the storekeepers, and the coordinators of the children's houses. A comparison of these is shown in Table 44. The three types of office

Table 44. Attitude patterns among office holders, by sphere of operation (percent)

	Ascetic	Life style	Situa-tion	Con-sumption	Total
Social (N = 19)	47	21	11	21	100
Economic (N = 32)	28	25	13	34	100
Service (N = 25)	20	—	32	48	100

holders are here distinctly ranked in a three-positional scale, with those operating in the social sphere being the most ascetic and those operating in the service sphere being the least; those in the economic sphere holding the middle rank.

These results are in full conformity with the theoretical analysis presented above. Office holders operating in the social sphere generally belong to the ideological leadership and are therefore more prone to uphold the original ascetic values. Those whose main preoccupation is with economic affairs tend to find more justification for a higher standard of living although they maintain the need for frugality. What they have in mind is a higher level of productive investment, with a resulting need for restricted consumer spending. The service functionaries represent the interests of the consumers: they are the main ones to suffer from the limited budget set aside for consumption expenditures and want to see these restrictions removed.

Further analysis demonstrated a variation in these findings according to ideological type of kibbutz. The social functionaries maintained an extremely ascetic attitude in all the kibbutzim included in the sample. In the economic sphere the results are ambiguous: the postulated tendency to greater asceticism was found only in the economic kibbutzim; in the pioneering kibbutzim the economic officers were only slightly more ascetic than the rest of the population, and in the consumer kibbutzim they shared the same attitude. Service functionaries were more conservative than the rest of the population only in the pioneering kibbutzim, while both in the economic and in the consumer kibbutzim they were much more reform-minded.

Comparison of men and women. In many areas of kibbutz life the women are the principal initiators of change. This stems largely from the way kibbutz functions are divided between the sexes. While the original reduction of family functions had little effect on the pater familias, it led to the profound change in maternal functions. Kibbutz women were taken away from family occupations and thrown into the communal labor market. What rankled was not only the disruption of the normal family pattern but the disappointing outcome of the change. Hopes that the division of labor would no longer be sex-linked proved false. Women continue to carry on the traditional feminine tasks, and rarely get beyond consumer service and child-rearing jobs. Economically such service jobs are valued less than the production jobs and since occupation is the main social-status criterion this is a major source of embarrassment and resentment.

It follows that there are two main reasons why kibbutz women are in the forefront of the consumption reform. One reason is job dissatisfaction. Most of the men, especially those engaged in production, derive satisfaction from their jobs. Not so the women, who are haunted by disappointment, confusion, and discontent to the extent that they cease to identify with the kibbutz and its ideals. Instead they begin to hanker after ease and comfort to replace the sense of creativity and fulfillment they have lost. The second reason has to do with the present division of labor. Most women work in the consumer services and have nothing to do with the production side. They naturally come to represent the interests of these services, especially since their daily work is rendered all the harder by the fact that so little manpower and so few resources are made available for this area. When the standard of living is raised they stand a better chance of pleasing the public in the performance of their duties.

All this leads us to the following hypotheses: that the consumer pattern will be more, and the ascetic pattern less, prevalent among women than among men; that the life style and the long-term situation patterns will be more prevalent among men, while the short-term situation pattern will be more prevalent among women.

Table 45. Attitude patterns among men and women (percent)

	Men (N = 220)	Women (N = 189)
Ascetic	35	30
Life Style	19	15
Situation		
Long-term	3	3
Short-term	8	6
Unspecified	6	7
Total	17	16
Consumption	29	39
Total	100	100

Our results are summarized in Table 45. Though the differences are small, they do support our main hypotheses. The ascetic and life style patterns are in fact more common among men while the consumption pattern is more prevalent among women. The attitude distribution in the situation pattern, however, is highly similar and our hypothesis is not confirmed: the short-term variant is slightly more prevalent among men.

Study of other areas of kibbutz life has shown that differences between men and women are most marked in the economic kibbutzim and less so in the pioneering and consumer kibbutzim. We found a kind of transition from conservative consensus in the pioneering communities to progressive consensus in the consumption-oriented communities. Yet in most of the sample kibbutzim the women were the initiators of change. We must therefore ask whether the same pattern will be repeated here and how the progressive attitude of the pioneering kibbutzim affects the male-female attitude distribution.

As Table 46 indicates, in the pioneering kibbutzim the men are slightly more conservative than the women, as may be seen particularly from the differences found in the life style and consumption patterns. In the economic-oriented kibbutzim too the men are more conservative than the women, and here the differences are quite pronounced throughout. In the consumer-oriented kibbutzim there is hardly any difference between men and women.

The general picture that emerges is the same as was found in respect to all the other aspects investigated, with one important exception. The similarity of attitudes in the pioneering kibbutzim is not due to their common conservatism but to their common innovative tendency. There is not much difference between men and women in the pioneering kib-

Table 46. Percentage distribution of attitude patterns, by sex and by type of kibbutz

	Ascetic	Life style	Situa- tion	Con- sumer	Un- known	Total
Pioneering kibbutzim						
Males (N = 51)	29	16	20	35	—	100
Females (N = 28)	29	7	17	47	—	100
Economic-oriented kibbutzim						
Males (N = 96)	44	25	13	18	—	100
Females (N = 95)	30	21	17	32	—	100
Consumer-oriented kibbutzim						
Males (N = 79)	27	14	18	39	2	100
Females (N = 60)	29	9	15	41	6	100

butzim and none in the consumer-oriented kibbutzim. Something close to consensus was found at both ends of the scale, based on a desire for reform. In the economic and pioneering kibbutzim the women appear to be the initiators of change.

The second generation. We now come to the last stage of our comparative analysis: attitudes among the second generation of kibbutz members. Here again two opposing influences are at work: the conservative influence of kibbutz education and the innovative influence of the institutionalization of the original kibbutz community. Generally we have found that the second generation occupies an intermediate position between the pioneering members of the new collective who are closest to the conservative extreme and the members of the first generation who are closest to the reform extreme. With regard to asceticism, however, the members of the new collectives seem to be more reform-minded than their elders. Moreover, the first generation members cannot be regarded as a single entity. While the older members turned out to be the most ascetic, the newer members are the most consumer-minded. Now the second generation members are the sons and daughters of the older members, who have undoubtedly tried to imbue them with their own spirit. Although these older members in many respects tend toward reform, they maintain a conservative attitude on the issue of austerity and simplicity and are inclined to reinforce the conservative influence of the educational institutions. This combined effect of parents and teachers is counteracted by the influences of the new kibbutz members and of the outside world. It seems, therefore, appropriate to ask whether the second generation maintains its usual intermediate position in spite of the fundamental changes that have taken place in kibbutz attitudes on the question of asceticism and whether their position is closer to that of the older or to that of the newer members.

Let us compare the second generation with the other kibbutz members separately for each attitude pattern (Table 47). The ascetic pattern

Table 47. Attitude patterns: second generation and other members (percent)

	Ascetic	Life style	Situa- tion	Con- sumer	Total	N
Old members of old kibbutzim	45	18	11	26	100	204
Second generation	19	32	22	27	100	137
New members of new kibbutzim	31	14	16	39	100	98
New members of old kibbutzim	14	13	27	46	100	70

appears weakest among the second generation and in this they are closest to the new members of the older kibbutzim and at variance both with the older members of the old kibbutzim and the new members of the new kibbutzim. In the consumer pattern a totally different picture is obtained. Here the second generation lines up with the older generation and, like it, is at variance with the new members both of the old and of the new kibbutzim. The life style pattern dominates among the second generation and is stronger there than in any other group. And a relatively high percentage appears in the situation pattern.

Thus the second generation, in turning away from the original asceticism, does not replace it with a consumer ideology but with one of the two compromise patterns which together account for over half of its responses. More members of the second generation chose these patterns than any of the others. Without going into the breakdown of the situation pattern we may note that here again the second generation takes a middle course, referring to the short-term variant slightly more often than the old members but less than the new members of either the old or the young kibbutzim.

Thus the younger generation does occupy an intermediate position, but in a different sense from what might have been expected. Its attachment to the original ascetic ideology is slight, with quite an extreme tendency toward reform, though not toward emphasis on consumption. Instead, the original asceticism has been transformed into an essential element of the kibbutz way of life or accepted as a mundane necessity. The parental tradition is not followed blindly, but also not abandoned outright, and priority is given to the neoconservative life style pattern.

CONCLUSIONS

Both our theoretical analysis and our empirical findings indicate that considerable importance should be attached to the compromise patterns which try to adapt ascetic ideals to new living conditions. The theoretical analysis leads to two complementary conclusions. From the relationship between asceticism and the structure and values of the kibbutz it must be inferred that austerity and restraint are an essential element of kibbutz ideology, and that the elevation of consumer desires to a higher priority is contrary to the fundamental tenets of this ideology and jeopardizes the rules of equality and cooperation. On analyzing the way in which the ascetic values are being transformed we found that the ascetic ideology contains many weak spots and is unlikely to survive intact. Its attenuation constitutes a process of internal change which is partly sanctioned by the original values, and is accelerated by the changes that take place in nonkibbutz society.

The compromise patterns stem from the need to curb consumer demands coupled with the difficulty of adhering to the former restrictions. The situation pattern derives the elements of thrift and self-restraint from the original ascetic ideology, while the life style pattern has taken over the original element of self-expression through one's way of life. In the ascetic pattern the values, goal, and formal emphases find equal expression. In the life style pattern the formal and values emphases alone are represented, while the goal emphasis has practically disappeared. The situation pattern is almost entirely goal-directed with only a few vestiges of the values element and none of the formal element. The compromises are thus the result of a process of selection, in which some of the original values are retained and others are rejected.

The compromise patterns strike a balance between investment in communal enterprises and concern for the people working in them. They mediate between the need to restrict consumer demands and the increasing desire for personal satisfaction and expression through consumption. The situation pattern puts greater emphasis on thrift and savings than the life style pattern, which leaves the way open for a gradual rise in the standard of living. The advocates of the situation pattern accept restraint and austerity as a necessary evil, an emergency measure, and do not look upon it as a positive element in their lives. The ethical basis of this pattern is weak, so that it is unlikely to be of help in shaping a way of life in which people will freely and willingly accept the need for restraint. It is, moreover, far from unambiguous, and sometimes its justification of thrift and frugality refers to a period long past.

The life style pattern, on the other hand, is firmly founded on lasting individual and collective values. Most of the elements of the original ascetic ideology have been retained, except that the stress has shifted. It is less collective, less values- and goal-directed than the ascetic pattern, but it is also less rigid. Stable yet flexible internal standards are provided. The commitment to simplicity does not negate the aspiration to a fair degree of prosperity, but forswears a constant escalation of the standard of living. The consumer institutions are thus protected against excessive and exorbitant pressures, but not relieved of the duty to give personal attention to their clients and to meet a diversity of needs with lenient circumspection. The ideal of moderation is likely to curb the tendency toward periodic peremptory demands for newfangled objects and amenities. Thus the life style pattern may help to eschew the dialectic consequences of the disparity between actual practice and official ideology, between what members want and what they get. Demands are complied with and curbed at one and the same time. Generosity is coupled with restraint, gratification with an educational ideal.

The style pattern is most prevalent in the economic kibbutzim and among the second generation. As in many other respects, here, too, members are looking for some modus vivendi that will help them bridge the gap between the original values and the living conditions that have developed. The compromise patterns have sprung up spontaneously, but they seem well worth promoting as the basis for a new official ideology.

A further conclusion to be drawn from our analysis and findings is that in all the kibbutzim examined the sense of mission that at one time imbued the kibbutz community is on the wane. Among those who espouse the new consumer values it has practically disappeared, but it is also much less strong among those who favor asceticism. We found considerable evidence of a close relationship between the attenuation of ascetic values and a dwindling sense of mission. In the absence of a religious sanction, the austerity and frugality required by the ascetic ideology are supported by the demanding yet rewarding pride that stems from a sense of mission. Once the confidence in that social mission is undermined, the inner motivation collapses. The limitations imposed by asceticism then become very difficult to accept. The sense of mission may contain a grain—or more—of a feeling of moral superiority, but it does help the kibbutz to abstain from blindly copying the outside world, and to develop and crystallize its own standards.

In concluding we should again point out that we have dealt here with asceticism only from the theoretical and ideological aspects. A concrete description of the nature and level of consumer aspirations is another subject. In this context several questions were designed to examine the limits and type of consumer demands. From the data available it appears that on concrete questions attitudes are less polarized than on matters of principle. The conservatives do not insist on any drastic lowering of the standard of living, while the reformers do not make any extreme consumer demands. Even among extremists who unhesitatingly rejected the need for asceticism, some barriers still remain: their concrete demands were generally quite modest. This is extremely pertinent to a proper understanding of the consumption tendency in the kibbutzim. It seems that kibbutz members are not perfectly secure in their consumption-oriented attitudes and themselves set limits to their demands and to the type and standard of consumption they would favor. The significance of this fact, which speaks volumes about the relationship between values and aspirations in kibbutz society, should not be lost in the search for new means of adapting collective principles and ideals to changing social conditions.

Appendix
References
Index

Appendix: The Sociological Study of the Kibbutz

The essays included in this volume are based on the findings of a research program carried out over a period of ten years, beginning in 1955, by the Research Seminar of the Sociology Department of The Hebrew University, under the direction of Professor Yonina Talmon and sponsored by The Hebrew University and the Federation of Kevutzot and Kibbutzim. The following description of the program and its methods was prepared by Mrs. Talmon upon completion of the first major phase of research.

TOPICS AND AIMS

The research program covered most spheres of kibbutz life. The main topics of research were: basic values, work, consumption, public life, the family, the second generation. We concluded that a comprehensive investigation of collective education would require the participation of psychologists and many years of follow-up studies, and hence could not be included in the program. In every one of the fields our investigation was designed so as to obtain the following.

1) A public opinion survey. The principal aim of this survey is to arrive at a statistically reliable statement of the attitude of kibbutz members toward the fundamental values and secondary norms which find their realization in various spheres of communal life. The findings will also include a comparative analysis of the attitudes of the main subgroups of this population. For this purpose a comparison will be made between the views of men and women, old-timers and new settlers, the young and the old, the first and second generations, those who are actively engaged in the various matters investigated and those who are not. A careful comparative study will be made of the views of members of different collective settlements. The survey will thus provide the kibbutz movement with a reliable and diversified picture of the attitude of its membership toward the accepted ideology and toward matters of topical interest.

2) A survey of principal insitutional patterns. This survey is to be based on a systematic follow-up on the operations and functioning of the various

kibbutz institutions, and a comparison of the institutional arrangements prevailing in the different collective settlements. We hope to locate the problems in each area, and to compare the various attempts made to solve them. The investigation is to be conducted with a view to pinpointing the internal drawbacks and advantages of each institutional set-up in order to assess the impact of any possible change in its functional pattern on other institutions.

3) A structural-functional analysis of kibbutz society. Our main task in this field consists of (a) examining overall coordination in the social structure of every kibbutz in the sample; and (b) comparing the main processes of change in different types of kibbutzim. The systematic pattern emanating from a comprehensive examination of social life in the kibbutz will help us in the sociological evaluation of our findings in the attitude survey and in the survey of institutional patterns, and will enable us to combine them into a meaningful whole. The structural analysis will outline the main variations in approach to certain focal problems taken by diverse sections of the kibbutz membership and by different types of kibbutzim. Only thus will it be possible to estimate the contribution made by each pattern to the stability of the individual kibbutz, and to examine the effect of each institutional pattern on kibbutz life in general.

METHODS

In the project we have used a combination of sociological and anthropological methods. Our first problem was the selection of a suitable sample. For our purpose two-stage sampling was required: first, a representative sample of kibbutzim was selected; second, from each of these kibbutzim a representative sample of members was drawn. The so-called stratified sampling method was used. We classified the seventy-one kibbutzim affiliated with the Federation of Kevutzot and Kibbutzim in 1955 (at the beginning of the project) into substrata by using various criteria of social stability. The kibbutzim representative of each substratum were drawn by lot, so that every kibbutz in each substratum had an equal chance of being selected.

It was our intention to obtain a range in the degree of social consolidation. As a by-product we also obtained a reasonably good range in kibbutz age and size. The sample comprised twelve kibbutzim, one sixth of the total number in the Federation. A preliminary test was carried out in two kibbutzim not included in the sample in order to assay the effectiveness, reliability, and validity of our instruments. When, following certain improvements introduced in the light of our experience, we found our methods to be satisfactory, we started investigating the kibbutz sample. For a more thorough and careful examination of our research hypotheses we used a subsample representing the main types of kibbutzim included in the full sample. By concentrating on a limited number of representative kibbutzim we were able to arrive at a precise formulation of our hypotheses before testing them on a larger scale.

The same stratified method was also used in the second sampling stage. After a thorough examination of its structure, the population of each kibbutz was classified into subgroups, by demographic and other criteria. The sample of members was drawn by lot from the total number included in each subgroup—with care being taken that the selection be random—at a proportional representation of one in four. The selection accordingly comprised 25 percent of the total population of the kibbutz sample, or 415 members.

In addition to the representative membership sample, some six to eight central kibbutz functions were also scrutinized. The roster of members subjected to intensive personal inquiry was augmented by the addition of a number of members who undoubtedly exerted substantial influence on kibbutz affairs, although they held no major public office at the time. These functionaries and key members were studied in addition to the sample proper because they were generally familiar with the problems of their kibbutz and affected the course of affairs to a considerable extent, and because we wanted to obtain a fuller picture of the more active members of the community. Thus, over and above the twenty-two members of this kind included in the general sample, we had an auxiliary sample of sixty-five functionaries and key members.

We used two other auxiliary samples which to some extent lay outside the scope of the kibbutz sample: the sample of members working in various capacities on behalf of the movement, and the second generation sample. The sample of movement functionaries comprised sixty-eight members. Of the second generation sample, where particular attention was paid to kibbutz children attending school beyond the elementary level, we have so far examined 124.

It should be stressed that the supplementary samples did not lead to any overrepresentation of these special categories, since only the general sample was used for the general statistical tabulations. These tabulations, which were designed to present a picture of public opinion prevailing in the kibbutzim, reflect only those functionaries and key members and those members of the second generation who happened to be included in the representative membership sample.

The structure we adopted—one major sample and a number of subsamples and auxiliary samples—was made necessary by the multitude of topics to be investigated. Our research was based mainly on the representative major sample, but we tried to achieve further depth and amplification by reducing or expanding the sample as circumstances required.

The main research instruments used were interviews and a factual information guide.

Interviews. Interviews formed the main basis of the attitude survey. The object of the interviews was to ascertain the subject's views on all matters comprised within the scope of this investigation, and to gather information on his personal behavior. It was decided from the start not to use a written questionnaire for this purpose. It was assumed that people doing hard work all day long, and not accustomed to writing down their thoughts and ideas, would not be prepared to submit their answers in writing or would do so carelessly and haphazardly. A written questionnaire might have been helpful in obtaining simple and relatively limited information, but it is doubtful whether it would have served our purpose, since we were looking for answers to complex questions requiring a considerable amount of concentrated thought and frankness. The mental effort required for serious, sincere reflection which would yet maintain the required degree of spontaneity seemed inconceivable unless through personal encounter, where responses and reactions are evoked in the course of conversation.

Having decided on a personal interview, we had to choose among three current methods. In the closed-questionnaire method, the subject is presented with questions to each of which a number of possible answers is assigned, and from these answers the subject is required to select the one closest to his views. This is the most convenient method for an accurate quantitative evaluation. At the opposite pole is the free-interview method, which allows the subject to talk at will, in his own way and at his own initiative, on matters which interest the investigator. This method is intended to limit to the absolute minimum any artificial direction given to the encounter. We adopted a middle course: an open interview based on "planned freedom." This combination gave us the advantages of both methods while minimizing their drawbacks. Our interview was guided by a questionnaire formulated in all particulars. The interviewer had to keep to the text of the questions and was not at liberty to vary their formulation and sequence. We insisted on uniformity in the text of the questions in order to avoid variations in replies due to differences in formulation. In this respect we accepted the rules of the closed-questionnaire method. In a number of instances where an unequivocal choice among alternatives could be offered, we did not hesitate to do so. Generally, however, we departed from the closed-questionnaire method in that we did not formulate replies in advance. We presented the questions without offering any ready-made replies, and gave the subject a free hand to answer as he saw fit. We encouraged him to enlarge upon the subject and to say all he had to say. He was given an opportunity to express himself fully and freely.

We paid special attention to the clarity and accuracy of the formulation of our questions and tried to give complete coverage to the problems investigated, in order to make sure that full information would be obtained. We tried to avoid anything too technical or conceptually difficult. We took care that the questionnaire spoke the same language as the members of the kibbutz, and addressed them in a conversational tone. In determining the sequence of the questions, we saw to it that all those relating directly to one and the same matter should appear together. Without disguising the investigative nature of the inquiry, we tried to ensure the associative and continuous development and flow of a conversation easily passing from one matter to the next.

A further principle that guided us in the formulation of the questionnaire was to refrain from invading the sphere of emotional problems. The interviews and the analytical procedures used were designed mainly to find out the subject's personal views on matters of ideology and practical problems of organization. We provided opportunity for the subject to vent his feelings and ideas, but we did not press him to talk about his personal problems if he did not wish to do so. On examination we found that intimate questions, rather than helping to reveal hidden secrets, prevented the growth of mutual confidence between interviewer and subject. We found that on certain matters kibbutz members found it easier to express their attitude during or following a general discussion. To avoid defensive withdrawals we asked many indirect questions and tried to learn about the subject's attitude from the manner in which he projected his personal views in discussions of principle and statements of fact. Most questions were formulated in a neutral and matter-of-fact way.

Another set of fundamental principles involved in constructing the questionnaire relates to the reliability of the replies. Here one of the primary rules was to avoid leading questions. Generally, any question was avoided which from the start indicated a bias. A second rule called for a partial overlapping of the questions for purposes of a reliability check. Repetition rendered the questionnaire bulky and cumbersome and tended to tire the subjects, but it was essential in checking for consistency. A third rule required a check to be carried out at different levels of abstraction. Sometimes unequivocal loyalty to the fundamental values of the movement and to accepted dogmas was found to be accompanied by an inclination toward change in intermediate norms. On the other hand we sometimes found that strict adherence to procedures and measures designed to translate ideals into everyday practice might be accompanied by a large measure of readiness for change in the realm of ideals and values. We had to be as wary of the tendency of kibbutz members to pay lip service to the declared ideology, as of declarations of loss of faith and disenchantment. Both were often only partly backed up by secondary resolutions. It is impossible to apprehend changing trends in value judgments without fully examining every such judgment in all its applications and at all levels of realization.

Regarding the recording method, which to a considerable extent determines reliability, we decided that notes should be taken during the interview. We found that this procedure had definite advantages as long as every possible care was taken that continual writing did not interfere with the conversation and the interviewer remained an active partner in the discussion. Immediate recording of replies makes for a more accurate report. And the procedure underlines the seriousness of the interview and confers on the subject a sense of importance. Many of the subjects themselves insisted on full and careful notes being taken. There were, of course, a few who were alarmed by the fact that their words were being recorded, or were embarrassed or hampered in their expression. In these instances the interviewer took care to write very little during the conversation but to record it immediately after the interview was over.

Our main target in constructing the questionnaire and in formulating the questions was to provide the investigating team with a sensitive instrument of research which would at the same time be both controlled and reliable. For the major representative sample we drew up a comprehensive questionnaire which was also used for the auxiliary sample of functionaries and key members of the individual kibbutzim. For the subsamples of members of the second generation and of members active in the movement we formulated two special questionnaires. In these we kept to the basic principles which guided us in the construction of the principal questionnaire. We departed from this practice only in the case of youngsters attending school beyond the elementary level, for whom we used a written semi-closed questionnaire.

The interviews took from four to thirty hours, averaging about twelve hours each.

Factual information guide. The interviews were designed to inquire into subjective attitudes and to furnish a description of personal behavior. Objective information on regular practice and everyday routine in the kibbutzim was obtained by means of a series of investigations set forth for the field workers in the factual information guide. These included the following.

1) A short factual questionnaire addressed to all members of the kibbutzim included in the sample; this was to be answered in writing. The questionnaire asked for full particulars of age, family status, number and age of children, country of origin, level of education, length of stay in the kibbutz and in Israel, and the amount of training received from the movement. In addition we requested full particulars on work and public duties undertaken during the preceding eight years. This was an important source of information and a primary and essential basis for all subsequent computations. Some of the kibbutzim had a well kept card index or other records which helped us to compile neat lists of the information we needed without having recourse to the questionnaire.

2) Information questionnaires on the daily routine and on members' behavior in all areas investigated. These questionnaires were addressed to the official liaison officer assigned by the kibbutz to the research team and to various kibbutz functionaries, each in his own sphere of activity.

3) Special guide for talks with members interested in the project and prepared to devote their spare time, whenever possible, to assist in the work. Everywhere we found a considerable number of members who followed our work with great interest, got in touch with the field workers, and tried to help them as much as they could. These volunteer participants, in trying to sum up the experience of their own lives, supplied us with information which was the result of many years of observation. There is no doubt that our infor-

mal contacts with these kibbutz members, and the conversations we had with them concerning the problems investigated, were essential in gaining necessary insight into kibbutz life.

4) A guide for direct observation, either passively from the outside, or through active participation in one of the spheres investigated. The main advantage of personal observation is that it affords an opportunity to study the subjects' spontaneous behavior. The investigator can with his own eyes observe the various interrelations and functions, and in the light of his personal experience over a number of months evaluate what his other research instruments have told him.

The importance of immediate observation is further enhanced by the fact that in the kibbutz strict limits are set to what the individual may regard as his own personal sphere, while most aspects of human life are publicly regulated and great prominence is given to open social meetings. Hence the extent and depth of this type of observation is much greater in the kibbutz than in a noncommunal society. When the province of private life is fenced off and completely barred from the eyes of the outsider, and social life is split up into a segmentary, intersecting pattern, there is not much room for direct observation. In most sociological studies, observation serves only for preliminary exploration, prior to the compilation of the questionnaire. However, in studying the communal society of the kibbutz, observation must be accorded a major place and must be systematically regulated.

5) Last in the series of research instruments was the systematic use of available written material. First in importance were the minutes of meetings of the various committees and the general assembly. The standard of reporting was not uniform, but in certain kibbutzim we found a faithful record of the principal proceedings of several of the major committees over many years. These records are a precious mine of information. Most problems arising in the kibbutz are defined as public affairs and discussed by one body or another. The proper utilization of this material helps in forming an independent view of the main changes that have taken place in the life of the kibbutz community.

Much was learned from a selective reading of the internal bulletins and publications of the collective movement. A proliferation of bulletins, pamphlets, journals, and papers of all kinds serves to ensure close contact between the members and institutions of the kibbutz and the movement. The internal press is the usual medium for the transmission of current information and creates a common platform for identification with the kibbutz and its values. It also serves as an important means for obtaining the active collaboration of members within the individual kibbutzim and within the movement at large, and affords to the relatively large number of those who have the ability an opportunity to express themselves in writing.

The kibbutz publications were our primary source of information concerning the declared ideology of the movement. Although it may also be used as a source of prevalent views and opinions, caution is indicated in this respect because the tendency to affirm loyalty to the movement and act as spokesman for its authority is stronger than the tendency to provide free expression for the uncensored views of all sectors of the public. Account also has to be taken of the considerable variation in the writing ability of different circles within the movement.

We attached considerable significance to the analysis of these publications. We did not accept the common trend of most anthropological and much sociological research of relying on field work concerned with the present state of affairs, to the exclusion or neglect of any analysis of written sources.

In summing up this description of our research instruments we would again point out that our overall project was designed to accomplish two equally important objectives: an attitude survey and a social behavior study. The interviews were chiefly designed to assess the kibbutz members' subjective approach at the time of the survey, while the fact-finding guide was intended to elicit and establish objective data concerning actual behavior in the past and in the present. In the attitude survey, stress was laid on opinions held and positions adopted; in the factual guide, on the collection on information about behavior and changes in principal behavior patterns. The functional division between the various instruments was not clear-cut; It was only natural that there should be some overlapping.

In designing and elaborating our research method we tried as far as possible to employ those instruments which were best suited to the special structure of kibbutz society. These we then developed and adapted to their special purpose. Among the methods thus evolved I would stress the importance of the participation of volunteers, the combination of interview and direct observation, and the systematic utilization of written material.

PATTERNS OF COLLABORATION

Our project team consisted mainly of trained research workers of the Department of Sociology, including undergraduates and graduates who were also members of kibbutzim. We valued the participation of kibbutz members closely acquainted with kibbutz life, and therefore tried, though with only limited success, to obtain the permanent participation of several sociologists who are also kibbutz members.

We attach much importance to the continuous contact between the representatives of the Federation's research committee and the research team, which helped us to keep in touch with the actuality of the movement and afforded us the advantage of a current critical response to our work.

Not all the kibbutzim in the sample showed the same degree of response, although in most of them we enjoyed full collaboration. Most of the kibbutzim gave their immediate consent to the project. Some were initially reluctant but eventually agreed. Two kibbutzim—one among the highest in the degree of internal social consolidation, and the other ranking among the lowest—were hostile to the project, and their attitude did not soften through-out the investigation. This was a considerable impediment to our work, but even in these two kibbutzim we were able to accomplish most of our pro-gram. About ten persons in the total membership sample—mostly in these two kibbutzim—refused to take part in the major interview. This figure is much lower than is common for studies of this kind.

While the number of absolute refusals to take part in the project was small, there was variation in the degree of response to the different questions. In most areas the rate of response ranged around the accepted norm in similar studies. Special difficulties arose in questions impinging upon the personal, or calling for complicated value judgments. Some kibbutz members were un-able to reply when powers of abstraction or nice distinctions were required; when asked to account for their decisions their answers were generally poor. It transpired that certain spheres of life in the kibbutz were practically un-known to various sections of the membership. Some of the female members, for instance, had no idea of what was going on in the field of production, and in public affairs. Peripheral subgroups were not integrated in public life and did not relate clearly to matters of principle and values.

Reluctance to participate in the project derived from several distinct sources. Here and there a strong undertone of disaffection with the institutions of the movement was noted, accompanied by an unwillingness to allow the movement a glimpse into the internal affairs of the kibbutz. In the main, however, reluctance was due to the suspicions harbored toward us as out-siders. A team consisting mostly of nonkibbutz members is suspect from the start as being foreign to the goals of the movement. Many doubted whether we, as outsiders, would be able during the limited time at our disposal to obtain a proper understanding of what was going on. Consciously or uncon-sciously, to a lesser or greater extent, there also came into play a disapproval of anyone who is not a member—a regular accompaniment of the sense of mission characteristic of all movements bent on the realization of a certain set of ideals and principles.

This reluctance to discuss basic values with an outsider was counterbal-anced by the great readiness and frankness shown by people who were familiar with the problems of the movement and who followed its develop-ment with interest and deep sympathy without actually being affiliated with it. Essentially the kibbutz movement is not an isolationist movement retiring from public life or objecting to all contact with nonmembers. We profited much from the great readiness for self-examination and the eagerness shown by many in their desire to help us obtain a true and faithful description of kibbutz society.

The ambivalent attitude toward the research was reflected in the actual carrying out of the project as well. Team members who were also members of kibbutzim were given preference in all that related to the collection of factual data. In carrying out the interviews, however, those who were not kibbutz members enjoyed a definite and striking advantage. With kibbutz members the interviews were frequently flat and stereotyped, for the matters inquired into had been discussed innumerable times among friends and in various meetings, and were therefore thought to require no explanation. With investigators who were not kibbutz members, such matters were not taken for granted. Contact with an outsider impelled the respondents toward renewed and sharper observation. They tried to explain the situation, to expand and enlarge upon it, and to define things as accurately as possible. Accordingly, the material obtained was richer in content, and the formulations were fresher and less worn.

The type of interviewer selected also had a direct effect on the amount of frankness shown by the subjects. We noted that a considerable portion of the members found it easier to talk freely when the interviewer came from a different milieu. When the interviewer was a member of the movement it was sometimes difficult to isolate and disentangle the interview from the entire skein of ties entwining them as members of a movement. On the other hand the neutral interviewer, although interested in and sympathetic to the problems of the kibbutz, is not given to judging and has no preconceived opinion, so that the encounter is purely investigational. This fusion of aloofness and affinity, of sympathy and objectivity, was a fructifying element.

References

1. Auerbach, H. A. "Social Stratification in Israel's Collectives," *Rural Sociology*, 18 (no. 1, 1953), 25–34.
2. Bachi, R. Marriage and Fertility in Various Sections of the Jewish Population (in Hebrew). The Jewish Agency Department of Statistics, 1944.
3. ———— "La Population juive de l'état d'Israël," *Population Studies*, 7 (no. 3, 1952), 405–452.
4. ———— "The Outlines of the Demography of Israel," *Israel Economist Annual*, 1952.
5. Bar Yoseph, Rivka. "The Patterns of Early Socialization in the Collective Settlements in Israel," *Human Relations*, 12 (no. 4, 1959), 345–360
6. Barnes, John A. "Land Rights and Kinship in Two Bremnes Hamlets," *Journal of the Royal Anthropological Institute*, 87 (1957), 31–57.
7. ———— "Marriage and Residential Continuity," *American Anthropologist*, 42 (no. 5, 1960), 850–866.
8. Beigel, Hugo G. "Romantic Love," *American Sociological Review*, 16 (1951), 326–334.
9. Ben-David, Y. Membership in Youth Movements and Social Status (in Hebrew), *Megamoth*, 5 (no. 3, 1954), 228–247.
10. Berger, B. J. "Comment on Slater's Paper," *Amercan Journal of Sociology*, 67 (1961), 308–311.
11. Bestor, A. E. *Backwood Utopias; The Sectarian and Owenite Phases of Communitarian Socialism in America*. Philadelphia, University of Pennsylvania Press, 1959.
12. Bettelheim, Bruno. "The Problem of Generations," in *Youth: Change and Challenge*, ed. Erik H. Erikson, pp. 64–93. New York, Basic Books, 1963.
13. Bion, W. R. "Experiences in Groups: III," *Human Relations*, 2 (no. 1, 1949), 13–22.
14. Bjerke, K. "The Birth Rate in Scandinavia during the 1940's" *Transactions* of the World Population Conference, Rome, 1954, vol. I, pp. 563–575.
15. Blood, Robert C. "A Retest of Waller's Rating Complex," *Marriage and Family Living*, 17 (1955), 41–47.

16. Bott, E. *Families and Social Networks.* London, Tavistock Publications, 1957.
17. Bredemeier, Harry C. "The Methodology of Functionalism," *American Sociological Review,* 20 (1955), 173–180.
18. Bryant, A. T. *Olden Times in Zululand and Natal.* London, Longmans, Green, 1929.
19. Caplan, Gerald. *Social Observation in the Emotional Life of Children in the Communal Settlements in Israel.* New York, Josiah Macy Jr. Foundation, 1954.
20. Chin, A. L. "Women in Communist China," in *Women in the Modern World,* ed. R. Patai, pp. 410–433. New York, The Free Press, 1967.
21. Coser, L. A. "Some Aspects of Soviet Family Policy," *American Journal of Sociology,* 56 (1951), 424–437.
22. Cumming, E., and D. M. Schneider. "Sibling Solidarity," *American Anthropologist,* 63 (1961), 498–507.
23. Davis, Kingsley. "Intermarriage in Caste Societies," *American Anthropologist,* 43 (no. 3, 1941), 376–395.
24. Diamond, S. "Kibbutz and Shtetl," *Social Problems,* 5 (no. 2, 1957), 71–99
25. Diels, A. E. "Ideas about Size of Family" (I and II), *Milbank Memorial Fund Quarterly,* 29 (1951), 163–170; 31 (1953), 124–130.
26. Donahue, W., ed. *Earning Opportunities for Older Workers.* Ann Arbor, University of Michigan Press, 1955.
27. Dore, Ronald P. "Function and Cause," *American Sociological Review,* 26 (1961), 843–853.
28. Drake, J. T. *The Aged in American Society.* New York, Roland Press, 1958.
29. Dunham, Vera S. "Sex—From Free Love to Puritanism," *Soviet Society,* eds. A. Inkeles and K. Geiger, pp. 540–546. Boston, Houghton Mifflin, 1961.
30. Eisenstadt, S. N. On the Sociological Image of Youth in Modern Society (in Hebrew), *Megamoth,* 2 (no. 1, 1950), 52–72.
31. ——— "Youth Culture and Social Structure in Israel," *British Journal of Sociology,* 2 (no. 2, 1951), 105–114.
32. ——— *Absorption of Immigrants.* London, Routledge and Kegan Paul, 1954.
33. ——— *From Generation to Generation.* Glencoe, Illinois, The Free Press, 1956.
34. Emmet, Dorothy M. *Function, Purpose and Powers.* London, Macmillan, 1958.
35. Erikson, Erik H. "The Problem of Ego Identity," in *Identity and the Life Cycle,* ed. E .H. Erikson, vol. 1, no. 1. New York, International Universities Press, 1959.
36. ——— "Youth, Fidelity and Diversity," in *Youth: Change and Challenge,* ed. E. H. Erikson. New York, Basic Books, 1963.

37. Etzioni, A. "Solidaric Work Groups in the Kibbutz," *Human Organization*, 16 (no. 3, 1957), 2–7.
38. Evans-Prichard, E. E. "Nuer Rules of Exogamy and Incest," in *Social Structure*, ed. Meyer Fortes. Oxford, Clarendon Press, 1949.
39. ——— *Kinship and Marriage among the Nuer*. Oxford, Clarendon Press, 1951.
40. Faigin, Helen. "Social Behavior of Young Children in the Kibbutz," *Journal of Abnormal Social Psychology*, 56 (no. 1, 1958), 117–129.
41. Fallding, Harold. "Functional Analysis in Sociology," *American Sociological Review*, 28 (1963), 5–13.
42. Firey, W. I. *Land Use in Central Boston*. Cambridge, Harvard University Press, 1947.
43. Firth, R., ed. *Two Studies of Kinship in London*. London School of Economics, Monographs on Social Anthropology, no. 15. London, Athlone Press, 1956.
44. Fortes, Meyer. *The Web of Kinship among the Tallensi*. London, Oxford University Press, 1949.
45. Fox, J. R. "Sibling Incest," *British Journal of Sociology*, 13 (1962), 128–150.
46. Freedman, R., D. Goldberg, and H. Sharp. "Ideas about Family Size in the Detroit Metropolitan Area," *Milbank Memorial Fund Quarterly*, 33 (1955), 187–197.
47. Friedmann, E. A., and R. J. Havighurst. *The Meaning of Work and Retirement*. Chicago, University of Chicago Press, 1954.
48. Friedmann, G. *Où va le travail humain*, rev. ed. Paris, Gallimard, 1953.
49. Gabriel, K. R. "The Fertility of the Jews in Palestine," *Population Studies*, 6 (no. 3, 1953), 273–305.
50. Geiger, K. "Deprivation and Solidarity in the Soviet Urban Family," *American Sociological Review*, 20 (1955), 57–68.
51. ——— "Changing Political Attitudes in a Totalitarian Society," *World Politics*, 8 (1956), 187–206.
52. Gil, B. Z. *Settlement of New Immigrants in Israel*. Jerusalem, Institute for Zionist Studies, 1954.
53. Gille, H. "Recent Fertility Trends in Countries with Low Fertility," *Transactions* of the World Population Conference, Rome, 1954, vol. I, pp. 615–634.
54. Glick, Paul C. "The Family Cycle," *American Sociological Review*, 12 (1947), 164–174.
55. Gluckman, Max. "The Kingdom of the Zulu," in *African Political Systems*, eds. M. Fortes and E. E. Evans-Prichard. New York, Oxford University Press, 1950.
56. ——— *Custom and Conflict in Africa*. Oxford, Basil Blackwell, 1955.
57. Golan, Shmuel. *Collective Education* (in Hebrew). Merhavia, Sifriat Poalim, 1961.

58. Goode, William J. *World Revolution and Family Patterns.* Glencoe, Illinois, The Free Press, 1951.

59. —— "The Theoretical Importance of Love," *American Sociological Review,* 24 (1959), 38–47.

60. Goody, Jack. "A Comparative Approach to Incest and Adultery," *British Journal of Sociology,* 7 (1956), 286–305.

61. Gough, Kathleen E. "Incest Prohibition and Rules of Exogamy," *International Archives of Ethnography,* 46 (1952), 81–105.

62. —— "The Nayars and the Definition of Marriage," *Journal of the Royal Anthropological Institute,* 89 (Part 1, 1959), 23–34.

63. Groenman, S. "Women's Opinions about Size of Family in the Netherlands," *Eugenics Quarterly,* 2 (1955), 224–228.

64. Havighurst, R. J. "Flexibility and the Social Roles of the Retired," *American Journal of Sociology,* 59 (1954), 309–311.

65. —— "The Leisure Activities of the Middle Class," *American Journal of Sociology,* 53 (1957), 152–162.

66. Hempel, Carl G. "The Logic of Functional Analysis," in *Symposium on Sociological Theory,* ed. Llewellyn Cross, pp. 271–307. Evanston, Illinois, Row, Peterson, 1959.

67. Herman, Robert D. "The Going Steady Complex," *Marriage and Family Living,* 17 (1955), 36–40.

68. Hill, Reuben, and Evelyn M. Duvall. *Family Development.* Chicago, J. B. Lippincott, 1957.

69. Hinds, W. A. *American Communal and Cooperative Colonies.* Oneida, New York, The Office of the American Socialist, 1878.

70. Holloway, H. *Heavens on Earth! Utopian Communities in America, 1680–1880.* London, Turnstile Press, 1951.

71. Homans, George C., and David M. Schneider. *Marriage, Authority and Final Causes.* Glencoe, Illinois, The Free Press, 1955.

72. Irvine, Elizabeth E. "Observations on the Aims and Methods of Child-Rearing in Communal Settlements in Israel," *Human Relations,* 5 (no. 3, 1952), 247–275.

73. Jolles, H. M. "Der Geburtenrückgang in Wien," unpubl. diss., Amsterdam, Vrije Universiteit, 1957.

74. Katz, A. M., and Reuben Hill. "Residential Propinquity and Marital Selection," *Marriage and Family Living,* 20 (1958), 27–35.

75. Kerckhoff, Alan, and Keith E. Davies. "Value Consensus and Need Complementarity in Mate Selection," *American Sociological Review,* 27 (1962), 295–304.

76. Kluckhohn, F. R. "Dominant and Variant Value Orientations," in *Personality,* eds. C. Kluckhohn and H. A. Murray. New York, Alfred A. Knopf, 1953.

77. Knani, D. *Batei Midot* (in Hebrew). Tel-Aviv, Sifriat Poalim, 1960.

78. Kreiselman Slater, Mariam. "Ecological Factors in the Origin of Incest," *American Anthropologist,* 61 (no. 6, 1959), 1042–1059.

79. Landshut, S. The Kvutsah (in Hebrew). Jerusalem, The Zionist Library, vol. 4, 1944.

80. Lea, H. C. *An Historical Sketch of Sacerdotal Celibacy in the Christian Church.* Philadelphia, Lippincott, 1867.

81. Leach, E. R. "Polyandry, Inheritance and the Definition of Marriage," *Man,* 55 (no. 199, 1955), 182–185.

82. Lévi-Strauss, Claude. *Les Structures elémentaires de la parenté.* Paris, Presses Universitaires de France, 1949.

83. Levine, Robert A. "Gusii Sex Offences: A Study of Social Control," *American Anthropologist,* 61 (no. 6, 1959), 965–990.

84. Levinson, Maria H., and Daniel J. Levinson. "Jews Who Intermarry," *Yivo Annual,* 12 (1958–1959), 103–129.

85. Litwak, E. "Geographic Mobility and Family Cohesion," *American Sociological Review,* 25 (1960), 385–394.

86. ——— "Extended Kin Relations in an Industrial Democratic Society," in *Social Structure and the Family Generational Relations,* eds. Ethel Shanas and Gordon F. Streib, pp. 290–323. Prentice-Hall, 1965.

87. Lorimer, F. *The Population of the Soviet Union.* Geneva, League of Nations, 1946.

88. ——— *Culture and Fertility.* Paris, UNESCO, 1954.

89. Mannheim, Karl. *Essays on the Sociology of Knowledge.* New York, Oxford University Press, 1959.

90. Mayer, John E. *Jewish-Gentile Courtships.* Glencoe, Illinois, The Free Press, 1961.

91. Merton, Robert K. "Intermarriage and Social Structure," *Psychiatry,* 4 (1941), 361–374.

92. Michelon, L. C. "The New Leisure Class," *American Journal of Sociology,* 59 (1954), 371–387.

93. Mishler, E. G., and C. F. Westoff. "A Proposal for Research on Socio-Psychological Factors Affecting Fertility," *Current Research in Human Fertility,* 1956, pp. 121–150.

94. Moore, B., Jr. *Political Power and Social Theory.* Cambridge, Harvard University Press, 1958.

95. Muhsam, H. V., and C. V. Kiser. "The Number of Children Desired at the Time of Marriage," *Milbank Memorial Fund Quarterly,* 34 (1956), 287–312.

96. Murdock, George P. *Social Structure.* New York, Macmillan, 1949.

97. Myrdal, A. *Nation and Family.* New York, Grove Press; London, Routledge and Kegan Paul, 1945.

98. Pareto, V. *The Mind and Society.* London, J. Cape, 1935.

99. Parsons, Talcott. *Social System.* Glencoe, Illinois, The Free Press, 1951.

100. ——— *Working Papers in the Theory of Action.* Glencoe, Illinois, The Free Press, 1953.

101. ——— "A Revised Analytical Approach to the Theory of Social Stratifi-

cation," in *Class Status and Power*, eds. S. M. Lipset and R. Bendix. Glencoe, Illinois, The Free Press, 1953.

102. ——— "The Incest Taboo in Relation to Social Structure and Socialization of the Child," *British Journal of Sociology*, 5 (1954), 101–117.

103. ——— "The Kinship System of the Contemporary United States," in *Essays in Sociological Theory*, ed. T. Parsons, pp. 177–196. Glencoe, Illinois, The Free Press, 1959.

104. ——— and F. Bales. *Family Socialization and the Interaction Process.* Glencoe, Illinois, The Free Press, 1955.

105. Philips, B. S. "A Role Theory Approach to Adjustment in Old Age," *American Sociological Review*, 22 (1957), 212–217.

106. Rabin, A. I. "Infants and Children under Conditions of Intermittent Mothering," *American Journal of Orthopsychiatry*, 28 (no. 3, 1958), 577–586.

107. ——— "Attitudes of Kibbutz Children to Parents and Family," *American Journal of Orthopsychiatry*, 29 (no. 3, 1959), 172–179.

108. Radcliffe-Brown, A. R. "Introduction," in *African Systems of Kinship and Marriage*, eds. A. R. Radcliffe-Brown and W. C. Daryll Ford. London, Oxford University Press, 1950.

109. Riesman, David. "The Search for Challenge," *Merrill-Palmer Quarterly of Behavior and Development*, 6 (July 1960), 218–234.

110. Rosenfeld, E. "Stratification in a Classless Society," *American Sociological Review*, 16 (no. 6, 1951), 766–774.

111. ——— "Institutional Change in the Kibbutz," *Social Problems*, 5 (1957), 110–136.

112. Rosenmayer, L. "Der alte Mensch in der Sozialen Unwelt von Heute," *Kölner Zeitschrift*, 4 (1958), 642–657.

113. Rosow, Irving. "Issues in the Concept of Need Complementarity," *Sociometry*, 20 (1954), 216–223.

114. ——— "Retirement, Housing, and Social Integration," *The Gerontologist*, 1 (no. 2, 1961), 25–91.

115. Sarell, M. The Second Generation in the Kibbutz—"Conservatism" vs. "Innovation" (in Hebrew), *Megamoth*, 11 (no. 2, 1961), 99–123.

116. ——— Adolescents in Israel's Collective Settlements (in Hebrew). Mimeograph, n.d.

117. Schapera, I. "The Tsawana Conception of Incest," in *Social Structure*, ed. Meyer Fortes. Oxford, Clarendon Press, 1949.

118. Schlesinger, R. *The Family in the U.S.S.R.* London, Routledge and Kegan Paul, 1949.

119. Schneider, David M. "Political Organization, Supernatural Sanctions, and Punishment for Incest on Yap," *American Anthropologist*, 59 (no. 5, 1957), 791–800.

120. ——— and G. C. Homans. "Kinship Terminology and the American System," *American Anthropologist*, 57 (no. 6, 1955), 1194–1208.

121. Seligman, Brenda. "Incest and Exogamy—A Reconsideration," *American Anthropologist*, 52 (no. 3, 1950), 305–316.

122. Shambough, B. M. *Amana—The Community of the True Inspiration*. Iowa City, Iowa, State Historical Society of Iowa, 1908.

123. Shryock, H. S., Y. S. Siegel, and C. C. Beagle. "Future Trends of Fertility in the United States," *Transactions* of the World Population Conference, Rome, 1954. vol. I, pp. 713–730.

124. Slater, Philip E. "Parental Role-Differentiation," *American Journal of Sociology*, 67 (1961), 296–308.

125. —— "On Social Regression," *American Sociological Review*, 28 (1963), 339–364.

126. Smith, R. *The Negro Family in British Guiana*. London, Routledge and Kegan Paul, 1956.

127. Smith Blau, Z. "Changes in Status and Age Identification," *American Sociological Review*, 21 (1956), 198–203.

128. Spiro, Melford E. *Kibbutz: Venture in Utopia*. Cambridge, Harvard University Press, 1956.

129. —— "The Sabras and Zionism," *Social Problems*, 5 (no. 2, 1957), 100–110.

130. —— *Children of the Kibbutz*. Cambridge, Harvard University Press, 1958.

131. —— "Is the Family Universal?—The Israeli Case," in *A Modern Introduction to the Family*, eds. N. W. Bell and E. F. Vogel, pp. 64–75. Glencoe, Illinois, The Free Press, 1960.

132. Streib, G. F. "Morale of the Retired," *Social Problems*, 3 (1955–1956), 271–280.

133. Talmon-Garber, Yonina. "Family Structure in Cooperative and Collective Settlements in Israel," *Transactions* of the World Population Conference, Rome, 1954. Vol. VI, pp. 813–827.

134. —— "The Family in Collective Settlements," *Transactions* of the Third World Congress of Sociology (Amsterdam), 4 (1956), 116–126.

135. —— Review of M. E. Spiro, *Children of the Kibbutz*, in *American Journal of Sociology*, 65 (no. 3, 1959), 324–326.

136. —— "Sex Role Differentiation in an Equalitarian Society," in T. E. Laswell, J. H. Burma, and S. H. Aronson, eds., *Life in Society*, Glenview, Illinois, Scott Foresman, 1965.

137. Tibbits, C. "Retirement Problems in American Society," *American Journal of Sociology*, 59 (1953), 308.

138. Timasheff, N. S. "An Attempt to Abolish the Family in Russia," in *A Modern Introduction to the Family*, eds. N. W. Bell and E. F. Vogel, pp. 55–63. Glencoe, Illinois, The Free Press, 1960.

139. Toby, Jackson. "Romantic Love," in *Social Problems in America*, eds. Harry C. Bredemeier and Jackson Toby, pp. 461–467. New York, John Wiley, 1960.

140. Townsend, P. *The Family Life of Old People*. London. Routledge and Kegan Paul, 1957.
141. Waller, Willard. "The Rating and Dating Complex," *American Sociological Review*, 2 (1937), 727–734.
142. Weber, Max. *The Protestant Ethic and the Spirit of Capitalism*. New York, Charles Scribner, 1958.
143. Weintraub, Dov, and Moshe Lissak. "The Moshav and the Absorption of Immigration," in *Agricultural Planning and Village Community in Israel*, ed. Joseph Ben-David, pp. 96–101. Arid Zone Research Series, no. 23. Paris, UNESCO, 1964.
144. Welpton, P. K., and C. V. Kiser, eds. *Social and Psychological Factors Affecting Fertility*. New York, Milbank Memorial Foundation, 1946–1954.
145. Westoff, C. F. "Differential Fertility in the United States," *American Sociological Review*, 19 (no. 5, 1954), 549–561.
146. ——— E. G. Mishler, and E. L. Kelly. "Preference in Size of Family," *American Journal of Sociology*, 62 (1957), 491–497.
147. Whyte, W. F. *Human Reactions in the Restaurant Industry*. New York, McGraw-Hill, 1948.
148. Winch, Robert F. *Mate Selection*. New York, Harper, 1958.
149. Yang, C. *The Chinese Family in the Communist Revolution*. Cambridge, Harvard University Press, 1959.

Index

Adolescents: on children's accommodations, 113–114; control of sexuality among, 156–157; communal vs. family life among, 157

Adoption: of new kibbutz by established one, 147; recruitment for youth movements through, 152

Affective rewards, 198–200

Age: and demand for family accommodations, 103–104, 109; and ban of in-group marriage, 141; attitude patterns by, 228–229

Aging, 166–180; sources of strain in, 166–176; redefinition of policy on, 176–180

Agriculture, prestige of, 168

Antifamilism: factors resulting in, 3–6; in bund, 34; in occupational placement, 137

Army, disruptive effects of service in, 153

Ascetic pattern, 214, 220–221; as conservative, 215n; motivation of, 216–221; contrasted with consumption pattern, 224; erosion of, 227–228, 237

Asceticism: of the kibbutz, 9–10, 210–213; Protestant, 203–204; and national renaissance, 205–208; weakening of, 209–213, 237; present attitudes toward, 213–216; ethical motivation for, 217, 219; socialist motivation, 217, 219, 220; national motivation, 217–218, 219, 220; rural motivation, 218, 219, 220; kibbutz motivation, 218, 219, 220; in different types of kibbutzim, 225–231; and office holders, 231–233; of men and women, 233–235; of second generation, 235–237

Attitudes: ascetic, 214, 220–221, 226, 231; life style, 214, 220–221, 231; situation, 214, 220–221, 231; consumer, 214, 226, 231; comparison of types of kibbutzim by, 225–231; by age, 228–229

Authority: within family, 26; reward of elite, 196

Bedtime, children's, 94–95

Birth rate, 6; economic consequences, 54–55

Border settlements, 151

Bott, E., 23n

Budgeting, 23

Bund: stage of kibbutz, 2; disruption of, 15; familism in, 34; women in, 39; norms of family size in, 66–67, 69–72; pioneering, 76, 83; family meals in, 84; collectivist pattern in, 118–119; parental influence on job placement in, 132–136

Bureaucratization: limits of, 43; of management, 188

Child care: parental part in, 13, 24; professionalization of, 49, 92; and age of child, 103–104, 109. *See also* Children's houses

Childhood, sexuality in, 155

Children: limited number of, 7; time spent with parents, 8; permissiveness toward, 11; influence of parents on, 13, 28; cause of emergence of family, 15; importance of peers to, 28; sleeping arrangements of, 84–117; relation of grandparents to, 171